THE FRENCH ARE COMING!
- 1805 -

The Invasion Scare of 1803-5

PETER LLOYD

I now consider the war between France and England....as an antipathy or national horror, after the same kind as subsists between the kite and the crow or the churchwarden and the pauper, or the weasel and the rat.

Rev. Sydney Smith

SPELLMOUNT LTD
Tunbridge Wells

© Peter Lloyd, 1991

First published in the UK by
Spellmount Ltd
12, Dene Way
Speldhurst
Tunbridge Wells
Kent
TN3 0NX

British Library Cataloguing in Publication Data

Lloyd, Peter
The French are coming - the invasion scare of 1803-5
I. Title
940.27
ISBN 0-946771-77-4

Printed in Great Britain by
Biddles Ltd
Woodbridge Park
Guildford
Surrey

For Susan

The French Are Coming!

In the Spellmount/Nutshell Military list:

The Territorial Battalions - A pictorial history
The Yeomanry Regiments - A pictorial history
Over the Rhine - The Last Days of War in Europe
History of the Cambridge University OTC
Yeoman Service
The Fighting Troops of the Austro-Hungarian Army
Intelligence Officer in the Peninsula
The Scottish Regiments - A pictorial history
The Royal Marines - A pictorial history
The Royal Tank Regiment - A pictorial history
The Irish Regiments - A pictorial history
British Sieges of the Peninsular War
Victoria's Victories
Heaven and Hell: German Paratroop war diary
Rorke's Drift
Came the Dawn - Fifty years an Army Officer
Kitchener's Army - A pictorial history
On the Word of Command - A pictorial history of the Regimental Sergeant Major
Marlborough as Military Commander
The Art of Warfare in the Age of Marlborough
Epilogue in Burma 1945-48
Scandinavian Misadventure
The Fall of France
The First Victory: O'Connor's Desert Triumph, Dec 1940-Feb 1941
Blitz Over Britain
Deceivers Ever - Memoirs of a Camouflage Officer
Indian Army of the Empress 1861-1903
Heroes for Victoria 1837-1901
The Waters of Oblivion - the British Invasion of the Rio de la Plata, 1806-07.
Soldier's Glory - being 'Rough Notes of an Old Soldier'
Craufurd's Light Division
Napoleon's Military Machine
Falklands Military Machine
Wellington's Military Machine
Commando Diary

In the Nautical List:

Sea of Memories
Evolution of Engineering in the Royal Navy Vol 1 1827-1939
In Perilous Seas

In the Aviation List:

Diary of a Bomb Aimer
Operation 'Bograt' - From France to Burma - Memoirs of a Fighter Pilot
A Medal for Life-Capt Leefe Robinson VC
Three Decades a Pilot-The Third Generation
Bob Doe - Fighter Pilot
The Allied Bomber War, 1939-45

MAPS AND DIAGRAMS

Introduction

This book tells a largely forgotten story. In the youth of Thomas Hardy, one of the greatest of English novelists and poets, the invasion scare of 1803-5 was still a vivid remembrance among Dorset folk. That period is only just out of living memory and there are plenty alive today who can recollect being told as naughty children, 'Boney will get you!' Nowadays though, most people only have a vague idea that Napoleon intended to invade and that the Battle of Trafalgar put an end to the idea. Those who have taken a look round the surviving Martello towers on the south coast, strolled along the banks of the Royal Military Canal or wandered about Dover's Western Heights, and been curious enough to find out about them, will know that the invasion threat was serious enough for the government of the time to do something about it. But of the three great plans to invade Britain in modern times, it is the Spanish Armada, with its anniversary recently behind us, and Hitler's Operation Sealion that generate the books, articles and television programmes.

It is easy to see why. Unlike Napoleon's flotilla the Armada actually sailed and, in national legend, was gloriously routed by swashbuckling sea-dogs. And though it is doubtful if Hitler really meant to invade at all, the idea of it still has a horrific fascination as we imagine with a shudder what life would have been like in Britain under a Thousand-Year Reich. Our particular bogeyman is still Hitler, half a century on.

In the following pages I have tried to do justice to a project infinitely better planned than the Armada or Sea Lion and charged with a steely commitment more than equal to the austere fanaticism of Philip II of Spain. For most of three years Napoleon subjected the problem of cross-Channel invasion to the full blast of his energies and the searchlight of his intellect. There was an expeditionary force to be trained and welded together out of the disparate armies of the Republic. On the maritime side, he started with virtually nothing, and had to create embarkation ports and a 2,000-strong flotilla from scratch. But the hardest nut of all to crack, over which he long brooded, was how to defeat and bamboozle the Royal Navy long enough to get his forces to the English beaches in safety. As the story unfolds, it is fascinating to see a great military mind feeling its way into the problems of sail, wind and tide about which it had hitherto known next to nothing. All in all, the whole thing can claim to be perhaps the single most ambitious enterprise of war on which the great Corsican ever embarked. If for no other reason it deserves to be better known.

Of course it came to nothing, as did all Napoleon's other attempts to subdue Britain. And yet. As this book goes to press, events irresistibly call forth an echo from the past. 'Britain is no more!' Napoleon issued this presumptuous rallying-cry from Boulogne in the dog-days of 1805, surrounded by his legions poised to embark for the Kentish shore. There are those in Britain of 1991 who would endorse the remark, but with a grim rather than happy anticipation as a tight little off-shore island girds itself for another long, half-reluctant step into the European embrace.

Napoleon would surely appreciate the joke. In a way, you might say he has triumphed at last; here is the arch-enemy sulkily capitulating to the idea of Europe, not through force of arms but by the endless haggling of the politicians and bureaucrats he so despised. Napoleon's view of Europe of course involved supervision by the man himself - was not the French way self-evidently the best? - but with his impatience with narrow, inward-looking nationalism it was not so very different. But the irony has an extra twist. When his invasion plans failed Napoleon built up his Continental System, an attempt to crush Britain by blocking her trade outlets. He knew, as we know, that commercial isolation would spell the inevitable decline of Britain. Plus ca change.

I should like to thank the following for permission to quote from published material: Dr N.A.M. Rodger of the Navy Records Society (The Keith Papers Vol.3) Mr M.Y. Ashcroft of North

Yorkshire County Record Office ('To Escape the Monster's Clutches') and Oxford University Press (The Wynne Diaries).

I should also like to record my thanks to: Peter Bloomfield, David Chandler and Malcolm Thomas for their helpful advice; Janet Adamson, Jane Ashworth, Alastair Brodie and Miss D. Sage for their prompt and efficient service; Stella Hurd for help with translations; John Chorley and Tom Hetherington for superlative photographic work; Marion Smith, doyenne of typists and exacting judge of my English; Ian Fletcher, a long-suffering and helpful editor; and Jack Bevan and Peter Roberts, true friends, for unstinting advice and encouragement.

Chapter One

The Weasel and the Rat

In March, 1802, Britain and France set their signatures to the Treaty of Amiens and thereby brought to an end nearly nine years of continuous war between them. Britain, the architect and last remaining member of the second coalition of nations to hold out against France, was alone able to negotiate with her on equal terms. On the Continent, France, under her First Consul Napoleon Bonaparte held undisputed sway: beyond Europe's shores, Britain's navy continued to hold the seas and oceans in its grip. The two nations were deadlocked, powerless for the time being to do each other significant harm. Bruised and weary, they now embarked uncertainly on an uncharted sea of peaceful co-existence. Yet before 1802 was out, the question was not whether the struggle was to be renewed but only when; five months into the new year, war had broken out once more, and Napoleon had begun to concert his plans for the invasion that was intended to be the endgame with the island foe. But before examining the events that tipped the old adversaries into a new war, we should first of all take a look at them as they stood eyeing each other warily on the threshold of peace.

Britain was no longer led by the statesman who had first taken her into the struggle with revolutionary France and presided over its conduct. William Pitt had dominated the political firmament since he had become Prime Minister in 1783 at the record age of 24. Like his father the Earl of Chatham, it was Pitt's fate to be a wager of war against France, though he lacked his father's genius and relish for it. His was an aloof, unendearing personality, his chief political characteristic ·being what he himself regarded as integrity but some saw as arrogance. Spending prodigal amounts of cash on foreign subsidies, he had laboured to construct and sustain two coalitions against France with fickle, selfish and mutually suspicious allies, only to see them both crumble before the onslaught of French arms. In February 1801, he resigned from office over the king's stubborn refusal to give way over his old *bête noire* of Catholic Emancipation, but by then Pitt had had enough of a war that had become futile and unwinnable; by the same token many had come to feel uncomfortable with this austere symbol of war without end and were not unhappy to see the back of him, at least for a while.

The new Prime Minister was Pitt's lifelong friend Henry Addington, the ex-Speaker of the House of Commons. The fact that Addington was the son of a physician was of much greater significance in that patrician age than it would be in ours. It was thought not quite proper, even by those who supported him, that the highest office in the land should be filled by a person of such lowly provenance. 'The Doctor', the half-contemptuous nickname by which he was known throughout his political career, is an indication that he was never taken entirely seriously by his colleagues, and any medical allusion in the Commons was a surefire occasion for mirth, particularly when made by 'the Doctor' himself.

> Windham attacked the minister most fiercely last night; in a speech of indignant self-defence, he asked if he had not given the House eight out of nine motions which the honourable gentleman supported? The idea of the Doctor having given the House eight out of nine motions tickled the patient so irresistibly that he was made quite angry.[1]

Philip Ziegler, Addington's modern biographer, has neatly encapsulated the innate weaknesses of Addington's premiership: he was not an aristocrat, he was not an orator, and he was not Pitt. His four-year term of office, bracketed by Pitt's first and second ministries, was essentially an interregnum lived out in Pitt's shadow and brought to an end by his action. It fell to Addington and his ministers, generally accounted a clutch of mediocrities by other leading politicians, to prepare the country to face the greatest threat to its existence since the Armada.

Britain alone had been able to assume the role of paymaster of the anti-French coalitions, since she alone packed the economic muscle to sustain it. Despite the punishing effects of war - inflation, violent price fluctuations, the closure of foreign trade outlets-the wealth she derived from world-wide trade and the engines of the new industrialisation continued to pile up. The conquest of enemy colonies had given a new boost to the lucrative re-export trade and the brimming rivers of British manufactured goods, finding the usual channels blocked, sought out new back-door routes into European markets. But there was a price to be paid in human misery for the double burden of war and headlong economic change. Dispossession, food shortages and impoverishment were visited on large sections of the artisan and labouring classes, creating a fertile seedbed for the new revolutionary gospel that menaced the old Europe. In response, the British ruling class closed ranks and came down hard on the desperate and disaffected with repressive legislation and show trials in the courts.

In August 1802, Napoleon Bonaparte, not quite 33, became France's Consul for Life, thus setting the seal on his position as undisputed master of France. The British visitors who flocked to Paris during the peace were able to see the new man for themselves, in his plain blue uniform of a colonel of Chasseurs, reviewing his troops in the Place de Carousel or presenting himself to the people on a balcony at the Tuileries. At this period he was losing the lean aspect of his youth but had not yet filled out to the portly figure of popular imagination. For a soldier, he was physically unprepossessing, particularly on a horse: but the twin-barrelled ranging of the blue-grey eyes betrayed the fire and steel beneath.

This scion of the Corsican *petite noblesse* was a true son of the Revolution. In 1789 he had been an obscure lieutenant of artillery with small prospects. The intervening years of upheaval and war provided opportunities for low-born talent to advance itself undreamt of in the old France, and Napoleon eagerly seized his chances. Within a few short years a series of dazzling victories in Italy and the conquest of Egypt had made him France's greatest captain. As he stacked triumph upon triumph, so his political ambitions began to grow. In 1799 he seized power in the coup d'état of Brumaire from the nerveless hands of a republican régime grown slack and corrupt, and in the following year returned to Italy to smash the Austrian army yet again at Marengo. France lay at his feet, but he quickly proved that he was no crude military dictator. For the first time, the wayward juggernaut of the Revolution felt the grip of a masterful hand. The conclusion of the Amiens peace saw him in the midst of the work - up to eighteen hours a day, dictating fistfuls of letters, memoranda and decrees, giving interviews, running meetings - that was to make France the best-governed country in Europe, and which has to this day indelibly stamped it with the Napoleonic mark. A Concordat had brought to an end the Republic's long wrangle with the Papacy and restored the primacy of France's ancient faith. Financial reform staved off the drift towards national bankruptcy. Far-seeing projects for the reform of education and the codification of the law were already under-way. A synthesis of Bourbon and republican forms of local government gave the First Consul the centralised control his autocratic spirit required.

Yet though Napoleon amply proved his credentials as a statesman, his instincts were first and last those of a soldier. He ran France like a vast army encampment in which everyone knew his duty and there was no questioning the general's orders. But most of the 28 million Frenchmen were realists; they were quite willing to settle for two-thirds of a loaf if the *égalité* of the Revolution's great rallying cry meant the consolidation of a social structure free of caste privileges, and *fraternité* a unified nation with a sense of pride and purpose. If the new régime showed little inclination to dispense much *liberté*, well, it was enough to be a proud citizen of the premier nation of Europe, able to enjoy peace, growing prosperity and efficient government.

In Britain, it fell to the new Addington government to take its cue from the national war-weariness and negotiate 'a peace which all men are glad of but no man proud of', as Richard Brinsley Sheridan described it in the Commons. Addington settled for the minimum terms that the dictates of national honour and interest allowed. He had no illusions about the durability of peace: on the other hand, France's First Consul had so far demonstrated only his considerable talent for war, otherwise he was something of an enigma, and would now have his chance to prove the sincerity of his pacific pronouncements; as far as Britain was concerned, the old enemy under its new ruler was on probation for good behaviour.

In some respects Napoleon saw things the same way. In seeking peace, he too was responding too an intensely pacific mood in his own country. Overseas trade had been virtually wiped out by the Royal Navy and manufactures severely dislocated. France's colonial empire was almost entirely in Britain's hands. Most importantly, the First Consul regarded a peace treaty as vital for the consolidation of his régime. But he was not inclined to forget that France had her destiny to pursue as the great power of Europe, and he put an even more decisive question mark than did Britain over the odds on a permanent peace.

> Between old monarchies and a young republic the spirit of enmity must always subsist. In the present situation every peace treaty means no more to me than a brief armistice; and it is my belief that, while I fill my present office, my destiny is to wage war continually.[2]

The terms of the treaty of Amiens required Britain to return all the colonial conquests taken from France, Spain and Holland with the exception of Ceylon and Trinidad, to return Egypt to Turkey and Malta to the Order of the Knights of St. John. For her part, France's principal concession was to pull her troops out of southern and central Italy. But from the beginning, when preliminaries were signed in October 1801, there lurked a central ambiguity about the treaty's terms of reference. Some months previously, France and

Austria had signed the treaty of Lunéville that brought hostilities on the Continent to a close; to Britain, there was a relationship between the treaties of Lunéville and Amiens that in French eyes did not exist. Although there was nothing in the Amiens agreement to say so, Britain maintained it implied a recognition by both parties that the situation in Europe should remain as fixed at Lunéville: as far as Napoleon was concerned, the two treaties were in no way connected, and what transpired between Continental powers was none of Britain's business. Nonchalantly he continued to tilt the Continental balance of power ever more in France's favour. Even before the two countries had signed a definitive treaty in May 1802, he had done enough to confirm existing British suspicions.

Negotiations were begun with Spain for the French acquisition of the Duchy of Palma and, in America, the territory of Louisiana. The despatch of an expedition to subdue the negro rebellion on San Domingo seemed to prefigure renewed French colonial ambitions. The Cisalphine Republic, a satellite state of France, renamed itself the Italian Republic, and requested its begetter, Napoleon, to become its president. There was more to follow. With unconvincing excuses, France kept postponing the military evacuation of Holland which under the terms of the treaty of Lunéville she was required to do. Piedmont, another Italian duchy, was annexed. By now, hope had long since died in Britain that the peace would bring about a revival of free trade with France and those parts of the European coastline under her control - Napoleon saw no reason to oblige in helping Britain repair her fortunes the better to fight another war. Relations between the two nations were not helped by Napoleon's perverse insistence on regularly reading translations of the British public prints in whose pages he found, to his rage, hacks vying with one another in scabrous vilification of himself and his family.

'Peace, Sir, in a week, and war in a month' had been the Earl of Malmesbury's prediction to the Duke of York. Even those who had initially held more sanguine hopes of a lasting peace now foresaw only a brief truce. The new year was barely a month old

when a new occasion for friction arose. A French agent, one
Colonel Sébastiani, had been sent on what was ostensibly a trade
mission into Tripoli, Egypt and Syria. On his return, his report was
published in the 'Moniteur', the government mouthpiece. It was the
Colonel's view that 'six thousand men would be sufficient to re-
conquer Egypt'. This was provocative stuff. If, as is possible, the
First Consul intended it to put pressure on Britain, he had badly
miscalculated: it had precisely the opposite effect, stiffening public
opinion and giving the British Cabinet the excuse it had lacked
heretofore for postponing its treaty obligation to evacuate Malta, a
base that looked ever more useful with the renewed French menace
in the Mediterranean. Meanwhile France was busy consolidating
her influence on her eastern border. An Act of Mediation frankly
proclaimed Switzerland's status as a French satellite state. An
Imperial Recess, masterminded by Talleyrand, Napoleon's Foreign
Minister, brought about a major re-distribution of several small
Rhineland and south German states to princes who now looked to
France rather than Austria as their patron.

As the British Cabinet now saw things, their initial distrust
of Napoleon's good faith seemed more than vindicated and the
refusal to evacuate Malta a wise piece of insurance. To Napoleon
it was Britain, with her perfidious refusal to fulfil her solemn treaty
obligation, who was the threat to peace. Her eagerness for war
seemed confirmed in French eyes by the king's speech from the
throne early in March, announcing that reports - false as it later
emerged - of naval preparations in French and Dutch ports left her
no choice but to respond by calling out the Militia and recruiting
10,000 extra seamen. The Cabinet considered itself to be acting
prudently in a deteriorating situation; if war was in the offing, the
ministers saw no reason to allow France to spin out the peace for
her own advantage. A wrathful Napoleon had already subjected the
British ambassador, Lord Whitworth - cold and unbending, the
very epitome of the aristocratic hauteur in British diplomats that so
maddened foreigners - to one of his violent rages, accusing Britain
of fomenting war, in language contemptuously described by
Whitworth as being:

....too trivial and vulgar to find a place in a despatch or
anywhere but in the mouth of a hackney coachman.

The Cabinet coolly stiffened its demands in what read increasingly
like a crescendo of ultimata. It had in fact correctly diagnosed
Napoleon's intentions: if there was no satisfying Britain's demands
short of humiliating compliance, then war it would have to be - but
not just yet. Events brought on by Britain's unexpectedly tough
stance were in danger of overtaking him before he could gird
France for a new round. A flurry of conciliatory proposals
designed to stall things was hastily thrown up by the French
Foreign Ministry, including a suggestion for Russian mediation.
But Britain was implacable. Whitworth demanded his passport,
packed his bags and left Paris on May 12th, still pursued by French
blandishments on his way to catch the Dover packet. Four days
later the king signed an order laying an embargo on French
shipping and issued letters of marque for privateering. Two days
after that, frigates of the Royal Navy captured two French
merchantmen off Brittany. Napoleon, incensed at this act of war
without formal declaration, ordered the internment of all male
British subjects on French soil, the bag, 10,000 in all, including a
brace of ambassadors in transit. Britain and France had embarked
on a further eleven years - to the month - of continuous war.

  Over the years, the responsibility for the rupture of the Peace
of Amiens has been regularly chewed over by historians. But
pinning blame on one side or the other can seem an irrelevant
exercise. The causes of war were relatively trivial, and it is not
difficult to imagine solutions arrived at if the will had been there
on both sides. We are left with an eerie impression of actors
mechanically going through the motions towards a well-understood
dénouement. In the end, and perhaps even from the beginning, the
only real point at issue was when war would begin: Britain wanted
it sooner, France later. The nub of the matter is best expressed in
Sidney Smith's melancholy prophecy of four years earlier:

  I now consider the war between France and England no longer
  as an occasional quarrel or temporary dispute, but as an

antipathy or national horror, after the same kind as subsists
between the kite and the crow, or the churchwarden and the
pauper, or the weasel and the rat.[3]

In Britain, everyone unquestioningly assumed that renewed war
would bring about a revival of French invasion plans. Well before
the Revolution, throughout the long struggle between Britain and
Bourbon France that stretched back over a century, the latter power
had ardently dreamt of how it might encompass the final downfall
of the arch-enemy. After 1793, the old rivalry over colonies and
trade was shadowed by a more ferocious ideological dimension and
republican governments pursued the invasion idea with a new
avidity. The French historian Desbrière, who made an exhaustive
survey of the subject, identified no fewer than seven invasion
projects in eight years, if we include those against Ireland. Most
were abortive or chimerical but by 1803 the British people already
had good cause to greet the new war with a fearful expectation. In
1796 an expedition had slipped out of Brest and, managing to evade
British squadrons, had reached the south-western coast of Ireland
and lain unmolested in Bantry Bay for over a fortnight, prevented
from landing troops only by bad weather and disorganisation. In
the black year 1797, when the country was shaken by financial
crisis and her fortunes were in eclipse on every front, people heard
with horror that French troops had actually set foot on the soil of
mainland Britain, at Fishguard. The landing itself was on a small
scale and rapidly turned into full-blown farce ending in the easy
round-up of the French by the stalwarts of the local Yeomanry, but
it was enough to cause a run on the banks. In the subsequent year
there was another attempt on Ireland, this time from Brest when a
thousand troops were put ashore at Killala Bay in County Mayo.
They came too late to assist in the '98 rebellion of the United
Irishmen, but vastly superior British forces had to be mobilised
before they were made to surrender.

Among the various novel schemes for invasion pondered at
this time was one advanced by a Swedish officer, Muskeyn, who,
familiar with the usefulness of light armed galleys for warfare in

the shallow coastal waters of the Baltic, managed to convince the Directory that a multitude of such craft might well be able to carry a cross-Channel invasion by sheer weight of numbers where a conventional fleet would fail to win through. In 1797 the first such flotilla was assembled in several Channel ports, to be used in conjunction with another flotilla of fishing smacks and a Dutch squadron located at the Texel. An 'Army of England' was created and General Bonaparte, fresh from his exploits in Italy, was appointed to its command. But the Corsican's mind was already elsewhere, on Egypt and the new destiny that awaited him in the east as the new Alexander. Not surprisingly his assessment of the prospects for success was studiedly cool, with a great deal made of the risks and difficulties. At all events, the destruction of the Texel squadron at Camperdown later in the year effectively spelled the end of the project. Then in 1801 Napoleon, now First Consul, created his own invasion flotilla. It consisted of some 630 small vessels, including 250 specially-built gunboats, based on a string of harbours from Flushing to the Morbihan but intended at the decisive moment to move on Boulogne, take on 30,000 troops and carry them across the Strait. However, though considerable alarm was felt in Britain, stimulating defence preparations on an unprecedented scale, the flotilla was mustered primarily as a diplomatic lever to push Britain towards the negotiating table.

It is easy in hindsight to dismiss most, perhaps all, of these projects as unworkable. Yet however half-baked and fantastical, they served a valuable strategic purpose. The narrowness of the watery divide separating Britain from the enemy, and the capital's proximity to the south-east coast meant that Britain could never afford to take even the appearance of invasion preparations less than seriously. Squadrons of the Royal Navy had to be disposed to watch enemy ports and guard the Channel, while troops that might be usefully deployed elsewhere were tied down at home.

But Napoleon's intentions in 1803 were directed towards no mere diversion. In March, when it became clear that war was more or less inevitable, he took steps to revive the invasion project, though as yet with no great urgency. He demanded a report on the condition of the flotilla craft laid up since 1801, issued a decree for enlarging the harbour at Boulogne and ordered a three-year construction programme for over 500 new vessels to be based at Dunkirk and Cherbourg, together with the stockpiling of materials to build a further 500.[4] But this leisurely timetable was soon swept impatiently aside. A week after hostilities were renewed, he was demanding a first instalment of well over half the initial total by the end of the year. Some days later, the deadline was pushed forward again, to September 23rd: 'Since it can be done, it must be done'.[5] In the next few months, as Napoleon harried his minions with fusillades of orders and exhortations, the reach of his thinking mounted to ever-dizzier heights. For the first time, France's long-cherished aspiration was harnessed to a cold and unsleeping resolve.

In Britain too the month of March saw the pace of preparation visibly quicken, especially in the navy's principal ports. The king's speech from the throne was the signal for the start of a 'hot press' - an intensive sweep by the navy's press-gangs to pull in large numbers of extra seamen, whether they had protection certificates or not. Plans were laid in secrecy to catch the birds before they could fly. On the day the king made his speech, the warrants received his signature and the Admiralty messengers were hurrying down the roads to the ports. On receiving them, the ports admirals straight away set the machinery into motion. At Plymouth,

....about 7pm the town was alarmed with the marching of several bodies of Royal Marines in parties of 12 and 14 each with their officers and a naval officer, armed towards the quays. So secret were the orders kept that they did not know the nature of the service on which they were going until they boarded the tier of colliers at the New Quay and other gangs the ships in Catwater, the Pool and the gin-shops. A great number of prime seamen were taken out and sent on board the Admiral's ship. They also pressed landsmen of all descriptions, and the town looked as if in a state of siege....One press gang

entered the Dock Theatre and cleared the whole gallery, except
the women.

Ships were despatched to intercept homeward bound merchantmen
and strip them of their prime hands, and scour ports as distant as
Yarmouth, Cork, Dublin and Waterford. At Portsmouth,

> ....it is with the utmost difficulty that people living on the point
> can get a boat to take them to Gosport, the terror of the press-
> gang having made such an impression on the minds of the
> watermen that ply the passage.[6]

In the pages of the 'Naval Chronicle' the Promotions and Appoint-
ments listings lengthened to several times their peace-time size,
gladdening the hearts of half-pay officers who had been languishing
on the beach for eighteen months or more.

Months before war was rejoined, Addington had anticipated
the revival of French invasion plans. The prospect did not dismay
him: on the contrary, it was the key to his strategy for the new
war. Looking across to the Continent, its principal powers resentful
of French hegemony but helpless to do anything about it, he saw
no possibility of a new coalition in the foreseeable future. Britain
stood alone, as she had done in 1801, though now her resolve was
stiffer and her economic sinews tougher. As then, the two adversaries were stalemated; but Addington calculated, correctly, that
this time Napoleon would find the situation past endurance:
maddened by Britain's defiance from her island fastness, he would
plan to lay siege to her shores. If the attempt was made Addington
was confident that it would fail, and such a reversal might well
inspirit the Continental powers into joining a coalition; if not,
Napoleon's army would rot on the Channel coast while Britain
grew ever stronger by her dominion over the seas.

In the course of the years 1801-3, the British ruling class
finally made up its collective mind about Napoleon Bonaparte.
There were those hardliners who had always so detested French
republicanism and all its works that they saw Napoleon simply as
another Jacobin, different only in being endowed with superior

talents and cunning. But there were others, Pitt and Addington among them, who yielded nothing to the ultras in repugnance for the new order or suspicion of Napoleon, but nevertheless felt that some kind of *modus vivendi* with him might yet be achieved. France had routed all her enemies in Europe, gained her natural frontiers and stood once more as much *la grande nation* as she had been under Louis XIV. Perhaps, it was hoped, her new ruler might now see the path of peace as the best means of securing France's status in Europe and his own position at home.

This fragile shoot of optimism was blasted long before war broke out again. By the time the Treaty of Amiens came to be signed, Napoleon had already done enough in the six months since the preliminaries to convince Pitt and many others

> ....that he was and ever would remain the same rapacious, insatiable plunderer, with as good little faith and as little to be relied on as he [Pitt] formerly found him to be....no compact, no covenant made with him could be secure.[7]

But coupled with the grim satisfaction of finding that the leopard had retained his spots was a conviction that the spots themselves were of an even darker and more sinister hue than had hitherto been suspected. The British had always regarded Napoleon as an unscrupulous political gangster: now Whitworth's despatches portrayed him as a deranged tyrant, of the same ilk as the late mad Tsar Paul of Russia. The more percipient began to appreciate with alarm the true nature of the new French régime, with the energies let loose by the Revolution now steered by a single untrammelled will. The ambition seemed insatiable, and the hatred of Britain unrelenting. Napoleon's metamorphosis in the British mind to full-blown bogeyman, both inhuman and superhuman, was now complete and beyond debate.

If Napoleon's reciprocal antagonism towards Britain did not have quite the same pathological edge, it was equally purblind. For him too, the brief interlude of peace served not only to confirm existing prejudices but also something more. As definitive proof of the remorselessness of their loathing of France, the 'English oligarchs' had revealed hitherto unsuspected depths of perfidy by breaking a solemn treaty obligation. On both sides, the carapace of blind antipathy had finally hardened, armouring each for a fight to the finish that Napoleon aimed to win with his knock-out blow.

As the full intimidating sweep of Napoleon's new invasion plan became known, the British upper classes cultivated, at least outwardly, the unruffled insouciance of Lord Grenville writing to his brother from his cherished new park at Dropmore:

> You will find me here very peacefully rolling my walks and watering my rhododendrons, without any thought of the new possessor to whom Bonaparte may dispense them.[8]

At the other end of the political spectrum, Charles James Fox claimed to be of the same untroubled mind when he wrote to his own brother in Ireland:

> We have just begun our harvest here, as some suppose for Bonaparte, but I am as stout as a lion. I believe he will not try, next that if he does he will be destroyed or at least driven back at sea, and lastly that even if he does land, he will frighten more than hurt us.[9]

Expert professional opinion, though rather more guarded, tended to concur. Lord Cornwallis, a senior soldier, wrote:

> The French have had fine winds and weather for their English expedition, and as they have not made use of them, I begin to think we shall not see them this year, and by next spring we ought rather to wish than to apprehend an invasion.[10]

But not everyone slept so easily in their beds; literally so in the case of the fashionable artist Joseph Farington, who confided to his diary:

> I had the last night the most distinct dream of invasion that could possess the fancy, of seeing the French boats approach in the utmost order, and myself surrounded by them after their

> landing....It seemed to me they came upon the country quite
> prepared, and met with no resistance....I could scarcely believe
> it a dream for a little time after I woke.[11]

And doubtless there were not a few who shared the more conscious
apprehensions of the man who confessed to a correspondent:

> I cannot subdue my anxiety when I reflect on the unprecedented
> good fortune of Bonaparte everywhere victorious.[12]

A Scottish lawyer believed that such fears were well-founded and
widespread, at least among the educated and well-informed:

> The utter security of this island ever since the blowing back of
> the Armada made the population treat actual invasion as a thing
> not to be seriously contemplated. But thinking men were in a
> great and genuine fright, which increased in proportion as they
> thought.[13]

Some unquiet spirits saw the approaching Day of Wrath as divine
retribution justly visited on a sinful nation, as had one doom
merchant, Samuel Coleridge, when he composed his poem 'Fears
in Solitude', a mournful meditation on the scare of 1798:

> We have offended, Oh, my countrymen....
> ....evil days,
> Are coming on us....

However, in 1803 his friend William Wordsworth who had long
forsworn the revolutionary sympathies that had inspired the
deathless line, 'Bliss was it in that dawn to be alive', was now
beating the drum with the rest of them, penning such strains as:

> No parleying now! In Britain is one breath;
> We are all with you now from shore to shore:-
> Ye Men of Kent, 'tis victory or death!

The fact that the national mood was not all unalloyed bullishness
is evidenced by the countless invasion rumours that buzzed about

the nation's ears throughout this period, many of them triggering off full-scale mobilisation in various parts of the country, some of which will be detailed in a subsequent chapter. Among ignorant and unlettered people in particular, the most grotesque *canards* could swiftly gain a hold. Eighty years or more after the event, Thomas Hardy, deeply knowledgeable about Dorset folk tradition concerning the invasion period that was still flourishing in his lifetime, wrote what he imagined to be an entirely fictitious 'Tradition of the Year 1803'. It was a tale supposedly recounted at a fireside by an old gaffer of how Napoleon himself came ashore one night at Lulworth Cove in Dorset to reconnoitre the invasion ground in person. Later, Hardy was to find to his astonishment that the story was, in fact, a local legend then still very much in circulation. Dorset rustics came up with another bizarre rumour that a community of local nuns had taken in one of Napoleon's brothers and were stock-piling arms and ammunition in preparation for a descent on the coast. The story gained such a hold that a magistrate was sent to investigate, though history does not relate haw he broached the matter to the ladies in question.[14] In the even more remote fastnesses of Wales, a gentleman on tour discovered that:

> They have got a strange notion....that Bonaparte has escaped from France and is lurking among the mountains so that they eye every stranger particularly; and (would you believe it?) absolutely took me for the First Consul and challenged my guide. I observed a great buzz among the women, and being informed of the cause went up to them, and assured them I was old enough to be Bonaparte's father. One of them fortunately observed that she had taken particular notice on my first entrance into the town of my eyes and that Bonaparte squinted. They say he was born in Wales, and that two of his brothers were transported.[15]

By 1803, the British radical agitation of the previous decade that had been inspired by the French Revolution was virtually dead, steam-rollered into the ground by government repression. Although the propertied classes could now afford to take a more relaxed and benign view of the lower orders, it was nevertheless realised that Napoleon might still be looked to by the underprivileged as potential deliverer from their chains. Hence a campaign was mounted, as studied and deliberate as any home front propaganda offensive in our own age of total war, to win the hearts and minds of the lower classes for the established order. A flood of what were known generically as 'loyal papers' - placards, songs, broadsides and handbills - appeared all over the country discoursing tub-thumping patriotism and its usual bedfellow, xenophobic rancour. The chief instigators were the London booksellers, who apart from disseminating material widely in the metropolis, advised, in the words of their advertisements, that:

> Noblemen, magistrates and gentlemen would do well by ordering a few dozen of the above tracts of their booksellers and causing them to be stuck up in the respective villages where they reside, that the inhabitants may be convinced of the cruelty of the Corsican usurper.

The nameless scribblers who churned out this stuff by the yard were not inhibited by considerations of wit, accuracy or finesse, and it all makes for tedious reading to the modern eye. The cruder the better, according to a Scotsman in London writing home:

> You should reprint the handbills that have had a great effect here; they are in general stupid and coarse, but it is the coarse souls which it is the most important to incite.[16]

The contents of the papers varied enormously. Some included artless caricatures which should, strictly speaking, be differentiated from the rarer, more sophisticated prints by such as Gillray, Rowlandson and Isaac Cruikshank. There were high-flown and windy addresses, haranguing variously 'Brave Soldiers, Defenders of Your Country', 'Men of England', 'Citizens of England', and in not one very pithy instance, 'To the infamous wretch, if there be such a one in England, who dares to talk of, or even hopes to find mercy in the breast of the Corsican Bonaparte, the eternal sworn foe of England, the conqueror and grand subjugator of France'. Doggerel was popular, sometimes serious, more often jaunty and humorous in a knockabout way, much of it being intended to be sung to such popular tunes as 'Britons Strike Home' and 'The Bluebells of Scotland'. More enterprising angles were taken by the authors of 'A Farce in One Act, called the Invasion of England. Principal Buffo, Mr. Bonaparte; being his first (and most likely his last) Appearance on this stage', and other spoof theatre bills in the same vein, together with those who drew up 'Bonaparte's Will', 'The New Moses or Bonaparte's Ten Commandments' and his 'Bonaparte's Epitaph'.

Although there was an assortment of formats, the messages hammered out were simple variations on the same two complementary themes: an assertion of British unity and fighting spirit, and vilification and ridicule of Napoleon, both coupled with a general debunking of the invasion threat. Much was made of the average Briton's good fortune, with his liberties and feasts of roast beef, compared to the miserable lot of the Frenchman. Even the wretched Irishman Pat, contentedly eating his potatoes, was co-opted by a generous stretch of the imagination into the general well-being. Ireland being a touchy point, Pat's appearances were always an occasion for emphasising national solidarity, lining him up with John Bull, Taffy and Sandy in a united front to face the invader. National symbols such as these figured large in both words and pictures. Britannia sometimes made her appearance, as did the king, who gained a new access of popularity at this time. But the most ubiquitous personification of the nation's will to fight was undoubtedly the figure of John Bull, often portrayed as a ferociously oafish plug-ugly, with a face appropriately resembling a side of beef, a huge leonine head and limbs like tree-trunks, often sporting a huge oaken cudgel that appeared to be fashioned from another one. His activities consisted largely of gorging on the fat of the land, hurling defiance and abuse at a diminutive Boney, or doing some kind of violence to his person.

Napoleon himself was equally closely stereotyped. In caricatures he is usually the poison dwarf, though he is also featured as a fairy, a moth, an earthworm, a monkey or orang-utang exhibited at a raree show, and the 'Corsican Fox' pursued by English hounds. The minuscule stature was always reassuringly in evidence, as was the ludicrous and comical nature of his appear-ance and antics: cadaverous, lank-haired, lantern-jawed, dwarfed by an enormous cockaded hat and sword, variously strutting about ranting in pidgin English, dancing with rage or gibbering with fear. A sub-species of the genre portrays him as Gulliver at the court of Brobdingnag, where he is usually being subjected to inspection through a glass by a curious George III.

While this approach employed the common device of drawing the sting of fear by heaping ridicule on its object, rather as Hitler was presented to a later generation of Britons at war, other writers preferred to make simple Britons' flesh creep by laying on the Grand Guignol. Here we encounter Boney the savage tyrant, violator of liberty and visiter of pillage and cruelty on the innocent. In particular, two episodes from Napoleon's Syrian campaign were harped on with relish and no little dramatic licence. These were the butchery of 1,400 Turkish prisoners at Jaffa and the alleged poisoning by opium of plague-stricken troops who were hampering his retreat from Acre. Lest the lurid recounting and embroidering of these and other samples of Napoleonic villainy should not make the point with sufficient force, one print featured 'An Invasion Sketch' in which was recounted a futuristic scenario of the French occupation of London, complete with violated British wives and daughters, desecrated churches, the levying of tribute, wholesale massacre and mass trials and executions of the nation's leaders, together with the final indignity, the re-naming of London as, inevitably, Bonaparte-opolis.

In the black-and-white world of the propagandist, a French descent on Britain could meet with no other end than wholesale rout, such as the *sauve qui peut* depicted in the famous Gillray cartoon. While the British troops, sometimes personified by John Bull in Volunteer uniform, were never less than in the best of fettle, prints such as Gillray's 'French Volunteers, marching to the conquest of Great Britain', showing a chained procession of emaciated ghouls in *bonnets rouges*, ridiculed Napoleon's hordes. But it is the aftermath of British victory that the papers preferred to dwell on most lovingly. The sadistic gloating in evidence here gives a disturbing insight into the kinship of human fear and hate. Again, Gillray's morbid imagination supplies the most strikingly gruesome depiction in his 'Buonaparte forty-eight hours after Landing', with an exultant John Bull holding aloft Napoleon's dripping head on a pitchfork. The decapitation motif occurs elsewhere, together with other wished-for fates: Napoleon skewered on a pitchfork, his body mutilated, hung on a gibbet and buried in a dunghill, or taken alive and led in triumph through the streets of London to be put on trial.[17]

Strangely, neither the output of invasion prints nor the concern about invasion as evinced in people's diaries and letters mirrored the growth of the threat itself. The torrent of prints gave out early in 1804, just at the time when Napoleon's design was first beginning to engage gear, and the British returned to their former preoccupations, men of affairs concerning themselves with the increasingly fluid political situation, the king's latest illness and his feuding with the Prince of Wales. It was as though the national psyche had undergone a purge of all its perturbation to emerge with a new calm indifference to the national peril. Significantly, when the danger was at its most acute, in August 1805, only one print appeared to commemorate it. But we are running ahead of ourselves. It is time to return to the First Consul in his office overlooking the Tuileries gardens, brooding over his plans to encompass the downfall of the island citadel.

Chapter Two

To Leap the Ditch

The First Consul was now dead set on a final and fundamental reckoning with Britain. Her stiff-necked oligarchs had shown the full measure of their obstinate hatred towards France: very well, it would be war to the knife. The outbreak of war was the trigger for a vast explosion of Napoleonic energy, driving invasion preparations ahead with white-hot intensity. Gradually, out of a blizzard of decrees, a more or less definitive plan began to take shape over the ensuing months. Two flotillas, one of 1,000 armed vessels to be specially built, the other of 600, later increased to 1,000, transports, were to carry across the Channel an expeditionary force of 115,000 troops together with horses, artillery and supplies.[1] This, it was clear, was to be an amphibious operation on a truly awesome scale that utterly dwarfed all previous armadas.

The most pressing priority was to initiate a flotilla construction programme more or less from scratch, since few of the vessels built in 1801 had survived storage. Shipyards in harbours from the Dutch to the Spanish border - Flushing, Brest, Lorient, Nantes, Rochefort, Bordeaux, Bayonne - rang to the noise of saw, axe and hammer. But building was not confined to the large ports, as the invasion craft were small enough to be put together in makeshift yards on river banks and in the tiniest harbour and inlet. 'There is not a creek or canal inland but what they are building at,' reported one British agent of his tour along the coast from Ostend to Boulogne. Yards proliferated along the Gironde, Loire, Somme, Oise, Scheldt, Meuse, Seine and Rhine. Napoleon took a particular interest in those established in Paris. On the Quais of Bercy, Les Invalides and La Rapeé, he ordered the construction of 60 vessels with labour conscripted from the surrounding *départements*, each to be named after one of the principal quarters of the city.[2] Holland was ransacked for naval stores - sailcloth, cordage, hemp and tar - and huge purchases were made from the main suppliers, Sweden and Russia, shipped to Holland and conveyed into France by inland waterway, while the forges of Liège, Douai and Strasbourg roared away at full stretch to turn out the thousands of new artillery pieces required to arm the multitude of new vessels.[3]

Within a few days of the outbreak of war, Napoleon had already put together an administrative framework to control the whole operation. The French coastline was divided into six maritime 'arrondissements', each under the supervision of a committee consisting of a naval officer, an engineer and an *administrateur maritime,* all supervised by Admiral Forfait, designated Inspector General, who was answerable directly to Admiral Decrès, the Minister of Marine.[4] The command of the flotilla itself was vested in Admiral Bruix. Napoleon drove his underlings unmercifully, ceaselessly prodding them to ever greater exertions. He wrote to Forfait:

> I do not know how to over-emphasise the need for the utmost despatch in the construction programme. The Minister has indicated to you only the minimum target for 22 September; work towards achieving double; there is no lack of funds.[5]

And to Bruix:

> At the moment we have enough gunboats under construction but not enough chaloupes or pinnaces, so if you can place a greater number in your arrondissement, do so; you have the authority. You have several places that could take them. I'm surprised there are none at Amiens.[6]

Much of the burden fell on Decrès, the very epitome of the grey, diligent yes-man whom autocrats like to have around them. His performance under the Consul's coldly vigilant eye was deemed somewhat less than satisfactory:

> Several parts of the Ministry of Marine are evidently neglected
> and I'm beginning to suspect that Admiral Decrès does not have
> the spirit of order and purpose which is the prime quality of an
> administrator.[7]

The idea of Napoleon, the personification of France's republican pride and martial spirit, throwing down the gauntlet to Britain, the great adversary, on the element she had made her own, sent a frisson through the nation. Prompted by a publicity campaign organised by the Second Consul, Cambacérès, the *départements* eagerly pressed forward with donations to the national coffers to finance a new naval resurgence. Seine-Inferieure made the first offer, to tax itself for the cost of a 74-gun frigate. Other *départements* were hard on its heels, as were numerous communes and corporations. The *départements* usually came forward with sums of between 300,000 and a million francs; larger towns financed a frigate, while cities like Paris, Marseilles, Lyons and Bordeaux could afford a ship of the line; smaller towns would often finance a flotilla vessel. Offers also came in from other quarters; the Senate and Capitol both voted the cost of a large ship of the line, several regiments in the army donated a day's pay, the Guard volunteered to pay for a flotilla vessel, the Italian Republic found 4 million livres for two frigates and a dozen invasion craft.[8]

The flotilla comprised a motley assortment of vessels. Our British agent quoted earlier identified eight different kinds. The transports, intended to carry most of the artillery and horses, wagons, rations and other supplies, were coasters and fishing smacks of various kinds; by December, over 600 had been hired, at a total cost of nearly 7 million francs. The majority of those that were specially built conformed to four specifications. The largest was the pram: 110 feet by 25 feet, with a draught of 8 feet, fully square-rigged and resembling a corvette, built to carry 12 24-pounder guns, a crew of 38 and 120 troops. The *chaloupe cannonier*, which the Royal Navy dubbed a brig, was 76 to 80 feet long, 17 wide, with a draught of 5 to 6 feet, carried a complement of 22 crew and 130 troops, and was armed with three 24-pounders and a mortar, two each at stem and stern. The *bateau cannonier* or gunboat was 50 feet by 14 feet, drawing 4½ feet, manned by a crew of six and intended to transport 100 troops and 2 horses, the latter in a stable amidships, and an artillery wagon on deck. It was armed fore and aft with a 24-pounder plus a mortar or light field piece. The smallest craft of all was the *péniche* or pinnace, about the same length as the gunboat but only 100 feet in the beam, with a draught of 3½ feet. Unlike the others it was open and undecked, and was equipped with oars and a light sail, carrying a crew of 5 plus 60 troops, and a small mortar by way of armament.[9]

They were none of them very handy vessels, to say the least. It was not that the French did not know how to build sea-worthy ships: on the contrary, their naval design was much superior to that of the British. The problem lay in the dual purpose that the vessels had to serve, as both seagoing transports and landing craft, and consequently they did not fulfil either role very well. Flat keel-less bottoms and shallow draughts, designed for grounding inshore on the shelving beaches of England's south-east coast, made for lubberly handling. Even with careful ballasting, none of the four types could sail at all close-hauled and their only reliable point of sailing was running before the wind. The pram was a notably ungainly performer, her high masts making her heel alarmingly far over with the wind. Both the pram and the chaloupe made particularly unsuitable landing craft, since with their deeper draughts they would have to be beached on a falling tide, so that the troops, laden down with musket, ammunition, several days' rations and paper cartridges (a load largely useless if wet) would be forced to wait for the tide to recede before it was safe to disembark. On the other hand, the shallower draught of the gunboat and pinnace made for better landing; but their low freeboards, which shipped water in anything heavier than a gentle swell, would have made a Channel crossing a nerve-tautening experience for their occupants. Also, Napoleon's insistence that the vessels should be armed led to their carrying too much weight for their size, and it was weight that was in the wrong places, making the vessels top-heavy and adding to their clumsiness in handling.[10]

> It is impossible to suppose for an instant that anything effective
> can be produced by such miserable tools, equally ill-calculated
> for the grand essentials in a maritime formation, battle and
> speed,

wrote Admiral Montagu with professional disgust after examining
the first specimen to fall into British hands.

> ....floored as this wretched vessel is, she cannot hug the wind,
> but must drift bodily to leeward, which indeed was the cause of
> her capture; for, having got a little to leeward of Boulogne
> Bay, it was impossible to get back and she was necessitated to
> steer large for Calais. On the score of the battle, she has one
> long 18-pounder, without breeching or tackle, traversing on a
> slide, which can only be fired stem-on. The 8-pounder is
> mounted aft but is not a fixture; so that literally, if one of our
> small boats was to lay alongside there would be nothing but
> musketry to resist, and those placed in the hands of poor
> wretches weakened by the effects of sea-sickness, exemplified
> when this gunboat was captured, the soldiers having retreated
> to the hold, incapable of any energy or manly exertion.[11]

It is not difficult to understand the Navy's unbudging scepticism
about the threat of what it called 'the mosquito fleet'.

Before long Napoleon grew impatient with directing his great
enterprise from afar and decided to take a look at things for
himself. On June 23rd he left Paris for Compiègne where he
inspected the yards on the banks of the Oise, afterwards proceeding
to others on the Somme at Amiens, Abbeville and St. Valéry, his
progress regularly punctuated by civic receptions and greeted by
cheering crowds. After a flying visit to Étaples he did not arrive at
Boulogne until late in the evening of the 29th. He snatched a few
hours' sleep, rose early and scrutinised the new port works, not
neglecting to rebuke those responsible for the lamentable state of
the main harbour battery and its lack of the wherewithal to heat
shot for firing at marauding enemy cruisers. Later he rode north
along the shore as far as La Crèche and inspected the first
contingents of the new Army of England to have reached the coast.

Next day he briefly visited Calais, and then finally Dunkirk, where he looked over the remnants of the previous flotilla, though no-one could steel himself to inform the First Consul that the vessels were in a sorry state of repair after two years' neglect. Throughout, a retinue of wilting secretaries took down a ceaseless flow of orders remedying derelictions, galvanising indolence and inertia, and cutting through red tape.

Yet for all the relentless goading, the continual to-ing and fro-ing of couriers and the lavish outpouring of resources, manpower and money - nearly 19 million francs by the end of the year - it soon became clear that Napoleon's timetable could not possibly be met by mortal men. Not until September did the first contingents of newly-built vessels begin a snail-like progress to Boulogne from Dunkirk and Le Havre. It was evident that too many vessels had been put on the stocks in the first place, with a result that a long interval elapsed before the first batches were ready. In October the order went out that no more should be laid down until all those under construction had been completed.[12]

Thus it was only after the turn of the year that flotilla vessels began to emerge from the yards in any quantity. But once the flow began it quickly gathered pace so that twelve months after construction work had begun, 1,100 were ready for service.[13] However, once a vessel was built it might still have to travel to its designated assembly port which might be hundreds of miles away, along a coastline patrolled by a vigilant enemy. Such a journey could be a long drawn-out affair, with protracted sojourns in safe anchorages along the way, so that by June 1804 fewer than half those ready for service had managed to reach their final destination.[14]

In all his enterprises Napoleon made sure that his allies pulled their weight. The invasion project was no exception, and the Dutch, with their long maritime tradition, were co-opted to do their bit. Though pleading near-bankruptcy, the Batavian government still managed to muster a slightly strained enthusiasm at the prospect. In June 1803, France concluded with the Batavian Republic one of those shamelessly exploitative agreements Napo-

leon was wont to impose on his satellite states. The Dutch undertook to supply France with 16,000 troops and pay the cost of a
French army of 18,000 men then stationed on Dutch soil; also to
make ready five ships of the line plus the same number of frigates,
sea transport for 25,000 troops, and a flotilla of 350 invasion craft
to take 36,000 troops and 1,500 horses. In return France
guaranteed the integrity of Dutch territory at home and overseas,
and undertook to win back the Dutch colony of Ceylon from
Britain. Lest they should think this a rather one-sided exchange,
Napoleon assured them that they were privileged to play their part
in such a historic mission. But privilege, he sternly reminded them,
entailed responsibilities:

> I count on the execution of the treaty by the Batavian govern-
> ment, and if great designs are frustrated by their derelictions,
> I have the right to complain to that government.[15]

The delivery date was to be January 1804; it was another of
Napoleon's impossible deadlines but the Dutch struggled manfully
to meet it. British agents' reports spoke of great activity at
Rotterdam, Amsterdam, Middleburg and Enkhausen, and the hiring
of civilian shipping. On December 5th, the Dutch ambassador was
forced to admit that despite herculean efforts his government was
able to supply only two-thirds of what was required. But Napoleon
was implacable: rejecting all excuses, he continued to insist on his
due and the Dutch toiled on until by the end of May they at last
managed to provide most of what was demanded.[16]

An amphibious invasion force needs harbour capacity for
assembly and embarkation. As in other aspects of the planning, it
took Napoleon some time to clarify in his own mind what exactly
he wanted. At the start he considered making use of a string of
harbours from Ostend down to Étaples, but then began to favour
a much narrower base of operations. There were sensible reasons
for this. The harbours north of Cape Gris Nez - Calais, Dunkirk,
Gravelines, Nieuport and Ostend - were on a coastline trending
north-east-south-west, while on the other side harbours like

Wimereux, Ambleteuse, Boulogne and Étaples lay on a shore that ran roughly north-south. This posed a problem in co-ordinating an invasion launch, since contingents north and south of Gris Nez could not leave harbour on the same wind; a fair wind for one would be foul for the other. Another consideration was the direction of prevailing winds in the Channel; being westerly to south-westerly, they favoured a departure from south of Gris Nez. Moreover, while advantageous for a crossing, westerlies would make it difficult for contingents of Lord Keith's North Sea command to clear their usual anchorage in the Downs and get across to the French coast. There were, in any case, solid advantages of communication and co-ordination to be derived simply from having the shortest practicable operational front. Everything plainly pointed to as concentration south of Cape Gris Nez.

An assembly harbour ideal for Napoleon's purposes would be secure from enemy attack, have the right capacity, and allow the exit of the maximum number of craft in a single tide. From Le Havre to Antwerp there was not one that answered all these needs. South of Gris Nez there were only a few insignificant tidal harbours, all small, shallow and prone to silting up. One of them, Boulogne, was in a rather less primitive state than its neighbours, since Napoleon had designated it as the chief assembly port for the short-lived invasion project of two years previously, when some 300,000 francs had been spent on new jetties, quays and embankments. It was here that Napoleon determined to create his centre of operations; it was eventually to hold half his flotilla, and its environs half the Army of England.

Boulogne lies on the Liane, a sluggish stream at that time nowhere wider than 40 metres, and in places only 20. Even when the harbour's sand and mud flats were flooded at full tide there was no great depth of water, and vessels of 6-foot draught were aground for eight hours in every 24. The entrance was a tricky one to negotiate especially in the prevailing westerlies, with perplexing tidal currents, a sand-bar in the main channel and a sand-bank on the western side. Gunboats and pinnaces could use the entrance for at most four hours in every tide, chaloupes and prames only three, and not at all during neap tides. A basketwork dyke had been erected on the eastern side of the channel beyond the harbour mouth as far as the low-water mark but the effect was to lengthen the channel rather than deepen it.[17]

Two months before the outbreak of war, Napoleon set aside funds for the excavation of a tidal basin behind a kilometre of new embankment on the left bank of the Liane, large enough initially to hold a hundred vessels. A dam with a lock and sluice was also planned to scour a deeper channel down to the harbour mouth. It was estimated that the new works would require the excavation of a million cubic feet of earth, and by the time war was renewed, 3000 men were already at work on the site.[18]

Étaples, a nearby harbour to the south, had also been considered for previous invasion projects, though it had never been improved. It too lay on a slow, narrow river, the Canche, only three or four feet deep at low tide, with a sand-bar at the junction of its two entrance channels, and vessels seeking a safe anchorage had to penetrate some two miles upriver as far as the town itself. Undeterred, Napoleon wrote to Bruix at the beginning of September:

> It appears that everything is underway at Boulogne. Now we have to see about Étaples......Have the piers been put into place? Is there a naval administration there, and have locations been found for the various naval and military establishments? Do all that is necessary for this harbour.[19]

Two other ports to the north of Boulogne, Ambleteuse and Wimereux, completed the new base of operations. Though intended to take smaller numbers, they too would require modification to suit them to their new role, and work on them also began in the latter part of the year.

It soon became apparent that the number of vessels intended for Boulogne - eight or nine hundred was the estimate by August - was too large, both for the capacity of the harbour and for the entrance to allow them all to get to sea in a single tide. However Napoleon believed that the difficulty could be surmounted by anchoring a proportion of the flotilla in the St. Jean road between La Crèche to the north and Le Portel in the south. This arrangement had been tried in 1801 by the then flotilla commander, Admiral Latouche-Tréville; the bottom had been found to give a secure hold for anchors, and troops sent aboard the vessels had had an opportunity to gain their sea-legs. The coastline, nearly three miles long, was fairly straight and offered no hazards in the form of shoals or banks. But protection had to be provided against the omnipresent enemy cruisers. An army engineer's report runs:

> It is necessary to defend the flanks by large-scale works. The terrain indicates the two points they should occupy: L'Heurt rock to the left, that of La Crèche for the right. These points are separated by a distance of 4,800 yards, quite adequate for anchoring a large number of vessels, but too long for the centre to be properly protected from the flanks; this necessitates the construction of an intermediate fort.[20]

While shore batteries offered ever-diminishing protection as the tide retreated, guns mounted on the two outlying rocks would both give good defence at low tide and threaten with enfilading fire any enemy ship venturing too closely inshore. The forts were to be permanent works, 53 yards in diameter, built in a semi-circular configuration. The intermediate outlying battery, a substantial structure designed to hold seven guns, was to be constructed on piles in front of the harbour entrance a little below low-water mark. Construction work went ahead slowly; it could only be carried out at times when tide levels permitted, and was delayed by bad weather and subject to harassment by enemy ships.

However, the need for coastal defence was not confined to the Boulogne road. Marauding enemy cruisers ranged along the entire French coast without let or hindrance, a perpetual menace to the passage of the flotilla vessels from the construction yards to the assembly ports. The Boulogne defences formed only the densest sector in a system that was to ring the thousand or so miles of shoreline from Nantes on the Atlantic right the way round to the Texel. With the zeal of a true artilleryman, Napoleon set about the creation and deployment of this vast panoply of ordnance. Gaspard Monge, his favourite scientific expert, was despatched to speed up output at the foundries. Twenty-four monster mortars of 12-inch bore were specially cast. Attempts were made to increase the range of conventional guns; 24-pounders were mounted on naval carriages, and pieces were staked down on the foreshore at low-water mark to provide advanced firing positions. Where it was difficult to site fixed batteries usefully, units of horse artillery were detailed to shadow the passage of flotilla contingents, their mobile field-pieces being able to take up firing positions right at the water's edge if necessary to lend the closest support possible.[21]

From the Seine to the Rhine there extended what Marmont called 'a coast of iron and bronze'. Within the three-mile stretch from L'Heurt to La Crèche alone were concentrated 143 assorted cannon, mortars and howitzers, one for every 35 yards of shoreline. 'I never saw a shore so covered with artillery in my life,' remarked an awe-struck British admiral. The shoreline between Calais and Lormel Point at the mouth of the Canche river bristled from end to end with 360 pieces of ordnance. To protect the Dutch flotilla as it rounded the danger point of Cape Gris Nez on its passage south, the headland was packed with 55 cannon and mortars mounted on timber platforms, all supervised by a general of artillery.[22]

As the first invasion craft were being laid down in the construction yards and the first spades were shovelling out the Liane mud, columns of summer dust could be seen hanging over roads all across France. The armies of the Republic were on the move, tracing an intricate pattern of movements across the face of the country, all master-minded by Berthier, Minister of War and *nonpareil* of military bureaucrats. Behind the vast outpouring of movement orders lay one great Napoleonic purpose: the creation of a unified French army, responsive to a single controlling mind. Soon to be dubbed the Grand Army, it was to become the most formidable fighting machine of its time. Six camps were set up at Utrecht, Bayonne, Brest, Ghent, St. Omer and Compiègne, the latter three, in the north-east corner, being designated as the bases for the Army of England. Together they formed a nodal point towards which many of the threads in the ever-shifting web converged; at the same time there were movements of dispersal to various points on the Channel and Atlantic coasts where units were assigned to flotilla vessels in which they would make the passage to the assembly ports. A contingent of one officer and 25 men was to form part of the crew, helping to work the boat on its journey. In some cases this would be a daunting prospect; the men of the 44th and the 66th, sent to Bayonne and Nantes, faced a particularly long haul via the inhospitable Brittany coast where many enemy ships lurked to add to natural perils.[23]

By the turn of the year the concentrations were well on their way to completion, with the three camps in north-eastern France holding about 70,000 men. Napoleon had decided to move the Compiègne and Ghent camps to locations nearer the coast at Montreuil and Bruges respectively. All three camps were now less than a day's march from the Channel, and commanders busied themselves assigning troops to the assembly ports, the infantry as labourers on the harbour works and novice deck-hands aboard the invasion vessels, while artillery detachments were detailed along the coast to defend the passage of flotilla contingents. After a further three months the concentration had reached a total of about 80,000, with a further 12,000 still dispersed with various units of the flotilla.[24] Each of the camps was commanded by one of Napoleon's most trusted paladins, all soon to be created Marshals of France, and all names that were to become indissolubly linked with that of the Grand Army.

The centre was entrusted to Soult, who only twelve years previously had been a lowly corporal of infantry; in eighteen months' time he was to clinch the great victory of Austerlitz for the master he was to outlive by thirty years. Soult's command comprised 23 infantry and two cavalry regiments, mostly located at Boulogne and Ambleteuse. Commanding the camp of the right wing was Davoût, the coldest of fishes and probably the best of Napoleon's marshals; he was certainly, as Napoleon's coeval, the youngest of the original eighteen. An aristocrat by origin, unprepo-

ssessingly short, bald and charmless, Davoût was to remain faithful
to his Emperor to the very last, when the rest of the marshalate had
forsaken him. He commanded 14 infantry regiments plus two of
cavalry, encamped at Dunkirk and to the right and left of Ostend,
'the healthiest spot in the area', as he informed Napoleon; and also
on the island of Walcheren, which by contrast was as unsalubrious
a station for troops as could be found anywhere in Europe; but
Walcheren needed defending as it commanded the approach to
Antwerp, Napoleon's newly designated naval base. Only the camp
of the left wing, now based at Montreuil a few miles inland from
Étaples, was still seriously under strength, with troops scattered in
penny packets along the Channel and Atlantic coasts all the way to
Bayonne. To this command Napoleon had appointed Ney, recently
returned from a mission to Switzerland. Ney was first and last a
cavalryman, the epitome of the dashing *beau sabreur*. Impulsive
and hot-headed, he was known to his men as '*le rougeaud*', the
red-head. Lacking the talents of a Davoût and the dependability of
a Soult, he nevertheless had the qualities necessary to hold together
the rearguard in the retreat from Moscow, that grimmest of
adversities, earning from his Emperor the epithet '*le brave des
braves*'.

Each camp comprised a *corps d'armée*, in effect a miniature
field army, able to manoeuvre and fight as an autonomous unit.
Each commander had his own staff, and in addition to contingents
of infantry, cavalry and artillery, each army was assigned detachments of engineers and other service troops. The system was not
new; French revolutionary commanders had long made use of it in
an *ad hoc* way, but it was Napoleon who had first deployed it
comprehensively during the Marengo campaign. From then on it
became central to his military thinking, giving him the flexibility
in the field that his practice of war required.

Thus by the end of the year Napoleon was well on the way
to forging the three components of his invasion weapon: a base of
operations, an expeditionary force, and the means of transit. Even
the most *recherché* details had not been overlooked. The First
Consul had found time to decree the formation of a special corps

of guide-interpreters, specifying how it should be raised - Irishmen considered - and the minutiae of the uniform. The Minister of the Interior had been entrusted with the task of commissioning an invasion song, preferably on the melody of the 'Chant du Départ', to be sung in the army camps and the theatres of Paris. Elated by the rate of progress, Napoleon was in sprightly mood.

> I have seen the coast of England from the heights of Amblete-use, as clearly as you can see the Calvary from the Tuileries. You can see the houses and the people moving. Here is a ditch that will be leaped by someone bold enough to try it.[25]

In its scale and complexity the great design was a worthy challenge to the great Corsican's talents - the dynamism of his will, his fixity of purpose, the reach and clarity of his intellect. As in everything, his imperious temperament demanded complete control. Subordinates were consulted but their advice was frequently ignored, and, as they realised, it was useless to argue. This was as much the case in nautical matters as in military ones. Though born of an island race, Napoleon knew little of the sea. Yet the sublime egoist is never one to be abashed by his own ignorance; equipped with a brain that could soak up ideas and information like a sponge, Napoleon always pursued his destiny in his own way. There was a kind of sense in this wilfulness. In the first place, he did not allow the planning to fall victim to the squabbles between army and navy that were to dog the German invasion plans of 1940 and many other amphibious expeditions throughout history. Moreover, Napoleon had few illusions about the calibre of most of his naval commanders; he realised that a decade of British naval supremacy had instilled in them an instinctive timidity that shrank from bold decisions.

The invasion coast now seethed with activity. Excavation work went ahead for twenty-four hours a day non-stop, with the town and harbour illuminated at night by torchlight. The army did most of the pick-and-shovel labour, digging out soil, loading it into wheelbarrows then into carts to be taken away for dumping. By January 1804, 13,000 men, 885 wheelbarrows and 28 wagons were

assigned to the Boulogne basin alone. At least the troops were paid
for their disagreeable toil, careful note being made in staff officers'
reports of what regiments had wages due to them. As the immediate locality was unable to supply enough skilled men like carpenters
and smiths, the prefects of neighbouring *départments* were ordered
to conscript extra workers. Wheelbarrows and carts were requisitioned locally while special consignments of axes, adzes and planes
were despatched from Paris. The nearby forests of Boulogne,
Desvres and Hardelot were pillaged for their timber to make
hutments, piles and planking. To interconnect the invasion ports
and link them to the camps and forests inland, other labour gangs
supervised by officers and engineers laid a network of new
roads.[26]

At the hub of it all was Boulogne, simultaneously a construction site, marine establishment and army cantonment. The aspect
of this hitherto obscure place and its environs underwent a sea-
change. The slopes around the town were patterned by steadily
advancing ranks of hutments which the troops built for themselves
out of mud, thatch and woodland timber. In time, the French
soldier's handiness in improvising a home from home gave the
encampments a permanent lived-in appearance. The huts, cosily
weather-proofed, each with its tiny vegetable plot, were arranged
regularly in avenues named after some famous victory or event. All
available buildings in the locality were requisitioned for conversion
into offices, workshops and hospitals. Barracks had to be built for
workmen brought in from outside, and stables filled the main
square to supplement the stabling provided by local convents and
churches, an indignity that only the town's principal church was
spared. In order to feed the newly swollen populace, magazines
were established for stockpiling the provisions that came in along
the inland waterways of north-eastern France - cheeses from
Holland, flour, rice, oats, salt provisions, wine and spirits.[27]

For the first and only time in the career of the Grand Army,
regular training figured large in the soldier's routine. Green
conscripts and old sweats drilled side by side to a pitch of effi-
ciency never seen in the hastily improvised hosts of republican

France. Troops also went through a programme of landing drill. Disembarkation exercises were conducted, troops being trained to sweep the shore with fire from the boats before landing. Moreover, nautical tyro though he was, Napoleon was aware that dizziness and seasickness could sap fighting spirit and lose him the battle for the beaches. He was insistent that every man should gain some experience aboard an invasion vessel, and parties of 25 at a time within each company took it in turns to live afloat both in harbour and out in the road. They helped the crew to work the boat and its guns, took swimming lessons, and, following the seven closely printed pages of the special manual (complete with glossary of nautical terms), learned how to row the smaller craft. Some of them were watched at their drill by a British agent:

> 'Tis curious to see them exercise the soldiers to learn them [sic] how to row; this takes place three times a day, and one hour each time, the officer standing in the stern with a speaking trumpet, giving the word of command. This marine officer teaches them first to handle the oars, second to bring them up on a levée together, third to make a stroke, fourth to bring the oar up again in a position for a second stroke; at all of which they practice continually.[28]

On November 4th 1803, at 3 a.m, the First Consul arrived at Boulogne for his second tour of inspection. In anticipation of the event, 39 vessels had left the harbour and formed a line in the St. Jean road. Before long, inquisitive enemy cruisers approached from the offing to investigate. The usual exchanges of fire took place, but nothing daunted, Napoleon, accompanied by Bruix and the Dutch admiral Verhuell put to sea in a pinnace to carry out his inspection. After some inconclusive skirmishing the British were driven off by the weight of artillery fire from the shore. It was one of many such desultory affrays but the author of the official account in the 'Moniteur' - was it, as often the case, the First Consul himself? - could not resist inflating it into a humiliating rout for the enemy.[29] The line held its station throughout the night; so far, so good. But the next day a stiff southerly breeze got up, later veering to a dangerous south-westerly, and the order to return to harbour was hoisted. In the ensuing scramble a vessel ran aground on the bank at the harbour entrance, thereby blocking it and forcing several others to spend a rough night out in the road. Others were driven out to sea where five were lost or forced round Cape Gris Nez to seek shelter in Calais. About this event the 'Moniteur' was silent. As usual Napoleon was ceaselessly on the prowl.

> On Friday I went to visit the harbour and arrived quite unexpectedly....at midnight I was still at it.
>
> On Sunday I spent the day visiting the new ports of Ambleteuse and Wimereux, making the troops there go through their manoeuvres.
>
> I spent the whole of yesterday at the harbour either on horseback or in a boat, so that I was soaked all day.
>
> Flotilla, port works, troops, coastal defences - all were subjected to sharp scutiny and there was no concealing the smallest error or omission.
>
> I went today to inspect the naval workshops in every detail; everything is in a most pitiable state. I've just had one of the barracks transformed into a naval arsenal and have to give orders about the most trivial matters.
>
> I notice that the soldiers have neither prickers, charge-extracators nor canteens on their knapsacks.
>
> With respect to one matter, no steps seem to have been taken at all - that is, the brandy that has to be loaded. We shall need 300,000 pints; forward half this quantity to Boulogne.

Mathieu Dumas, a Councillor of State, who was present at the debacle in the road later wrote, wise after the event, 'You might say that Fortune gave Bonaparte one of those premonitions she lavished on him before forsaking him'.[30]

It cannot be said that Fortune stinted her premonitions. When Napoleon made his next visit on New Year's Day 1804 conditions were too rough for the craft to venture out of the harbour. In subsequent months, when the worst of the winter was over, further attempts to keep a line permanently in the road were repeatedly frustrated by the weather. Even in the most favourable period, from May to October, it was only thought safe to venture out for 75 days in all.[31]

The lessons were plain. In the first place, Napoleon could no longer cherish any illusions about the magnitude of the gamble he was contemplating; his armada could well meet its doom at the hands of the Channel weather without the necessity for a solitary Briton to prime a single musket. More immediately, he would have to follow the advice of Decrès and Bruix, hitherto ignored, and increase the capacity in Boulogne. Most significantly of all it was now clear just how dangerously protracted an operation the crossing would be. It was never possible for more than 200 vessels to clear the harbour in a single tide, which meant that a total of six tides - 72 hours - would be needed to get the entire proposed Boulogne contingent of over 1,100 out to sea.[32]

Like others before and since, Napoleon had begun to realise that the invasion of Britain was not as straightforward as it appeared. Of all the operations of war, seaborne landings are among those most prone to disaster, as the names of Gallipoli and Dieppe in our own century remind us. For the would-be invader of Britain the problem presents itself in its most intractable form, since the Royal Navy was in secure command of the sea and possessed a long-established strategy for blocking all such attempts. Despite his involvement in two previous projects, it is doubtful whether Napoleon had hitherto given much thought to what was involved.

From the time when Muskeyn's project for a flotilla invasion was first seized on by the Directory, it remains an abiding mystery why French planners persisted in the delusion that the operation could succeed without naval cover; even more baffling is the enthusiasm of the French marine, who should at least have known better. Such wishful thinking can only be explained by the mystical conviction that revolutionary *élan* would somehow carry an army across the Channel in the face of enemy squadrons rather as the same commodity had swept all before it on battlefields across Europe. Despite the navy's involvement, it was clearly conceived as a military operation that would happen to be conducted at sea, rather like an ambitious river crossing; indeed, Admiral Lacrosse, the commander of the Boulogne flotilla, confidently affirmed that, given the right conditions, a Channel passage would be as straight-forward as traversing the Rhine or any other large river. Whether this opinion sprang from genuine conviction or a servile compliance with the master's perceived wishes is difficult to know. Equally hard to fathom is whether Napoleon himself ever really believed it. Certainly the initial planning was for an unescorted crossing, with discussions on the relative merits of favourable conditions - a calm day, or fog, or darkness. 'Eight hours of darkness favourable to us,' Napoleon pronounced, 'would decide the fate of the world.'[33]

But though such cloudy thinking may have satisfied his predecessors, it could not long survive Napoleon's scrutiny. The implications of what had been learned at Boulogne were not to be ignored. There was virtually no possibility of his vast armada being able to cross the Channel without being annihilated by enemy squadrons, if only because it would have to take the form of six 'waves', one each tide over a 72-hour period. He was driven to recognise what generations of British seamen had always known, that the key to the invasion of Britain was the command of the Channel. Incredulous British commanders could not bring themselves to believe that an attempt would be made without it. Whilst in charge of a special anti-invasion squadron in 1801, Nelson had written, 'This boat business may be part of a great plan of invasion; it can never be the only one.' 'We may rest assured that the enemy have no intention of invading us without a superior sea force,' pronounced Lord Keith in 1803. 'It is a mere farce to suppose that we are to be taken by fishing boats and hoys.'[34]

Thus Britain's hold on the Channel must somehow be loosened. To achieve this by an overall challenge to her maritime supremacy was very much a long-term proposition as the French navy of 1803 was only a third the size of its adversary. It would entail a huge programme of expansion that Napoleon himself estimated would need a decade to fulfil, and even then would probably require the co-opting of the navies of allies such as Holland and Spain decisively to overtop British naval might. Napoleon did not shrink from such an undertaking; if flotillas failed, Britain must be challenged and crushed with her own weapons on her own element. Indeed, since the renewal of war, a start had already been made, with Antwerp earmarked as the new great French naval arsenal. But all this lay in the future. In the short run another way had to be found by using the inferior means to hand.

At the beginning of December 1803, Napoleon's correspondence shows a flicker of interest in an idea that showed a way forward. When asked for an assessment of the feasibility of a surprise crossing, Admiral Ganteaume, the naval prefect of Toulon, counselled against it. Instead, he offered an alternative; a small fast squadron might be able to slip through the British blockade, lay a false trail to lead enemy forces astray and hold the Channel long enough for an invasion to take place. This kind of proposal was far from new. In the period after the Seven Years' War, the governments of Bourbon France, smarting from defeat at the hands of Britain and bent on revenge, had worked up a whole catalogue of intricate diversionary ploys all with the same object of dissipating the enemy's naval strength away from the Channel to prepare the way for invasion. 'Citizen General Ganteaume, you have anticipated my intentions,' was the reply.[35] Whether or not this was true - Napoleon did not like giving the credit to others - a chord had been struck. Here was something he understood: the subtle contrivances of deception lay at the very heart of his practice of war. But the initial spurt of enthusiasm quickly died, and the notion apparently joined the many thousands of speculative fancies that flared briefly in that teeming brain before being tossed aside. Shortly after the turn of the year the invasion project was thrust into the background by other events. However, the germ - the co-ordination of flotilla and fleet - was not forgotten but filed away in the infallible Napoleonic memory to await disinterral when the moment was right.

The matter that thrust the invasion and all else from Napoleon's attention was the very survival of his own person and régime. The Consulate was the government of a single man, and one who did not lack enemies: on the right the Royalists, for whom he was the embodiment of a hated republic; and on the left the Jacobins, who detested him as the tyrant who had betrayed it. One August night in 1803, a squat, barrel-chested Breton was secretly put ashore from the Royal Navy brig 'Vincejo' at the foot of cliffs near Biville, between Dieppe and Tréport. His name was Cadoudal, but he was more commonly known as Georges. The name already possessed a fearful significance for Napoleon. Georges was the agent of the Comte d'Artois, the younger brother of the executed Louis XVI and presently ensconced at Holyrood House on a British pension. His mission was financed by British secret service funds and its objective was to draw together royalists and Jacobins in a conspiracy to 'kidnap' the First Consul and restore the monarchy. However, there is little doubt that it was, in fact, as assassination plot; Georges was a ruthless and dedicated killer who had come within an ace of blowing up Napoleon's coach in a Paris street on Christmas Eve, 1800. In the view of monarchist Europe, Napoleon was a parvenu: his régime had no legitimacy, and the code of behaviour between rulers simply did not apply in dealing with him; even so, complicity in such thuggery shows how the invasion threat had lent a paranoid intensity to British fear and loathing of the Corsican ogre.

The ceaseless snooping of Napoleon's police soon revealed that something was afoot. Two of Cadoudal's henchmen, interrogated under torture, spoke of a plot involving 'a prince' and two republican generals. Meanwhile the net closed inexorably around Georges, and he was arrested in March 1804. Napoleon's mounting anxiety provoked a vengeful rage. 'Am I a dog to be beaten to death in the streets?....They attack my very person. I'll give them war for war.' The thinnest of evidence appeared to identify the Duc

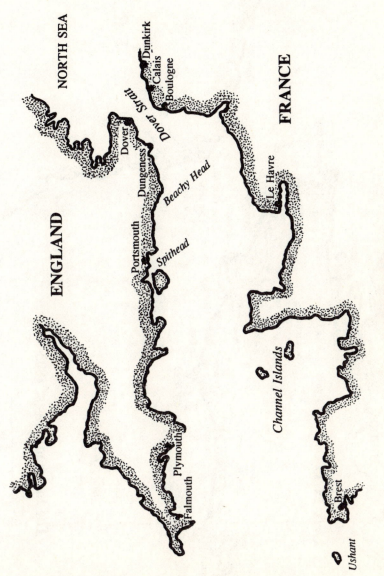

NORTH SEA

Dunkirk
Calais
Boulogne

FRANCE

Dover

Dover Strait

Dungeness

Beachy Head

Le Havre

ENGLAND

Portsmouth

Spithead

Channel Islands

Plymouth

Falmouth

Brest

Ushant

The English Channel

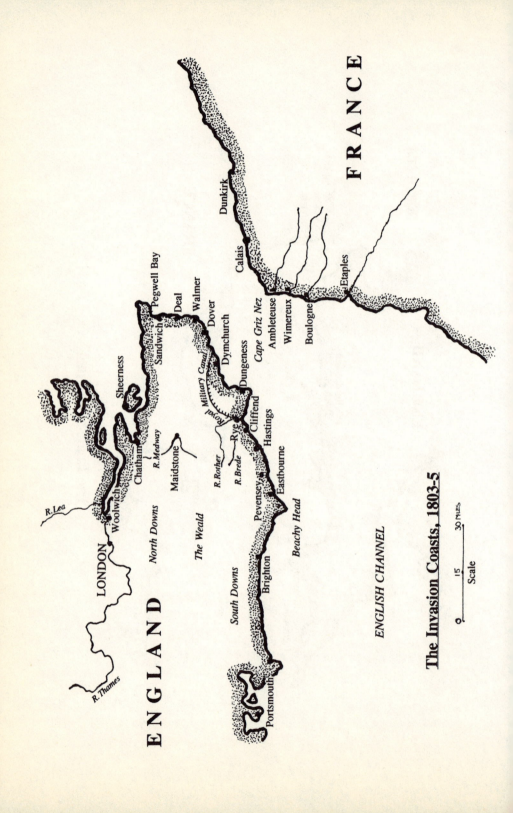

FRANCE

ENGLAND

LONDON

R. Lea

R. Thames

Woolwich

Sheerness

Chatham

R. Medway

Maidstone

North Downs

The Weald

South Downs

Brighton

Portsmouth

Beachy Head

Eastbourne

Pevensey

Hastings

Cliffend

Rye

R. Brede

R. Rother

Royal Military Canal

Dungeness

Dymchurch

Cape Griz Nez

Dover

Walmer

Deal

Sandwich

Pegwell Bay

Dunkirk

Calais

Ambleteuse

Wimereux

Boulogne

Etaples

ENGLISH CHANNEL

The Invasion Coasts, 1803-5

0   15   30 MILES

Scale

d'Enghien, the grandson of the Prince de Condé, as the 'prince' and in the early hours of March 14th a detachment of French dragoons crossed the Rhine and kidnapped the hapless Bourbon from his home in the nearby principality of Baden. Despite clear indications that the evidence linking d'Enghien with the plot was garbled, the First Consul was set on teaching the royalists a lesson they would never forget. Within the space of a few hours d'Enghien was hauled before a military commission on charges of being an emigré in British pay and bearing arms against France, found guilty and shot in the ditch of the Château of Vincennes. At the time the incident sent a frisson of horror through the courts of Europe but only one ruler's voice was raised in public condemnation, that of Tsar Alexander of Russia. In France itself, on the other hand, the liquidation of a scion of the house of Bourbon actually strengthened Napoleon's position. It was seen as a final slamming of the door on any compromise with the royalists and the whole episode gave a powerful impetus to the burgeoning call for a hereditary Napoleonic monarchy. 'We have done more than we hoped,' Cadoudal is supposed to have said as he awaited execution, 'we meant to give France a king, and we have given her an Emperor.' Whatever the Breton's share in it, by a senate decree of May 1804, the government was entrusted to Napoleon I, Emperor of the French.[36]

With the vessel of state once more set fair, Napoleon returned to unfinished business. On May 25th, a lengthy, elaborately detailed set of orders was drawn up - the scrawled signature is now 'Napoleon' instead of 'Bonaparte' - for Admiral Latouche-Tréville, the commander of the Toulon squadron. Latouche was Napoleon's favourite admiral, who had the fire and resourcefulness, rarely to be found in his colleagues, that were required for the execution of an audacious new plan. As the first essay of Napoleon the strategist, it is worthy of note. In essence it was the one of three alternative schemes earlier put to Ganteaume that the latter had most favoured. Speed and timing were the key. Latouche was to break out of Toulon, pass the Gibraltar strait and head north for the Channel, picking up the Rochefort squadron on the way. The combined force would then skirt Ushant to avoid Cornwallis, who would be held to his station by simulated preparations for an Irish expedition. Finally, Latouche would take temporary control of the Channel and protect the invasion corridor while a crossing was made. The Emperor was hazy about nautical details but specified minutely the means of misleading the enemy about when and where the squadron was to sail, the admiral being urged to take every opportunity of laying false trails to keep the enemy guessing.[37] All thoughts of a winter crossing were now abandoned; this had to be a summer operation as bad weather would wreck the fine timing necessary for the conjunction of fleet and flotilla.

The beginnings of comprehensive invasion strategy can now be discerned. Britain's navy was large because it had to be; it was entrusted not only with the nation's security but with the multifarious task of protecting her far-flung commercial interests to which any sizable French squadron at sea posed a dangerously unpredictable threat. A force leaving Toulon unobserved might have one of several objectives: to the east the possibilities included Sicily, Sardinia, the Morea and Egypt; westward, once past the Gibraltar strait into the Atlantic, it might go south to the Cape, west to the Caribbean, or north to England or Ireland. A bemused enemy would be tempted into dispersing his strength in chasing shadows. Handled with boldness and cunning - and, it must be admitted, blessed with a generous helping of luck - the squadron might be able to exploit the situation long enough to accomplish its mission.

In July Napoleon began another five-week tour of the invasion ports to assess the general state of readiness on the spot. It was his first visit as Emperor and the arrival at Boulogne was elaborately stage-managed to accord with the new imperial dignity. With every street and vessel bedecked with flags and the massed port batteries thundering their salutes, Napoleon made his way through cheering crowds along a street newly named Rue Impériale, passing under twelve triumphal arches each symbolising one of his victories to a specially erected Temple of Immortality. Boarding a boat, he went out to inspect the new forts and a line drawn up in the road, flirting with disaster at one point by rashly insisting on proceeding north of Wimereux in the face of an approaching squall and enemy ships loitering in the vicinity.

That evening a north-westerly wind set in and rapidly rose to gale force. The return signal went up and everything in the road ran for the harbour entrance. Many did not make it. By the time the gale had blown itself out just before dawn, 13 vessels had been lost, nine run aground and others driven south were forced to seek shelter in Étaples and St. Valéry. The official estimate of men lost was 40, but it is probable that the figure was much higher. The Emperor himself, pacing the foreshore in impotent fury, was a witness to the whole débâcle. Characteristically he was coy about the scale of the losses. In one letter he mentions only two vessels lost, and an account sent to Josephine was all hazy self-dramatizing:

> The wind having got up during the night, one of our gunboats in the road dragged her anchor and had been driven on to the rocks a mile from Boulogne. I thought it would be lost with all hands but we managed to save everyone aboard. It was an impressive scene; the boom of the alarm guns, the shore lit up with flares, the sea roaring in fury, the whole night spent in suspense over the fate of those poor wretches. My soul was poised between eternity, the ocean and the night. At five in the morning it all cleared, everything was saved and I went to bed with the sensation of an epic, romantic dream. It was an experience that would have drawn me into pondering my inescapable loneliness had not fatigue and a thorough soaking wiped out all needs other than sleep.[38]

The light of day revealed the aftermath to the more prosaic gaze of a British cruiser:

> ....the entire coast between Boulogne and Portel was covered with wagons and soldiers, clearing away wrecks, and an immensity of small boats were engaged in dredging the bottom for different articles. In the space of fifty yards close under

Portel, there was a gun-brig and four luggers dashed to pieces.[39]

Once more 'the ditch' had issued an even louder warning growl to the would-be invader, this time in high summer as if to rub in the lesson the more unmercifully. It is likely that about this time Napoleon had the dies made in Paris for a new commemorative medal. On one side it bore his laurel-wreathed head in classical profile and on the other, a representation of Hercules (France) throttling a sea-god (Britain) together with the legend "Descente en Angleterre, Frappé à Londres en 1804'. The Channel had given its own devastatingly ironical reply to this extravagant piece of Napoleonic presumption. But the Emperor was never one to brood on reverses or ponder ironies. Once more he threw himself into his usual hectic round of inspection.

Napoleon had set up his invasion headquarters in a château at Pont-de-Briques, a village a few miles inland from Boulogne, but he would often avail himself of the more basic comforts of a modest wooden pavilion specially built for him on the edge of the cliff of the Tour d'Odre, from which vantage point he could survey the harbour, roadstead and camps below. In a busy programme the Emperor allowed himself one piece of grand ceremonial on August 16th, the day after his 35th birthday, to make presentations of his new-fangled Legion of Honour. In a natural amphitheatre above Boulogne near the spot where the column of the Grand Army still stands in commemoration, the entire Army of England was drawn up by columns in a fan-like formation stretching away to the rim of the slope. At the focal point stood the historic throne of Dagobert garlanded with the army's banners, on which Napoleon took his place shortly after midday to the noise of fanfares and cannonades. As their names were read out, those to be honoured came forward to the throne. The Emperor recited the oath, to which all chorused with a main voice, 'We swear it'. Then each received the modest enamelled star with its red ribbon from the Emperor's hand. It was a thrilling piece of theatre put on by a consummate though unillusioned master of the genre. 'It is with such baubles that men are led,' was his cynical justification for the institution of the Republic's greatest honour.

Offshore, the Royal Navy kept its usual vigil and, finding itself engaged in hotter and more frequent engagements than usual, correctly surmised the reason:

> For three successive days about the middle of August we were warmly and closely engaged each day with an immense force of the enemy's flotilla....The enemy, although he did not venture from under the shelter of his batteries, was unusually bold, and boats having officers of rank on board them were seen frequently to pass along their line. From these circumstances it was thought, and not without probability, that Bonaparte was present at the time and that, under the eye of their newly-elected emperor, they fought with a resolution and boldness unknown to them before.[40]

Napoleon found himself observing one of these skirmishes from an unexpectedly close quarter. When Bruix sent out a detachment from the line to chase away a sloop hovering provocatively nearby, waiting British ships immediately pounced. Having watched all this with mounting excitement from the shore, Napoleon set off in a pinnace with Berthier, Bruix, Decrès, Mortier and Soult towards the scene of the action. The British broke away to attack the line not far from the Emperor's boat, from which he sent an urgent signal to press home the attack. Eventually the British vessels broke off and retreated with the loss of a cutter. After his first whiff for some years of the genuine smoke of battle, Napoleon was fired with euphoria.

> The information I have states that the enemy had 60 wounded and 12 to 15 killed. The frigate was badly knocked about.
>
> The minor engagement in which I was involved on the eve of my departure from Boulogne has had an enormous effect in England. It has produced real alarm.[41]

Though, in truth, hardly likely to set their lordships of the Admiralty trembling in their shoes, the incident did at least go some way to offset the disaster in the road that had earlier cast its shadow over the visit.

By the time he left Boulogne for a tour of the Rhineland on August 26th, it is likely that Napoleon had already received the news that Latouche-Tréville had died of fever aboard his flagship 'Bucentaure' in Toulon six days previously. In effect, this spelled the end of hope for invasion in the foreseeable future, since no name exactly leapt out of the uninspiring list of French flag officers as a replacement. Latouche's death had a further significance. It underscored the uncomfortable fact that responsibility for the success of the Channel crossing was now in the uncertain hands of a navy in which the late admiral's qualities were thin on the ground; the chances of even the greatest army in Europe and an armada 2,000 strong prevailing without a commander in the Latouche mould were far from encouraging.

The fact that for all practical purposes the invasion was in abeyance did not inhibit Napoleon from dreaming up a grandiose new design in the following month involving the French and Dutch fleets in simultaneous invasions of England and Ireland, combined with forays to the Caribbean and West Africa for good measure. Such a fantastical farrago prompts speculation about some ulterior purpose, and there is indeed evidence to suppose that some deep game was in play to feed disinformation to the enemy.[42] Nevertheless, for all its absurdity, it can be seen as marking another step on the road towards a fully-fledged invasion plan. We observe for the first time the deployment of more than one squadron, and actual thrusts rather than feints at secondary targets to draw the enemy's attention away from the main objective. We shall see how these elements were woven into the finished invasion strategy that was to emerge in a few months' time.

Napoleon's chief preoccupation in the last few months of 1804 was with his status as Emperor of the French. There was an imperial court of an appropriate splendour to create, with its protocol, aristocracy and army of functionaries. The attitude of the other courts of Europe had to be canvassed at least for form's sake, though Napoleon himself was largely indifferent to the reaction of his peers. He had to deal with the clamorous importunings of the Bonaparte clan for ever more honour and wealth, and decide the knotty question of the succession. Moreover, he was determined from the start to secure the imprimatur of the Papacy on his title. Content with nothing less than a coronation in Notre Dame in the presence of Pope Pius VII himself, it was only after long haggling with the Vatican that Napoleon got his way. On December 2nd, a chilly but clear winter's day, he rode resplendent with Josephine in a gilded coach through cheering crowds to Notre Dame where, at the climax of a magnificent three-hour ceremony, he crowned himself with the gold laurel wreath and then - the moment immortalised in David's famous painting - placed the Empress's crown on Josephine's brow. The old monarchies of Europe were stonily unimpressed; having hitherto despised Napoleon as an upstart they now regarded him as an usurper to boot, and the British government used the first available opportunity to get in a calculated snub. When the Emperor sent a New Year peace proposal to Britain, addressed, much to the king's indignation, to 'Monsieur Mon Frère', the rebuff that came back was signed by the Foreign Secretary, and addressed, as ever, to 'The Head of the French Government'.

Meanwhile, on the invasion coast all was quiet. During the autumn progress on the port works slackened and, with the onset of winter, things ground to a complete halt. The works were still nowhere near completion. As winter gales buffeted the Channel, its encroaching sands stealthily infiltrated the freshly-dug tidal basins, reversing the labours of eighteen months. The routine monotony of the Royal Navy's vigil was broken but rarely, though one December day provided a welcome diversion in the form of the coronation celebrations ashore - the crash of saluting artillery, the flotilla and camps aflutter with banners and flags, and illuminations and fireworks lighting up the night. Otherwise there was little activity to be seen with only a thin trickle of invasion craft continuing to slip into the assembly ports. The process of moving the Dutch flotilla to Ambleteuse came to an abrupt stop with Verhuell's command dispersed between Flushing, Ostend and Dunkirk. On shore the troops read the signs and dug in for winter. The ills that afflict an army first sharpened up for action and then condemned to sit indefinitely on its collective backside soon began to surface. Discipline slackened and despite tough punishments desertion lists grew longer, while a rash of duelling broke out among officers. It became increasingly difficult to get unwilling troops on board vessels going out into the road and once there to prevent them, officers included, from sneaking ashore. All the naval and military commanders left their posts at the approach of the coronation and stayed in Paris throughout the long festivities. In Forfait's words, 'No-one believes in the invasion any more'.[43]

The standstill on the invasion coast appeared to endorse the view of a growing school of thought in European capitals that Napoleon was in reality intent on a Continental war rather than an invasion of Britain. A convinced exponent of this belief was the Prussian ambassador, who as long ago as May 1804 had written to Berlin, 'A war on the Continent would redeem his prestige, compromised by the invasion project which had been announced with such a flourish'. In December he opined, 'A continental war offers both the general and the statesman opportunities much less risky than a seaborne attempt on England'.

A marked increase in tension between France and Austria appeared to confirm prognostications. There was no good cheer in Napoleon's New Day message to the Austrian ambassador: 'I answer threat with threat. If the Emperor Francis arms, so shall I'. And if we are to believe a not entirely reliable witness, the Emperor finally revealed all with a theatrical flourish to the Council of State on January 17.

> To be able, in peacetime, to assemble such an army, to have 20,000 artillery horses and complete baggage trains, some pretext had to be found to concentrate them without alarming the continental powers, and this was provided by the project for the invasion of England....I have not been able to tell you this in the last two years, but now you can see my point.[44]

All along then, if the Emperor is to be believed, the invasion preparations had been nothing but a blind, a cover for a long-laid plan to strike against Austria. The Austrian diplomat Metternich declared that Napoleon made the same claim to him several years later. But we should not take this disclosure of god-like far-sightedness too seriously. With an army equally well placed for a thrust across the Channel or the Rhine, it was natural for Napoleon to exploit the double threat for all it was worth by deliberately promoting uncertainty about his intentions - it was, after all, an oft-noted ploy in the master's repertoire.

With the invasion preparations at a stand, the pressure on Britain relaxed. But letting his opponents off the hook was not Napoleon's way. Of all the rag-bag of operations concocted in September, the most promising appeared to be an expedition to the Caribbean with the object of striking at this vital limb of Britain's commercial empire. In the last months of 1804 the squadrons at Toulon and Rochefort were made ready for sea. Latouche-Tréville's successor to the command of the Toulon squadron was Pierre Charles Jean Baptiste Silvestre, Comte de Villeneuve. It was an appointment made very much *faute de mieux* and appears to have owed more to a lifelong friendship with Decrès than any manifest merit. In an otherwise undistinguished career, Villeneuve's sole claim to distinction lay in making good the escape of the rear division of the French fleet from the havoc of Aboukir Bay six years previously.

On January 11th 1805, Admiral Missiessy slipped out of Rochefort under cover of thick snow. A week later, after a three-week delay due to headwinds, Villeneuve left Toulon with 21 ships of the line while Nelson was sheltering from westerly gales under the lee of Sardinia. But disaster quickly struck; a gale got up during the first night and in Villeneuve's words:

> My ships looked well enough in Toulon but when the storm rose, things suddenly changed. The seamen were not used to storms: they were lost amongst the mass of soldiers: these lay about the decks stricken with sea-sickness. It was impossible to work the ships, so that yards broke and sails were carried

away. Our losses were due as much to clumsiness and inexperi-
ence as to defective materials supplied by the arsenals.

The squadron was scattered and Villeneuve took the decision to
return to port. The abortive sortie had a depressing predictability:
the poor-quality dockyard supplies that had bedevilled the French
navy since the Revolution, inexperienced and unseasoned crews,
and an admiral all too eager to scurry back to safety. It did not
bode well for the grand design that was perhaps already ripening
in Napoleon's mind. As Nelson wrote:

> Bonaparte has often made his brags that our fleet would be
> worn out by keeping the sea - that his was kept in order, and
> increasing by staying in port; but now he finds, I fancy, if
> Emperors hear truth, that his fleet suffers more in one night
> than ours in one year.[45]

Chapter Three

The Wooden Walls

Whenever Napoleon happened to look down on Boulogne and its surrounding cantonments from his cliff-top eyrie on the Tour d'Odre, unsettling presences were nearly always at hand to spoil the picture somewhat for him. Even when the Channel mists closed in, he knew they were still present. On a reasonably clear day, there they lay in plain sight - the sloops, brigs and cutters of the Royal Navy's Boulogne squadron ceaselessly on watch just out of artillery range, waiting to swoop in for the kill if any French vessel should stray incautiously beyond the cover of the shore batteries or standing insolently close in to spy on what was happening ashore.

If it was one of those days when the Channel is free of haze and the cliffs of Dover are etched in gleaming outline on the other side of the Strait, the Imperial gaze could pick out, about ten miles out to the north-west, the tiny flecks of white indicating the squadron's main body, ready to move in if the French dared to sally forth in strength. Only when the hardest westerlies blew down the Channel did they disappear and run for the Downs or Dungeness, knowing that the gales from which they sheltered would safely bottle up the invasion flotilla in its harbours until their return. Since the renewal of hostilities, these ships had watched the tide of troop encampments lapping over the slopes around the town, the ant-like swarms transforming the face of the port and the steady flow of invasion craft arriving to swell the throng within. As the Royal Navy's probing point they served as a nagging reminder to Napoleon on his Channel sojourns of the instrument that he had to beat or outwit before he could storm the island citadel.

For a dominant sea-power like Britain, blockade of the enemy coast is the natural, indeed the inevitable, choice of strategic weapon and by 1803 the Royal Navy had had nearly nine years of continuous war to perfect its workings. Within weeks of the renewal of hostilities, from Toulon to the Texel, British ships were once more in place outside the enemy's principal harbours and ranging the coastline in pursuit of his commercial shipping. But the kingpin of Britain's defence against invasion was to be found, not in the Channel under Napoleon's eye but far to the west, in the storm-beaten waters off the Brittany coast where Channel and Atlantic meet. This was the Channel fleet. The fleet's chief duty, fixed half a century previously by Lord Anson, was to guard the approaches to this vital seaway. The job was doubly essential to Britain's survival, as the Channel was not only the likeliest avenue for invasion by an enemy fleet but a busy conduit for merchant shipping. In these waters half of Europe's trade dispersed or made landfall to and from the Mediterranean, the Caribbean, the Cape and points east - and most of it was British. The fleet's station was off the chief French naval arsenal of Brest, whose location on the southern approach to the Channel posed the most immediate threat to British control of her home waters, and thus made it, of all the French ports, the prime focus for blockade.

In 1800 the traditional method of blockading Brest had been radically overhauled by a new commander, Lord St. Vincent. Hitherto, the main body of the fleet under his predecessors Lord Howe and Lord Bridport had been stationed at Spithead 150 miles to the north-east, with only a small contingent cruising off Brest itself, though well out to sea, and a light squadron close in to the entrance. The fallibility of this easy-going arrangement had been embarrassingly shown up more than once. At the end of 1796, a French expedition to Ireland had escaped from Brest on a south-east wind that kept Bridport and half his fleet struggling to work up the three miles from Spithead to St. Helens before it could make its way down-Channel, by which time all contact with the enemy had been lost. In 1799, when an even larger squadron was once more allowed to slip away and Bridport duly set off in pursuit in the direction of Ireland, his quarry was meanwhile making good his escape south towards the Mediterranean. St. Vincent's aim was to put a stop to such mishaps with a close blockade by the entire fleet. Flying in the face of conventional Service wisdom that conditions off Brest were too arduous for line-of-battle ships to maintain a continuous presence, it demanded all the iron will with which St. Vincent had earlier shaken up the Mediterranean command.

There was no denying that these waters were the most pitiless of stations for both ships and men. Brest itself lies within a deep cavity in the coastline that provides a vast reach of deep-water anchorage. Leading from the harbour road to the open sea is a passage bounded by high cliffs known as the Goulet, along which nowadays the nuclear submarines of the *force de dissuasion* nose discreetly in and out. At its seaward end the Goulet widens into two capacious anchorages, Bertheaume Bay and Camaret Bay, where shipping assembled prior to sailing. Beyond, the coastline opens out to the 22-mile-wide gape of the Iroise Channel, the main approach to the port. At each extremity of the Iroise, two narrow channels, the Passage du Four to the north and the Passage du Raz to the south, thread their way between the mainland and a maze of offshore islets and shoals.

St. Vincent kept an inshore squadron at the mouth of the Goulet, with frigates standing well into the entrance while the main body patrolled between Ushant and the Black Rocks some eight miles to the south. A 20th-century edition of the Admiralty's 'Channel Pilot' gives seafarers a crisply-worded warning about the area:

> Sailing vessels should in all circumstances give Ushant and its dangers a wide berth. Mariners approaching Ushant should be on their guard against the danger of being set eastward of their reckoning, and must exercise the greatest caution in rounding it. That island is surrounded by dangers in all directions; rocks are numerous and some lie far from land; fogs and thick weather are not uncommon; the tidal streams are strong, and the extent of their influence seaward undetermined.[1]

To compound this daunting catalogue, the prevailing westerly winds made the Brittany coast a dead lee shore.

To pit clumsy line-of-battle ships against such a conspiracy of elements needed the highest degree of seamanship and endurance. The strain was unremitting; strong tidal currents forced ships to keep under way 24 hours a day, while all around lurked uncharted rocks and shoals unknown even to the conscripted French pilots. Though ferocious Biscay storms taxed ships and men to the limit, captains' requests to put up for Torbay for repairs were granted grudgingly, and only if the work could not be carried out at sea. Six days was the maximum period allowed in port unless a mast needed shifting, while officers were forbidden to spend the night ashore or go further than three miles from the beach. Otherwise ships kept their station with the fleet, fed and watered by victuallers and water hoys from the south-western ports, an unfailing supply line which together with other measures to maintain seamens' health succeeded in keeping sick-lists short throughout the long months at sea. By the time St. Vincent took charge of the Admiralty in 1801 and handed over his command to Admiral William Cornwallis, he had demonstrated that with discipline and organisation what had hitherto been regarded as impossible could actually be made to work.[2]

As Britain prepared for war in the spring of 1803, nowhere was the tempo more hectic than at Portsmouth and Plymouth, the fleet's bases. By the middle of April the big two-and three-deckers were beginning to congregate in Cawsand Bay as they completed refitting and taking on stores. On the 17th, Cornwallis sailed from Torbay with five ships to resume his old station, leaving orders for the rest of the fleet to follow as soon as they were made ready. The blockading regime was as punishing as ever:

> ....we know they have four- or five-and-twenty great ships, which makes it necessary to be alert and keep our eyes open at all times, [wrote Vice Admiral Collingwood, commanding the inshore squadron], I therefore bid adieu to snug beds and comfortable naps at night, never lying down but in my clothes....I take the utmost pains to prevent all access, and an

anxious time I have of it, what with tides and rocks, which
have more danger in them than a battle once a week.[3]

Within a few months Cornwallis had the chance to show the steel
that proved him a worthy successor to St. Vincent when the
Channel was battered by a series of fearsome gales during the
winter of 1803-04. While the inshore squadron was able to ride out
the worst in Douarnenez Bay to the south of the Goulet, the
majority of the main body was forced back in driblets to Cawsand
or Torbay with stove-in gunports, wreckage up aloft and pumps
hard at work. By the end of 1803, the average number of ships off
Brest was down to as few as half-a-dozen and even Cornwallis
himself made brief appearances in Torbay in the course of
December and January. The Admiral's determination to keep such
sojourns as brief as possible had earned him his nickname of 'Billy
Blue' after his habit of keeping the Blue Peter flying, signalling
imminent departure the moment the weather moderated. Yet while
westerlies lashed the Channel, the enemy's ships were blockaded
even more securely than was possible by the best efforts of the
Royal Navy. The strategic advantage to France of Brest's location
was offset by the severest of drawbacks in the age of sail: the
prevailing westerly winds on the Breton coast were foul for leaving
port, and any succeeding change that allowed the French to sail
would also bring the Channel fleet out of its temporary refuge back
on to its station.

Though the blockade of Brest was as tight as human
contrivance and tenacity could make it, Cornwallis and his
colleagues were aware that it could never be infallible. The
enemy's *chasse-marées*, loaded with naval supplies, continued to
slip past the inshore squadron into the Goulet. As regards the
chances of a successful enemy sortie, seamen, knowing their
element to be a fickle mistress, were not by nature given to
complacency. Collingwood observed,

To block them up in this port effectually I do not think is
practicable. In the varieties of weather which at this season are

becoming more common, opportunities will occur in which no vigilance can prevent their escape.[4]

Lord Keith concurred:

> Brest has been watched by great officers, and in general meritoriously, but it is impossible to prevent an enemy from slipping out a force from a place which is defended by rocks and has three passages.[5]

In particular, a commonly-feared eventuality was that Cornwallis might be blown out to sea by persistent easterlies that would allow a French squadron to make good its escape unseen before he could return to his station. If the French track was up-Channel, Lord Keith pointed out that they were in a better position than hitherto to co-ordinate such a move.

> The times are different since the days of Elizabeth; our enemy is more active; there is a telegraph from Brest to the Texel; the fleet quitting port might be announced along shore in five hours.[*]
>   ....On its appearance with a fair wind on any part of the coast, passing up-Channel, the intelligence might be carried with equal rapidity; and a continuance in the Downs or Margate forty-eight hours would enable a great force to be sent across the water and take a situation until more arrived.[6]

Furthermore, once the enemy had broken out, his objective might well be far from clear, as the Admiralty warned Cornwallis:

> ....it is probable that they will endeavour to mislead you by adopting in their outset a course different from their ultimate intention.[7]

---

[*] Keith was not quite correct. Signal stations on the French coast did not form a continuous chain. Signal communication from Brest to the eastern end of the Channel, though speedy enough, was indirect - initially along the telegraph line to Paris, thence along another line terminating at Boulogne. [Wilson: The Old Telegraphs. (1976).]

Life aboard the Channel fleet was a mind-numbing round of boredom and fatigue, enlivened only by the occasional expedition to cut out an enemy vessel or demolish a signal station. Yet commanders had to be forever on the *qui vive*, as hardly a month went by without reports of enemy activity brought in by the cutter that daily penetrated into the Goulet, or gleaned from some other intelligence source. We have already seen that the British presence outside his chief ports did not inhibit Napoleon from concocting ambitious naval plans, if only to perpetuate a war of nerves. Throughout the latter half of 1803, preparations in France's Biscay ports kept an invasion scare on simmer in Britain for several months, while early in the new year Napoleon toyed with another Irish expedition to sail from Brest with a contingent of United Irishmen. The Irish card was kept in play throughout 1804, to form part of the bizarre multiple operation of September mentioned in the previous chapter.

Continuous blockade aggravated the French navy's inadequacies, a decline which Napoleon was well aware of. The proud traditions of the Bourbon navy that had wrested control of the seas from Britain during the American war and made possible the independence of the rebel colonies were no more, having been snuffed out in the early egalitarian frenzy of the Revolution. The élite corps of seaman-gunners had been disbanded and the officer corps savagely purged, its members dismissed, guillotined or driven into exile. To fill the gaps junior officers were thrust up to flag rank and warrant officers and merchant marine officers found themselves commanding ships of the line. The arsenals were neglected so that French ships, ironically superior in design to their British counterparts, were forced to put to sea with poor quality masts and yards, canvas and cordage. French matelots tended to be of inferior quality compared to their British counterparts, since the Royal Navy had swept the seas clean of France's merchant shipping and so deprived her of her nursery of seamen. The sorry record of the republican navy, a chronicle of reversals and defeats, redeemed only by a dogged bravery in adversity, was the inevitable consequence.

When Napoleon came to power in 1799, the navy was included in his overall drive to remedy the derelictions of previous republican governments. A new system of administration for the navy arsenals was introduced, a start was made on replenishing the stocks of dockyard supplies and the officer corps was overhauled.[8] Yet for all Napoleon's dreams of a great renaissance in French naval power priceless reserves of esprit de corps and expertise, once thrown away, could not easily be replaced. Perhaps the greatest casualty of revolutionary upheaval, and one the blockade intended to corrode further, was morale. The greater skill and experience that bred an easy self-confidence in the British Navy tended to inculcate a corresponding timidity in their French opponents. Long confinement in port not only perpetuated this sense of inferiority but also gave it objective substance. Ships were not tested at sea, while officers and crews were denied opportunities to gain the sea-going and fighting experience that alone would redress the balance.

Within the Channel itself, the Navy spread its blockading forces to cover the entire reach of the enemy coast as far as the Texel. To the south-west a squadron based at the Channel Islands, watching Le Havre and the Seine estuary, formed a link between the Channel and North Sea commands. This latter, running from Selsey Bill to the north-eastern tip of Scotland and thus including the crucial invasion sector, was the responsibility of Admiral Lord Keith. Keith, a dour Scot who had amassed a vast fortune from prize-money, was one of Britain's many supremely professional seamen whose accomplishments were of the kind that did not attract public acclaim. When he hoisted his flag in May 1803, the Admiralty put at his disposal a total of 38 ships, mostly frigates and smaller vessels, with a few ageing ships of the line to be used as blockships in the Thames estuary. His headquarters was at the Downs, where he flew his flag on 'Monarch', though he spent most of his time ashore at his house at East Cliff near Margate. From there he deployed his forces in accordance with his instructions: to keep watch on the enemy coast from Le Havre to the Texel, blockade it, prevent the passage of traffic along it and generally do everything he could to frustrate invasion preparations. In addition, he was required to draw up a contingency plan to deal with invasion; supervise the volunteer coastal defence force known as the Sea Fencibles; concert anti-invasion measures with the Army; and organise the routine duties of convoy escort and other means of protecting merchant shipping against the enemy privateers that swarmed in the waters under his command.[9]

To meet an invasion attempt from across the Narrow Seas, the Navy had built a triple-layered defence in depth. Off Boulogne, Calais and Dunkirk, Flushing and the Scheldt estuary, Hellevoetsluis and the Texel were stationed forward squadrons based at Dungeness, the Downs and Yarmouth, equipped with a preponderance of small vessels suitable for inshore work. On the other side, in the Downs, was Keith's reserve of 24 ships, ready to protect this vital anchorage or move across the Channel in support. Finally, on the English coast itself, a multitude of small craft manned by civilian volunteers and commanded by regular officers were charged with the task of intercepting the flotilla on its landing approach. These, known as the Sea Fencibles, set up five years previously, were recruited from the ranks of the seafaring fraternity to man specially armed shallow-draught vessels such as snows, colliers, fishing boats and coasters of various kinds, supplemented by custom-built gun-boats supplied by the Admiralty.

The Fencibles had always been one of the Admiralty's headaches. Seamen were rough, independent types who did not take kindly to being organised by officialdom. Many enrolled just to dodge the Press and the ballots, and they had a lamentable habit of not turning up for training sessions. Moreover, an alleged insufficiency of coastal defence craft provided a useful stick with which the government's critics, led by Pitt, could belabour ministers in Parliament. A despairing St. Vincent declared that the money voted for the Fencibles was 'of no other use than to calm the fears of the old ladies, both within and without [Parliament]'.

The main workaday business of Keith's offshore squadrons was the interception of shipping sailing to, from and along the enemy coast, whether invasion vessels on their way to the embarkation ports or merchant traffic. Even fishing boats, traditionally left to ply their trade in peace, were now to be taken when it was found that Napoleon was requisitioning them for his flotilla. Neutrals were not exempt; they too were waylaid and searched, and if enemy cargo was found it was confiscated, to the impotent fury of governments like the United States. Yet despite every effort, the Navy was unable to stamp out the enemy's coastal trade and nimble *chasse-marées* continued to slip from harbour to harbour, many of them carrying the timber and other supplies needed by the flotilla.

Keith had a standing instruction that attacks on enemy vessels within shore range should be made only if there was some obvious advantage in it, insisting that the priority must be to maintain readiness for meeting the enemy if he came out in force.[10] Sheltered though they were by their shield of shot and shell, the French always moved with caution. First checking by telegraph that the coast was, literally, clear, they would edge along from one anchorage to the next, taking advantage where they could of poor visibility, and using oars to move in windless conditions that immobilised the opposition. British ships for their part would wait about off capes, headlands and promontories where shore artillery would find it difficult to bring converging fire to bear if they approached close in. Negotiating a headland like Gris Nez could be a tricky manoeuvre for a coasting vessel, especially coming south in the prevailing westerlies. A misjudged tack could run her aground or push her out into the offing, to be jumped on by a waiting enemy. Another dangerous area was the Seine estuary; the Royal Navy's grip there was so tight that, after a year, more than two hundred vessels were stuck in Le Havre. On the other hand, they could move relatively undisturbed further north along the stretch from the Scheldt estuary as far as Ostend, where sandbank and shoal were strewn so thickly that the British were forced to keep a safe distance offshore.

In this running game of cat and mouse it was seamanship that counted above all; most of the losses on the French side and not a few on the British were due not to enemy action but the hazards of manoeuvring close in to the shore. French ships would often end up aground, sometimes deliberately in obedience to Napoleon's order to avoid capture at all costs, but determined British commanders would send out boats to pull off the stranded vessel or, in the last resort, burn it. When British ships found themselves stuck, it was a point of honour to prevent the stricken vessel from falling into enemy hands. In one of many such incidents reported in the pages of the 'Naval Chronicle', a party of brigs and cutters engaged a Dutch contingent that left Ostend in October 1804. But the tide was falling, and '....in Lieutenant Ormsby's gallant zeal to close with the enemy,' the 'Conflict' brig:

> ....took the ground and the tide left her so rapidly that every endeavour....he used to get her afloat was unsuccessful, and he was under the necessity of quitting her with his people.

However,

> ....as I considered it my duty to make every attempt to save the king's ship or at least prevent her falling into the hands of the enemy,

the commander of the detachment twice sent out boat parties which were beaten back with heavy casualties, and this time the ship had to be abandoned.[11]

The Dutch, bred to a more robust nautical tradition than the French, were more inclined to give as good as they got. At dawn on May 15th 1804, the Dutch Admiral Verhuell left Flushing on the first leg of a passage to Ostend with 68 invasion vessels, one of the biggest contingents ever assembled for such an operation. They had not gone far before they were set upon by two sloops, and the squadron commander Sir Sidney Smith hastened to the scene in the frigate 'Lively' together with two other frigates. A running fight went on all day, with the shore batteries laying down a heavy fire and the Dutch putting up a spirited resistance. As usually happened, the British were forced to retreat on the ebb tide. They had not managed to sink a single Dutchman but nine vessels had been beached in the mêlée. During the next few days, watched by an audience of troops on shore, Smith's brigs did their utmost to get close enough in to destroy them, but each time they were driven back by shore fire and despite continued harassing, most of the Dutch managed to reach the safety of Ostend.[12] Napoleon never stinted his commendation of fighting spirit: he awarded Verhuell the Legion of Honour and a promotion, together with promotions for several of his officers and men.

> Reading your letter has given me the liveliest gratification; I felt a true joy in your success. You have shown much boldness and ability. You did not have a quarter of the enemy's fire-power. The event has filled our enemies with confusion and presages the return of happy days to our cause. You have reminded me that you are in the line of Tromp and de Ruyter.[13]

For the Royal Navy, this sort of outcome - a withdrawal forced by an ebbing tide, with nothing much to show for their efforts - was frustratingly common. Captures and sinkings were rare; in two years the French reckoned that only nine flotilla craft had been taken or sunk, with another 17 lost or wrecked for other reasons. Napoleon's artillery concentrations amply proved their worth in creating a safe transit corridor, and the Navy was forced to realise that the most it could do was delay the inevitable.

But for most of the time there was little else to do apart from look at what was happening ashore. One captain had precious little to report in May 1804:

> The view of the French coast is novel and interesting. We cab see everything they are about and every person that is walking on the sands, and they have now, as I am writing, 42-gun brigs and about 85 of their lugger-rigged gun-boats all moored in one line along the coast and all moored at equal intervals, all with their colours flying and a broad pendant on one of them. A chain of mortar and large gun batteries immediately on the heights above them, with people constantly attending them in case they see any of us coming inadvertently within the range -

the heights for miles to the northward and southward of the town are covered with huts, which seem built large and commodious, and we can count from the ship 1,000 or thereabouts, but the range is often intercepted by hill and mounds of land. But what is very remarkable, they all seem uninhabited....so that one would suppose they all had marched away somewhere else or for some other expedition. I have seen troops of horse on the beach and some trains of artillery, but never but a few straggling companies of recruits (I suppose) excercising here or there where you would expect legions - and in all camps you can see groups of soldiers idling about but here never, for which I can't any way account. In and around the town and shipping everybody is busy and strings of twenty carts going along at a time, and the gun-boats increase in number every tide but really don't think they have anybody yet to fill them.

At least one English civilian - 'Mr Squier' of Dover - crossed the Strait with some MIlitia officers in a hired boat to take a look for himself and found himself under fire from the Calais batteries when they ventured too close, 'and might easily have been taken prisoners if the French had manned a boat and come out of the harbour armed for that purpose'.[14]

The Navy's constant presence off the enemy coast gave it a role in another, less overt but equally important, campaign. Because of the nature of seaborne invasion, intelligence figures larger than in other operations of war. In such a high-risk undertaking, accurate information about the size and deployment of enemy forces in the possession of either side could significantly tip the balance of advantage either way. Furthermore the preparations, necessarily elaborate and protracted, cannot easily be concealed from the eyes of the enemy. In 1944 it was these considerations that led the Allies to fake a full-scale expeditionary force in southeast England to persuade the German High Command that the assault on Fortress Europe would take place in the Pas de Calais rather than Normandy. We have seen that in the intelligence war of 1803-05 too, the invader had his own diversionary threats to make things difficult for the defender but, unlike the dummy gliders and assault craft and inflatable rubber tanks of 1944, they were only too real - the squadron at Brest and another at the Texel together with an army 23,000 strong.

Although Napoleon's foreign intelligence service, constantly fed by a vast army of spies, infiltrated every corner of Europe and beyond, it probably had far fewer agents in Britain than elsewhere. Yet they did exist, sending back accounts of varying accuracy about possible landing sites, coastal defences, troop strength and deployment, and other matters. One French agent reporting his impressions of the Volunteers may serve to corroborate the cynical view that spies tend to supply their masters with what they believe they want to hear.

> I observed the Volunteers closely; the first moment of enthusiasm brought them out in large numbers to dress up in elegant uniforms; workmen, the middle classes, the upper class - it was a matter of who was turned out most splendidly. But when they had to do duty on the coast, it was different. These gentlemen needed carriages, coffee in the mornings, tea in the evenings, a comfortable bed. Despondency is widespread and only if compulsion is used will these men of goodwill come forward.

Similarly rose-hued tidings were retailed by another agent in the momentous month of August 1805.

> Three-quarters of the populace are disaffected. If the French land an army of 60,000 at different points and win a position they could hold for three weeks, that would be enough to secure victory.[15]

To offset such fanciful make-believe, it was as well that there were more reliable sources of information easily to be had. In fact the job of the foreign spy in Britain was something of a sinecure; far from risking his neck having to work at ferreting out nuggets of information piecemeal, he was provided with a generous flow of news about every aspect of defence preparations by a range of public prints totally unfettered by censorship. We shall see that when Napoleon at last activated his invasion design in 1805, his best sources about the movements of not only the enemy's ships but his own were British newspapers smuggled across the Channel by his agents.

By contrast with Napoleon's systematic approach to intelligence the British effort was casual and makeshift. The only official provision for clandestine operations abroad was an Act of 1782 which put a Secret Service fund at the disposal of the Foreign Secretary and the Admiralty. Incredibly, the Duke of York, as Commander-in-Chief, had no official access to intelligence gained thereby and had to make do with what was passed on to him by the Cabinet. Secret Service subventions financed not only intelligence activity but also more nefarious work such as the Cadoudal conspiracy. Indeed, the British government found itself with egg on its face when the inept shenanigans of two of its representatives in Germany with a French double agent enabled Napoleon gleefully to proclaim the depths of its complicity in the plot. The Navy, always within sight of enemy shores, was no less deeply involved, organising its own covert operations. One of its leading spymasters was the senior British naval officer on Jersey, Philippe d'Auvergne, Prince de Bouillon - one of the more exotic names on the Navy List - who was responsible for running a long-established royalist intelligence network inside France, putting agents into the country and funnelling arms and cash to rebels in Brittany and Normandy.[16]

On less of a cloak-and-dagger level, the Navy's inshore detachment collected information on what was happening in enemy harbours, commanders routinely sending ships close in to spy out activity on land. Close-quarter scrutiny of the invasion coast had its not inconsiderable perils as, haze-free conditions being rare, ships often had to go in within range of enemy shore batteries to get clear sightings. A teenage midshipman aboard the Boulogne commander's frigate recalled an uncomfortable trip when the ship took on three distinguished passengers - two lords and a general - who wished to inspect the coastline from Cape Gris Nez down to Cap d'Alprech at a distance

> ....nearer than was pleasant, saluted the whole way by shot and
> shell from all the batteries, with a constancy and rapidity that
> almost told they had divined the noble cargo with which the
> 'Immortalité' was freighted.[17]

Besides its own offshore inspections the Navy used every other
potentially useful source of information to hand - escaped prisoners
of war, captured enemy seamen, neutral skippers. There was even
a case, reported by the naval prefect of Brest, and doubtless not
unique, of a British naval party coolly landing on the mainland to
question the locals. But data of this kind tended to be fragmentary.
For a fuller picture of the invasion preparations in particular, it was
necessary to send across agents briefed beforehand to report back
on specific things. Since such characters should be able to slip
easily and unobtrusively to and fro across the Channel, the Navy
often recruited them from the shady end of the seafaring fraternity.
One example is a Scot from Dundee named Robb, alias John
Brown, whose name makes tantalisingly fleeting appearances in the
correspondence of senior naval officers. With a heavy hint of a
wink, one officer who met him opined to a colleague, 'He is
certainly a KNOWING fellow'. Interviewed by Keith, Robb reveals
a way of life that showed scant regard for frontiers.

> He says that he has resided in Holland for 30 years, subject to
> occasional absence; particularly that in 1800 he sailed in an
> English privateer from Folkestone. His wife is an English-
> woman and keeps a shop in Flushing. He says that he can
> return with perfect safety to Holland, but not openly.[18]

Keith also learned that Robb's wife sold tea and other items to
smugglers, and that he was 'a kind of agent for smugglers and goes
a trip now and then'. Robb was not the only smuggler so
employed; indeed, both sides used them for intelligence work on
a regular basis. Napoleon declared that those based at Dunkirk and
Gravelines carried his spies to and fro across the Channel and
sheltered them during their stays in England, as well as bringing
him his supply of English newspapers.[19] With their cross-Channel

contacts and long practice in giving officialdom the slip, smugglers made ideal agents. Slippery is the word; Napoleon suspected many of them of playing a double game and Keith once complained to Sir Sidney Smith that without his knowledge the wily Robb was feeding disinformation to 'the French General at Flushing' provided by 'some branch of HM Government through you'.[20]

At the time Smith was a key figure in cross-Channel intelligence operations. Then commander of the Flushing squadron, he had become a national hero second only to Nelson after leading the successful defence of Acre in 1799 and thus inflicting on Napoleon the first defeat of his career. Smith's popularity with the public did not extend to naval circles. Heartily disliked by his superiors from St. Vincent downwards, he was often referred to as 'the Swedish knight', a snide reference to the fact that his title had been conferred by a foreign potentate. Fretting at the routine of North Sea blockade duty, Smith occupied his time by playing spymaster on the side, running a string of at least six agents in and out of the North Sea ports based on contacts he had made after his daring escape from prison in Paris in 1798. Lord Keith was far from impressed with his subordinate's new-found hobby, noting that, 'I consider all this a mere humbug; it flatters the vanity of the man, which I suppose the nation is made to pay for.'[21] All kinds of tell-tale data - estimates of troop strength, reports of troop movements, numbers of vessels under construction in the yards, numbers in harbours and their state of readiness for sea, the comings and goings of important personages - fitted together to build an ever-shifting picture that gave a comprehensive survey of the enemy's doings. An astute agent could find things out by seemingly innocent inquiry, like the one who learned from a conversation with a Flushing baker that he baked 15,000 bread rations a day for the troops aboard the invasion vessels; or simply by keeping his eyes open, as did the one who noted the Dutch government's advertisements for horse-forage contractors. The veracity of intelligence material is always notoriously variable. 'All that which is good comes by neutrals and people not interested to tell lies' - every intelligence chief would give an 'amen' to Admiral

Markham's pronouncement. In particular, informants were too
eager to take seriously the various simulated invasion preparations
staged specially for their benefit: on the other hand, it is clear that
the Admiralty was always in possession of fairly accurate estimates
of the vital statistics of troop strength and flotilla size. At least one
of Smith's agents compiled a long report on his mission from
Ostend to Boulogne that was a model of its kind, listing with keen-
eyed exactitude the numbers and dimensions of the various kinds
of invasion craft, and crammed with detail so sharply observed that
I have been unable to resist quoting him more than once.

Espionage in countries under Napoleon's control demanded
a low profile and steady nerves. France in particular crawled with
policemen and a host of informers, whose findings were scrutinised
by the cold eye of Fouché, the sinisterly omniscient Minister of
Police. They were often read by Napoleon himself, who was quick
to act on information received. Alerted by reports of enemy spies
operating on the invasion coast he ordered police reinforcements to
be rushed to the area, urging Soult to crack down hard:

> ....the English have their agents everywhere; they are making
> great sacrifices to achieve their ends. Set up a military commis-
> sion composed of energetic men and make a few examples of
> people. At Boulogne you are inundated with spies.
>
> There is no doubt that you have a band of assassins organised
> at Boulogne. Be ruthless - seize them and have them shot. You
> have gendarmes d'élite; they should cover the town in plain
> clothes.[22]

Anyone suspected of being in contact with the enemy was liable to
be harshly dealt with.

> Have the crew and gear of the fishing boat that had contact
> with the English arrested at once. Make the skipper speak....if
> he is unforthcoming, you can follow the procedure for dealing
> with spies, and crush his thumbs under the hammer of a
> musket.

And proven spies were given short shrift:

> The military commission had condemned to death the one
> known as Franqueville, native of Andouville, arrondissement of
> Boulogne, département of Pas de Calais, found guilty of
> espionage and criminal contact with the enemy; this sentence
> will be carried out on the 6th of this month.

Suspicious eyes were everywhere. The all-pervasive system of
official surveillance is described by Smith's agent 'No. 6':

> 'Tis impossible to describe the watchfulness of the government
> respecting strangers. The moment you enter the French
> territories you are visited by a gendarme who demands your
> passport, where you are going and where you intend to sleep;
> which having answered, he writes it down and sends it forward
> to the next stage, so they know you are coming before you
> arrive. When you arrive at a town and mean to sleep there, the
> master of the hotel takes you in person to the Commissary of
> Police, who also demands your passport and obliges you to
> bring two persons who are inhabitants to prove you are the
> person the passport points out; this being done, he takes your
> passport and gives you a printed receipt for it. On returning
> this, you obtain your passport and proceed on your journey.
> This takes place in every town you stop at so that you must
> travel in the character of a negociant, and must take some small
> purchases, whether you want them or not, to prevent suspicion
> and detection.[23]

On one occasion, part of Smith's network was blown and one of
his agents was forced to go to ground.

> Mr ---- arrived from Zerickzee at Deal on the 9th and had been
> sent to Sir Sidney Smith with whom he communicates. He says
> that on the 22nd ultimo, Du Berne, the landlord of the St. Luke
> at Amsterdam, to whom he had letters, was taken up and sent
> to Paris, and that a Mr. Muschel, to whom he also had letters,
> is in hiding, and the police in quest of him. He says that when
> he went to the post office at Amsterdam to enquire for letters,

he found that things were blown; that he immediately fled and
secreted himself nearly three weeks.[24]

One Hamon, a renegade French pilot who went into Brest on a
mission for the Navy, was another agent who found himself in a
tight corner when the boat that was supposed to pick him up failed
to make the rendezvous:

> By reason of which, after walking some time on the beach, and
> being fired at, at random in the dark, I suppose by the patrols,
> I was obliged to return again to the town of B[rest].

He tried to reach the inshore squadron by boat but his crew of two
boys, fearful of a rising sea, insisted on turning back. Keeping his
nerve, the intrepid Hamon bought the boat from them and set off
on his own down the Iroise.

> About four o'clock the next morning, they saw me from the
> 'Culloden' and sent a cutter, which picked me up about two
> miles from the ship; and I verily believe but for this fortunate
> circumstance, I should have died of thirst and fatigue, for the
> boat, being leaky, was occasionally to be baled out with one of
> my boots, and what with that, my anxiety and sculling upwards
> of fourteen hours without so much as a drop of water to refresh
> me, I dare say my being nearly exhausted does not surprise
> you.[25]

One wonders whether the exhausted Frenchman considered the £50
the Admiralty paid him to be a decent recompense for his nerve-
wracking escapade.

In the years 1803-5, the Royal Navy performed a testing and
thankless job with smooth professionalism. But it was a frustrating
time, with its squadrons condemned to month after weary month of
routine sentry-go outside enemy ports, powerless for the most part
to thwart the steady massing in the invasion harbours. As they
studied the intelligence reports, the men at the Admiralty were
loath to stand by and do nothing. They began to think of ways of
striking at the very heart of the monster.

Chapter Four

Two Fiascos

In the 1580's and 1940, when invasion threatened Britain's shores the enemy shipping concentrations became prime targets for pre-emptive strikes. Not surprisingly, the intention that sent Drake to 'singe the King of Spain's beard' at Cadiz in 1587 and the Blenheims and Wellingtons of Bomber Command to attack the barges assembling for Hitler's Operation Sea Lion was also in the air at the Admiralty in 1803. But Napoleon's invasion harbours presented the Navy with a hard nut to crack.

The usual way of mounting an assault on a port is to land a force on a nearby, less well-defended part of the coast rather than attack the target head-on. But in 1803 the density of the shore artillery and the huge troop concentrations all along the embarkation sector more or less ruled this out. A traditional expedient, bombardment with high-trajectory mortars from bomb ketches, was tried on a few occasions but the effects were inaccurate and desultory. Then when vessels began to venture out of Boulogne to form a line in the road, cutting-out expeditions were mounted. This was one of the Navy's specialities, but time and again, daring sorties would be frustrated by tides and alert defences and meet the same profitless end. A typical episode occurred one July night in 1804, when Lieutenant McLean with a party of two midshipmen and thirty seamen in two boats set off:

> ....to go into the harbour and cut out a fine gun-brig which was moored not far distant from our squadron. The attack was commenced with characteristic spirit, and our brave tars succeeded in the first instance after a smart conflict in boarding

the vessel and cutting her adrift. The flood tide however running very strong, the gallant captain could not row out their prize, which unfortunately drifted among the whole line of brigs that was moored in the road, where she was exposed to the fire of several of them, and after a spirited resistance, was retaken by the enemy. One of our boats effected her escape with the lieutenant and 12 of the seamen on board, besides two killed and wounded; and we lament to find that the two midshipmen and 18 of their brave companions were either killed or taken prisoners.[1]

Faced by the ineffectiveness of the usual methods, the Navy was driven to consider less orthodox solutions. There was certainly no shortage of these, pressed on the Admiralty by their enthusiastic inventors. Most were notable more for fiendish ingenuity than practicality, like the fearsome Heath Robinson contraption devised for aeriel bombardment by one hopeful, involving the launching of balloons carrying combustibles over the harbours, which would, so their optimistic contriver claimed, descend on the flotilla 'like a flight of locusts'.

But one scheme was thought to offer at least some measure of success. It was put forward by two decidedly louche characters, by name Etches and Mumford. Richard Cadman Etches, an American, was a smuggler and a secret agent, professions that as we have seen sometimes went together; his partner 'Captain' Mumford, another smuggler, claimed also to be a merchant skipper. It was Etches, the front man and evidently a persuasive talker, who sold their idea to Lord St. Vincent himself.

> Mr. Etches, [the First Lord told his cabinet colleagues] is a very intelligent man and has been much employed by government, and we all know the smugglers are capable of great enterprise....In our hands, there would not be the remotest possibility of the success he so sanguinely holds forth; but if the smugglers will undertake it for a given reward, play or pay, it may be worth attending.[2]

It seems odd that St. Vincent, a hard-headed seadog of vast experience and no mean judge of men - he was one of the few of Nelson's superiors who could handle that prickly genius - should have swallowed the idea so readily. Such an uncharacteristic lapse of shrewdness in the canny old First Lord can most likely be explained by illness and overwork, since at the time he was plagued by dropsy and battling to push through his radical and ill-advised purge of dockyard corruption. Etches explained that the idea first came to him when he saw some Dutch East Indiamen stuck in the sand at the entrance to Middleburg harbour.[3] Straight-forward enough, at least in theory, the plan was to seal up the entrance to Boulogne by scuttling blockships laden with 'piers' - massive slabs of Portland stone held together in iron cages - whose weight would hold them fast in the sandbank at the harbour mouth. In fact, it would be a far from easy operation. Boulogne was - still is - a difficult port to approach, with a tricky tidal pattern running at right angles to the entrance at speeds of up to four knots. Fine timing was crucial; the blockships would have to be sent in at three-quarters flood tide, across the current, and strike the target - the edge of the sandbank on the western side of the entrance - with pinpoint accuracy to ensure success. But here Mumford was to come in, billed as having a deep knowledge of local navigational conditions.

The 'Stone Ships Expedition', as it came to be known, began to get under way. Three dilapidated ships were found on the London river and in the middle of February 1804 were despatched to the Downs together with barges laden with 600 tons of stone. However, the more the Navy got to hear about the plan the less they liked it. Keith pointed out that the French, anticipating a repeat of Nelson's unsuccessful attack of 1801, had thrown a barricade of chains and booms across the harbour mouth like that which had foiled the previous effort. Moreover, even if the ships were accurately placed Keith was not convinced they were immovable; give the French three weeks working with explosives only at low tide, he predicted, and the entrance would be cleared. He distrusted the undeflatable confidence of the two smugglers:

'[Etches] seems of a speculative disposition and both are more sanguine than I am'.[4] Even St. Vincent had some reservations of his own:

> I hope and trust your Lordship will not hazard Captain Owen
> in it, for the speculation is not worthy of the risk of so valuable
> life as his, and the blame of the miscarriage may be thrown on
> him should he have the direction of the measure.[5]

Yet despite forebodings all round, the operation trundled on, with the Navy resignedly going along with it. Meanwhile the chances of success had already seriously been jeopardised. Everything depended on secrecy, but long before the public prints had picked up waterfront gossip and uninhibitedly set about acquainting readers with as many facts as they could uncover. Such information had a habit of finding its way across the Channel and on to the First Consul's desk within a week, and only a few days after the first report appeared in the 'Morning Herald' - ironically a government mouthpiece - early in March, Ney was informing Soult of an enemy plan to run ships aground at the entrance to Boulogne to be used, so he thought, as batteries.[6]

When the expedition arrived at the Downs, Keith found his suspicions only too well substantiated. He reported that there was 'not a pilot or a plan', suspecting that Etches and Mumford had cynically 'projected nothing but to put money in their pockets and leave us to execute an ill-concerted plan'.[7] Despite St. Vincent's concern for his career prospects, Captain Edward Owen, the commander of the Boulogne inshore detachment, found himself supervising the operation and was soon complaining bitterly about blown security, chaotic organisation and the apparent cluelessness of Mumford, the purported expert on the tides.[8] The whole thing was rapidly shaping up as one of those misbegotten ventures of war that assume a seemingly unstoppable momentum of their own. Finally, with everything ready, there ensued a long interlude at the Downs while Mumford dithered over the weather. The enforced idleness finally brought the bad blood between the Navy and the projectors to a head, and on March 23rd a violent row erupted, with accusations lustily hurled back and forth - Mumford's fondness for the bottle was brought up, while Etches complained of the Navy's 'jealousy and counter-action'.[9] Ripples from the disturbance reached the Admiralty and a concerned St. Vincent asked Keith to go and make the peace.

When the expedition managed to get to sea on March 30th, it was promptly driven back by rough weather. It finally reached the French coast on April 2nd but returned to port with nothing accomplished. As day broke on the 12th Owen's frigate 'Immortalité', together with bomb vessels, brigs, cutters, a Deal hoveller and the three 'stone ships', once again left the Downs and crossed the Strait. By now the French were on their guard, forewarned by the previous loiterings and the regular bulletins helpfully purveyed by the 'Morning Herald''s correspondent aboard one of the ships of the squadron. All available troops had been stood to and batteries were on full alert. While the British stood watching, a line of vessels was hurriedly marshalled across the harbour entrance and, as night fell, lights ashore showed that the French were very much awake. Then, with everything in place, Owen, convinced that he had a potential shambles on his hands, ordered the firing of the two rockets that signalled cancellation. The expedition hung about off Boulogne for another three days to no purpose until on the 16th the wind stiffened to gale force and Owen decided to call everything off and return to Dungeness. As the expedition sheltered from the westerlies in the lee of the promontory Owen penned a long indictment of the whole wretched scheme. He underlined the uncertainty of trying to hit a narrow target from a half-mile distance, probably under fire, across a fierce tidal current.

> It must require much practice, much coolness and judgement. I really consider Mr. Mumford unequal to the task. I do not think that he has the knowledge and his is certainly without judgement.

In the unlikely event of the blockships' hitting the target, Owen reckoned that the obstructions would be cleared in a week and, even if this proved impossible, the river would simply find another way round them. If on the other hand they were incorrectly placed, the French might well be able to turn them to advantage as foundations for more offshore batteries. He was insistent that Mumford did not know what he was doing, and had evidently been conducting some investigations of his own:

> If I remember correctly [Mumford] was described to your Lordship as the master of a packet boat. It was not so, my Lord; I've learnt that he was employed in the packet from speaking English to procure them passengers, and had no charge whatever in the navigating of the packet, of which I believe he was part-owner.[10]

Though the operation had by now assumed something of the character of comic opera, St. Vincent still clung to his faith in the cunning of the smuggler. Reassured by another dose of salesmanship from the ever-confident Etches, he wrote,

> Messrs Etches and Mumford persevering in their enterprise and having recently affirmed their confidence in the success of it, there does not appear to Lord Hobart and me just grounds for abandoning it.[11]

But to proceed further was so manifestly futile that the good sense of Owen and Keith at last prevailed and, to the Navy's relief, the 'stone ships' were laid up and left to rot at their moorings. Thus ended one of the less glorious episodes in the annals of the Royal Navy -

> ....the ever memorable Stone Expedition, known to every waterman on the river long before it was attempted in vain to be carried out....,

leaving the Admiralty to foot a bill for £16,000 and the two smugglers to disappear into the murky milieu from which they had emerged.[12]

Yet even as the Stone Ships project was limping towards its inglorious end, another plan for a strike against Boulogne was already on the table. In May 1804, a tall, lean American in his late 30's crossed the Channel in secrecy. His arrival in London was eagerly awaited, being the outcome of long negotiations in Paris and Amsterdam between a British government agent, 'Mr. Smith', and the mysterious American. The latter was known as 'Mr. Francis' but his real name was Robert Fulton, and he was no stranger to Britain. Fulton was an inventor, though his career in Britain had so far shown more imagination than worldly success. During the previous decade he had experimented with a steam boat and, it being the heyday of canal building, had invented an inclined plane and an excavating machine, but none of these projects had come to anything. By 1797 Fulton's fortunes were at a low ebb and in the belief that the new France might prove more fertile soil for the entrepreneur, had taken himself off across the Channel.[13]

Later that year, Fulton approached the French government for funds to develop an ambitious new project, a submersible boat. He propositioned his prospective patrons with a shrewdly angled case. The submersible, so it was boldly claimed, could become France's longed-for equaliser against British naval might; launched against the Royal Navy it would achieve nothing less than the complete overthrow of the arch-enemy. By sweeping the seas of their warships, the overseas trade on which Britain's prosperity depended would be wiped out, thus fomenting economic chaos and social unrest, and so facilitating invasion. The Directory evinced only a fitful interest in this alluring prospect and Fulton had to wait until the advent of the Consulate before the project won more solid backing. July 1800 finally saw the launching of Fulton's prototype, the 'Nautilus'. The vessel was 21 feet long with a 7-foot beam, built of copper sheeting rivetted to iron frames. She was a true submarine in every particular: like today's nuclear boats she could run, if only slowly and clumsily, both on surface and underwater, was equipped with a conning tower and hydroplanes to adjust her angle of dive, and could keep her crew alive beneath the surface. Contemporary drawings show a sleek, bulbous configuration that affirms her kinship with the modern submarine symbolised in the continued use of her name up to the present day. Her armament, a type of mine which Fulton called a 'torpedo' after the *torpedinae* class of fish, better known as the sting-ray, was towed on a lanyard threaded through an eye at the end of a beak projecting from the hull. The beak was driven into the hull of the target, the mine was drawn up against it by the lanyard and detonated by a jerk when the submarine was a safe distance away.[14]

Despite an opportunity to plead his case in an interview with the First Consul himself, who expressed polite interest, Fulton began to realise that though the new régime had shown more generosity than its predecessor, its commitment still remained limited. As his disenchantment deepened with a similar lack of interest in his revived steamboat project, Fulton was in the mood to give a ready hearing to approaches from another quarter. The British government had soon learned of the existence of 'Nautilus', so that when she was undergoing trials in Bertheaume road outside Brest in September 1800, Cornwallis took care to order guard boats posted around his ships near the Goulet as a precaution against possible attack. By the time hostilities were renewed the Admiralty were in possession of highly accurate intelligence about the submersible and took seriously the threat it posed, as is evident from their despatch to Lord Keith:

> Mr. Fulton, an American resident in Paris, has constructed a vessel in which he has gone down to the bottom of the water and has remained there under for the space of seven hours at one time. That he has navigated the said vessel under water at the rate of 2½ miles per hour; that the said submarine vessel is uncommonly manageable and that the whole plan to be effected by means thereof may easily be executed and without much risk; that the ships and vessels in the port of London are liable to be destroyed with ease, and that the channel of the river Thames may be ruined, and that it has been proved that only 25lbs of gunpowder was sufficient to have dashed a vessel to pieces off Brest, though externally applied.[15]

Exaggerated though this was, British disquiet was understandable and the Addington ministry concluded that the best way of scotching the new menace was to buy over its begetter. Probably

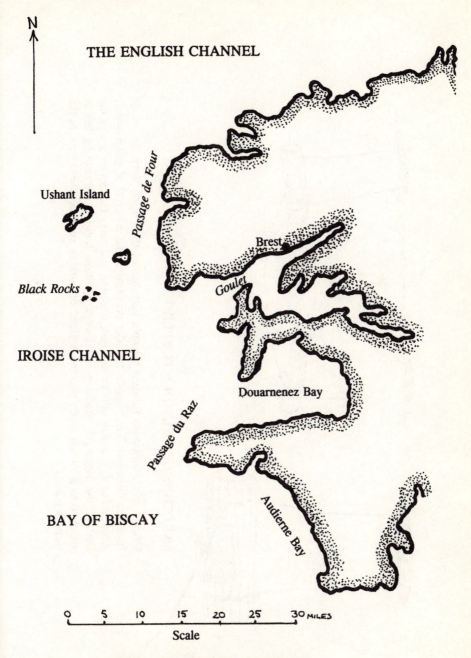

N

THE ENGLISH CHANNEL

Ushant Island

Passage de Four

Brest

Black Rocks

Goulet

IROISE CHANNEL

Douarnenez Bay

Passage du Raz

Audierne Bay

BAY OF BISCAY

0   5   10   15   20   25   30 MILES

Scale

The Approaches to Brest

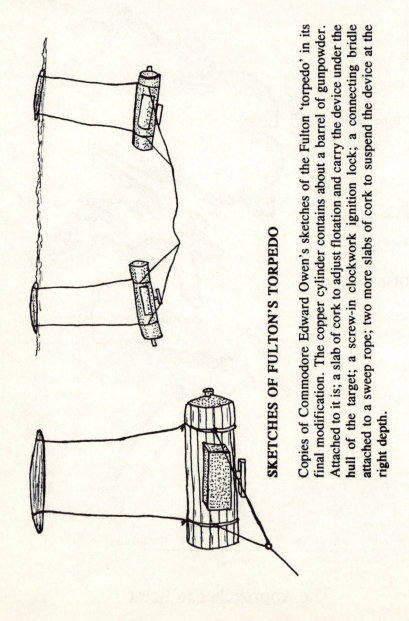

SKETCHES OF FULTON'S TORPEDO

Copies of Commodore Edward Owen's sketches of the Fulton 'torpedo' in its final modification. The copper cylinder contains about a barrel of gunpowder. Attached to it is; a slab of cork to adjust flotation and carry the device under the hull of the target; a screw-in clockwork ignition lock; a connecting bridle attached to a sweep rope; two more slabs of cork to suspend the device at the right depth.

at the instigation of Lord Temple, Fulton's former patron, the Foreign Secretary Lord Hawkesbury despatched a secret agent to Paris with instructions to negotiate with Fulton. His lack of success in France did not make the American a soft proposition.

> I agreed on certain conditions and Mr. Smith set off for London to give my terms. I then met him in Amsterdam in December with the reply, which not being satisfactory, he returned to London with other proposals and I went on to Paris.[16]

Eventually in March 1804 Fulton agreed to terms sent out in a letter from Hawkesbury. On his arrival in London in May he found a new government in office, but it was just as keen to do business and a contract was duly signed.

Fulton was to be paid a retainer of £200 a month plus a generous expense allowance and he was given the run of the nation's dockyards and arsenals. He was to be awarded half the estimated value of any vessels destroyed under his supervision plus a quarter of the value of any destroyed by others using his devices during the following 14 years. Four commissioners, two appointed by each party, were to scrutinise them and if a majority opinion judged them to be worth purchasing he would be paid £40,000. If they were not used, a majority opinion that the devices were as effective as their inventor claimed would still entitle him to the same sum. These were generous terms - even better than those he had tried to negotiate with the Directory, which were strictly on the basis of payment by results. By this new contract, Fulton had a great deal to gain and nothing to lose, having bound himself only to refrain from divulging his ideas to any other government for 14 years. It was a testimony to both British anxieties and Fulton's entrepreneurial audacity - no other-worldly inventor he. A quartet of pundits were soon found to serve as commissioners: Sir Joseph Banks the President of the Royal Society, the chemist Henry Cavendish, William Congreve, no mean inventor himself, and John Rennie the civil engineer. Together with Captain Home Popham, then considered the Navy's leading technical expert, they examined

Fulton's ideas. However, the contract shows that British interest was not the same as that of the French. The pressing need was not for another means of attacking enemy navies but for a weapon that promised better results against the invasion harbours than the useless Stone Ships, and it is possible that the initial overtures had been made to Fulton with the latter application in mind. There was much more interest in the mines than the submarine. Indeed, laying the mines did not necessarily entail employing the submarine; Fulton himself had always maintained that the mine was the essence of the thing, the vessel being only what in modern parlance would be called a delivery system.[17]

It is quite likely that the explosive systems were what the British had been after all along and their interest in the submarine was to deny its use to the French rather than develop it themselves. Or it may have been that development was considered and then dropped because it was thought to be impracticable or too long-term. Certainly while the invasion concentrations proceeded apace, rapid applicability was the main concern and the explosive devices promised quick results. For his part Fulton, with a lucrative contract in his pocket, was content to follow his employers' bidding. At any rate no British progeny of 'Nautilus' were built, and another early chapter in the evolution of the submarine thus came to a close.

It is easy to understand British eagerness to lay hands on Fulton's clandestine engines; it would need only a few planted in the crowded French harbours to wreak wholesale execution on the close-packed lines of invasion vessels. It remained to devise a simpler alternative to Fulton's submersible that would do the same job of delivering the devices to the target unobserved. Fulton and Popham set to work and came up with a contrivance at first called, misleadingly, a 'plunger', but it seems clear from accounts that it was the same, or a similar, device to that later known, less confusingly, as a 'catamaran'. This consisted of:

> ....two pieces of timber about nine feet long and nine inches
> square, placed parallel to one another at such a distance as to

receive a man to sit between them on a bar which admitted his sinking nearly flush with the water and occasionally immersing himself so as to prevent his being seen in the darkness or by moonlight.

As we can visualise from the description a sort of crude catamaran was clearly what it was, and the inventor was probably Popham, who had seen extensive service in the Eastern Seas where the twin hull originated. Trials took place at Lymington, where visibility was Popham's main concern:

It veered astern about ten o'clock last night, and although there was a considerable glare from the moon, it was scarce perceptible at 25 fathoms, and quite out of sight at 35, nor could any trace be discerned half-way up the main rigging.[18]

At the same time, Fulton's original mine was undergoing radical modification. The final result was known variously - more confusing nomenclature - as a carcass, coffer or torpedo.

I may compare them [wrote 'an officer engaged in the experiment' in the 'Naval Chronicle'] to a large log of mahogany, formed like a wedge at each end. The coffers are made of thick plank lined with lead. A plank is left out for filling in. When filled the plank is put in, nailed and caulked, paid all over with tar covered with canvas, and paid with hot pitch. Some of them when full weigh two tons....There was a line affixed to one end, with something like an anchor. This line and anchor were floated with pieces of cork, intended to hook their cables, that the coffer might swing round and lay alongside. The other line is the towing line. The coffers were weighted with shot, so as only to float, by which means they could scarcely be struck of any shot in the water and could pass undiscovered.[19]

The carcasses were not the only product of Popham's and Fulton's combined know-how.

We have tried an experiment with a tin lantern made in a particular way, having a tube fitted with a slow fire composition and put in a cask charged with gunpowder and combustible balls; the cask has ballast boxes below it to keep it steady, and each boat may carry tow to throw overboard when it may be judged expedient to do so. They are about the size of a forty-gallon cask and will, I think, do a great deal of mischief.[20]

Despite snags encountered in making the carcasses watertight Popham was able to report to Keith in the middle of September that 'the new curiosities will be finished by the 21st' and, a few days later, Fulton informed him that he was:

....now occupied in loading, balancing and arranging five large coffers, five small and ten hogsheads, in the whole 20 pieces, which I hope will be sufficient to enable your Lordship to give a good account of Boulogne. If not, we have materials to repeat the operation.[21]

A further innovation was the detonating device fitted to all the engines of destruction, Fulton's simple trigger having been discarded in favour of a clockwork delay mechanism attached to a gunlock and set in motion by the removal of a pin.

Meanwhile however, the original plan to place the devices in amongst the press of shipping within Boulogne harbour itself had been dropped, as the entrance was judged to be so well defended that there was little hope of slipping in unobserved. The line moored in the road was decided on as an alternative, though it offered a much less promising prospect of a holocaust as enemy vessels had more room for manoeuvre and were much less numerous. With this more modest objective, the operation was arranged for the night of October 2nd-3rd. For good measure the carcasses and casks were to be supplemented by 'explosion vessels', old ships packed with combustibles and gunpowder, making a more lethal variant on the traditional fireship.

Evidently not having learned their lesson from the Stone Ships episode, the Navy once more imprudently signalled their intentions well in advance; a participant sardonically observed:

For several days prior to the attack, there was a great display
of our force before Boulogne amounting to between fifty and
sixty vessels of all kinds, for no object that I can conceive
except to put the enemy on his guard and give him timely
notice of our intentions.[22]

Keith himself was present, as was no less a personage than Lord
Melville the new First Lord of the Admiralty - testimony to the
hopes entertained at the top. Once more the French braced
themselves for another attack: every vessel in the road was
provided with its own guard boat, the line kept station as far
inshore as possible, regular patrols were set up and boats assigned
the unenviable duty of towing the fireships clear.

The operation began shortly after nine o'clock in the
evening. The wind, a moderate south-westerly breeze, was set fair
and the high spring tides favoured inshore work. The volunteer
crews, some specially trained for the wet and sweaty work of
rowing the clumsy catamarans, donned their black guernsey
waistcoats and trousers and masked their faces with black caps.
Officers in charge were briefed to bring back the activating pins as
proof that they had set the clockwork locks in motion. The
catamarans together with their carcasses and boats loaded with
casks set off for the shore, while brigs positioned themselves to
cover the retreat or move in to tow off the assault force if the wind
freshened or veered on to the coast.[23]

But the French were ready and waiting. Alerted by the
suspicious splashes of casks being dropped overboard, the guards
immediately opened fire.

Our leading boats were soon descried. The enemy's sentinels
hailed and discharged their muskets nearly at the same moment;
and long before the carcasses could be set adrift, the whole bay
was lit up by vivid flashes of musketry that was soon increased
to noonday brightness by a blaze of artillery from the flotilla
and batteries which continued to pour heavy though happily
with few exceptions, harmless showers of grape in the direction
of the boats.[24]

Captain McLeod, commanding the explosion vessel 'Amity', was in the thick of it:

> I set sail towards the shore at the turn of tide at one a.m. and run in among the brigs at anchor a little east of Boulogne when under a heavy discharge of musketry, howitzer shell and shot, I left the vessel in the midst of them for explosion and retreated offshore in the boat....Full twenty minutes under their shot and shells and not a man hurt, although from their directed fire, they evidently kept the boat or brightness of her wake in view throughout the time of being within range.[25]

Most of the devices, 19 in all, detonated on cue and the pyrotechnics could be seen by Pitt and Harrowby watching across the Strait from Walmer Castle. But the French had reacted coolly, manoeuvring to allow the devices to drift ashore where they exploded harmlessly. Incredibly, the only casualties on either side were the unfortunate crew of a French pinnace who were trying to deflect an explosion vessel when it blew up, killing all 40 of them. On the British side, a report in the 'Naval Chronicle' demonstrated a shameless invention worthy of Napoleon's propaganda machine. Speaking of hundreds of French being lost, it claimed:

> The enemy had no expectation of [the attack] and were completely astonished. The tremendous explosions and blazes struck them with panic....Eleven ships were at one time counted on fire and it is supposed about 40 were destroyed.[26]

Even Melville was ready to swallow improbable intelligence reports from the other side.

> I have the satisfaction to tell you, [he wrote to Pitt] that by information received from France which I have this morning received, the alarm created everywhere by the operations at Boulogne exceeded everything we had ever supposed....and the panic has laid hold of the army intended for the invasion at every place from whence it was intended to have come.

But the object had been rather more than to send a ripple of fear along the enemy coast: the fact was that there was virtually nothing to show for a large outlay of effort, ingenuity and courage.

A month or so later, another minor attack using the devices as static charges against the forts commanding the approaches to Boulogne and Calais proved a completely damp squib. Two operations with no result; in the Commons, Sheridan from the opposition slyly referred to a speech by Canning as being 'of the catamaran species, plenty of noise and little mischief'. Keith began to voice reservations; he thought the unhandy catamarans were impossibly difficult to steer and the carcasses too heavy for towing. Even Pitt and Melville now began to have second thoughts, and no more operations were planned. Fulton, with a by now practised nose for sniffing official apathy, resolved to force the issue. In August 1805 he challenged the government either to renew their commitment or scrap the whole thing, in which case, he darkly hinted, he would go off and sell his ideas elsewhere.[27] The bluff worked, and new contracts were approved for the manufacture of improved carcasses made of copper. This time Sir Sidney Smith was put in charge, and another attack was mounted on the line in Boulogne road on September 30th. All the carcasses detonated successfully but, as before, there was yet another embarrassing absence of observable effect.[28]

By now Fulton's credibility was dangerously near rock bottom, so an experiment was arranged in the Downs to prove the case one way or the other. The next month, October, a mock attack was mounted off Deal on a 200-ton brig, the 'Dorothea', in front of a sceptical audience whose attitude was exemplified by the reported remark of an army officer who complacently averred that 'if a torpedo were placed under his cabin while he was at dinner, he should feel no concern for the consequence'. At 3 pm, Fulton tied a handkerchief to the tip of his cane and waved it. Two gigs, each towing a carcass, released them under the brig's bow; Fulton coolly pulled out his watch and remarked to his companion, Hester Stanhope, "Fifteen minutes is her time". The result, almost bang on cue, was described by the 'Naval Chronicle''s astonished correspondent:

> ....the explosion seemed to raise her bodily about six feet; she separated in the middle and the two ends went down; in twenty seconds nothing was to be seen of her except floating fragments; the pumps and foremast were blown out of her; the foretopsail yard was thrown up to the cross-trees; the forechain plates with their bolts were torn from her sides....the mizenmast was broken off in two places.[29]

The point having been made in spectacular fashion, the government concluded that it owed the devices one more chance and the experiment was repeated against a flotilla vessel in Boulogne road. The carcass exploded satisfactorily but no damage could be confirmed.[30]

October 1805 was a momentous month in naval history and Nelson's victory at Trafalgar on the 21st blunted the urgency of anti-invasion operations. Fulton realised that his hour was past and set about winding up his business arrangements to maximum advantage. Cheekily bargaining hard to the last, he made explicit his previous innuendo of blackmail, threatening to hand over 'to the weaker maritime powers advantages over the stronger which the stronger cannot prevent'. Despite this piece of effrontery and the by now well-proven ineffectiveness of his devices, he received a handsome final pay-off of £16,000. But if ministers believed they had thereby concluded a gentleman's agreement to buy his silence, they were mistaken;

> ....my situation now is, my hands are free to burn, sink and destroy whom I please, and I shall now seriously set about giving liberty to the seas by publishing my system of attack.[31]

By now he was eager to return to his American homeland. Once there, he tried, again without success, to market his 'torpedoes', continued to tinker with submarine design and was eventually to find his long-sought fame and fortune with his steamboat project.

The question remains why Fulton's devices performed so disappointingly. The 'Dorothea' experiment, in Captain Owen's words,

> ....placed the power of the weapon beyond dispute and left the means and policy of using it the only questions.

The difficulty was exact positioning; unless the device could be wedged hard against the underside of the target hull the force of the explosion was not sufficient to do damage. It was a drawback of which Fulton and his collaborators were well aware, and stimulated radical modifications to the prototype. To make things more problematic the French had unwittingly equipped themselves with a static version of something like the modern paravane technique of mine-sweeping, flotilla vessels being moored by four small anchors, two each fore and aft, which snagged the device's tow rope, thus holding it well clear of the hull as it detonated. Ultimately, the fact was that, like other abortive inventions before and since, the weapon had run up against the technological limitations of its time, in this case the relatively feeble destructive effect of gunpowder. Fulton's ideas ultimately had to wait nearly a century and a half to come to fruition, when the midget submarines of the Second World War, in many respects the true descendants of 'Nautilus', sneaked into enemy harbours to blow up shipping; but by then magnetic charges were available for attachment to steel hulls and in any case the enhanced power of explosives made contact with the target less critical.

Chapter Five

'Bonaparte May Pass This Way'

Baby, baby, naughty baby,
Hush, you squalling thing, I say,
Hush your squalling or it may be
Bonaparte may pass this way.
                    (Contemporary lullaby)

On the last day of November 1803 George III wrote from Windsor
to his old friend and tutor the Bishop of Worcester, '....we are
here in daily expectation that Bonaparte will attempt his threatened
invasion'. The old king contemplated the prospect with sceptical
equanimity.

> The chances against his success seem so many that it is
> wonderful he persists in it. I own I place that thorough depend-
> ence on the protection of the Divine Providence that I cannot
> help thinking the usurper is encouraged to make the trial that
> his ill-success may put an end to his wicked purposes. Should
> his troops effect a landing, I shall certainly put myself at the
> head of mine and other armed subjects to repel them.

All the same, the worst had to be anticipated:

> As it is impossible to foresee the events of such a conflict,
> should the enemy approach too near to Windsor, I shall think
> it right the Queen and my daughters should cross the Severn
> and shall send them to your episcopal palace at Worcester.[1]

The evacuation of the royal family was only part of the government's contingency plans for a last-ditch fight if London fell to Napoleon's legions. The nation's gold deposits were to be entrusted to Sir Brook Watson, the Commissary General, whose responsibility it would be to convey them in a convoy of thirty wagons, guarded by a relay of twelve Volunteer escorts, across the Midlands to join the royal family at Worcester. The artillery and stores at Woolwich arsenal, together with the contents of the Ordnance Board's powder magazines at Purfleet, were to be transported inland up the Grand Junction canal to the new ordnance depot under construction at Weedon in Northamptonshire. Arrangements were made to pay troops in gold rather than paper money. As to the king's intention to take the field, his words were no mere blimpish fire-eating. One of his courtiers wrote:

> The king certainly has his camp equipage and accoutrements quite ready for joining the army if the enemy should land, and is quite keen on the subject and angry if any suggests that the attempt may not be made....God forbid he should have the fate of Harold.[2]

The intention was that if the enemy landed in Essex the king would move to Chelmsford with Addington and the Home Secretary, and set up a seat of government; if Kent was invaded he would proceed to Dartmouth and do the same. In the event of the capital falling, he would retreat into the Midlands accompanied by his ministers and use the final mainstays of sovereignty - treasure and arms - to keep up the final struggle.[3]

The king was not alone in his confidence that an invasion attempt would fail; most of the experts, naval and military, shared it, though on more material grounds than His Majesty's assumption that God was an Englishman. Even so, when the ultimate threat was at hand common sense dictated a concentration of minds on the worst possible scenario. A glance at the map revealed not just Britain's narrow moat but another equally ineluctable fact of geography. In a speech addressed to his colleagues, a member of the French tribunate put his finger on it by drawing a telling contrast between the situations of the two countries.

> If, as I speak, you were told that the English had made a landing on the French coast, who is there among you who would not wish them to be allowed to advance deeper so that their entire destruction would be the more certain? Compare your reaction to that which would spread throughout England with the arrival of the French army, its crossing doubtless more difficult but its effect far more devastating....She can wound us lightly: we can reach her heart.[4]

That heart was of course, London. Time and chance, ever the begetters of ironies, have since brought about the fall of Paris more than once while London has luckily managed to escape the occupier's heel. But in 1803 Britain's defence planners were not endowed with foresight and uneasily contemplated what the Duke of York called 'this original defect in our position'. As one of his many biographers, J.M. Thompson, observed of Napoleon, 'Capitals always drew him on', and this one held a special allure. To gain his primary objective he did not need to subjugate the whole country but merely to take possession of the metropolis. Apart from its being the centre of the British economy, London's world-wide network of trade, finance and credit generated the wealth that had sustained two coalitions against France. A knockout blow against the powerhouse of opposition to French supremacy would achieve a result unparalleled since Rome destroyed Carthage - a classical parallel Frenchmen were fond of making.

Those in charge of Britain's defences could at least be fairly sure that wherever else the invader might strike, it would not be up the Thames. Rivers are not easy avenues of invasion since like any other narrow pass they are too easily defended. Although in 1667, during the second Anglo-Dutch war, a Dutch fleet had penetrated the estuary as far as the Medway, blockading the capital for a whole month, there was little likelihood of another such coup in 1803. The Nore Squadron stood guard off the entrance to the Medway, and the navigable channels that thread between the sandbanks of the estuary were sealed tight by blockships positioned by Lord Keith in consultation with Trinity House, whose pilots alone knew all the river's secrets.[5]

England's soft underbelly and London's real insecurity lay elsewhere, along the south-east coast. Kent and eastern Sussex offer several lengths of open shore ideal for a flotilla-borne landing, with few offshore rocks or shoals to obstruct an approach and no cliffs or other obstacles to bar the way inland. Once the invader had managed to secure a *logement* there or north of the Thames estuary on the Essex coast, he would find himself no further than seventy miles or so from the capital; that is, a week's march or perhaps less, since he would necessarily have to come without most of the paraphernalia - supply wagons, artillery - that slowed an army down. Napoleon, a legend in his own time for rapid marches, claimed in later years that he would have managed it in four days.

> Before you would have had time to arrange your defence, I should have been at your doors, and the terror of such an army would have paralysed your exertions.[6]

Though Napoleon often liked to indulge Latin taste for hyperbole, an estimate by someone who, in 1805, managed to move an army from the Rhine to the Danube in 17 days should not be lightly dismissed as exaggeration.

In 1803 Britain's military supremo was Frederick, Duke of York, the army's Commander-in-Chief. The king's second son, he has the best claim to exemption from the Duke of Wellington's verdict on all seven of the royal male brood as 'the damnedest millstones'. For a long time the Duke had a bad press. His dismal record as a commander in the field during the Low Countries campaigns drew harsh criticism from the likes of Sir John Fortescue, and incidentally perpetuated his memory as a nursery joke - the grand old Duke of York', who, bafflingly, 'marched his men to the top of the hill and marched them down again' in some of the flattest terrain in western Europe. Moreover, his career was ignominiously cut short in 1809 as the result of allegations of corruption laid against him by a conniving ex-mistress. More recently his career has been re-assessed.[7] His failures in the field have been viewed with more sympathy, perhaps in the light of the experiences of his successors in two world wars who as commanders of British contingents in allied armies also found, like Frederick, that they were not always masters of their own fate. Due recognition has also belatedly been given to the vigorous policy of reform that marked his period at the Horse Guards.

Since his appointment in 1795, successive invasion scares had caused the Duke and his planners to bend their minds in some depth to the subject of defence strategy, but never before had there been the same urgency to get it right. Like his opposite number, the Duke knew that the key factor was time, and he intended to co-opt it as his own ally.

> The line of operations against the capital is the shortest which can be undertaken. No case ever more strongly demanded the protection of a great army aided by every assistance which can be derived from the resources of military science. To impede the march and thus gain time upon the invader should he not be defeated on landing, is the only remedy for this original defect in our position, and may be said by the operation of delay to lengthen the line of approach. Thus we may hope to occasion the waste and dissolution of the enemy's forces and gain the necessary time for collection of our own.[8]

The Commander-in-Chief's strategy, then, is clear. Britain's weakness lay in the short approach from the south-east coast to the capital: this could be significantly offset by her vast superiority in manpower. Even if Napoleon managed to get across the Channel the 167,000-strong force that the flotilla was eventually capable of carrying - and that must rate as the most conditional of 'ifs' - it would still be dwarfed by the 580,000-strong host that Britain had in arms. The great majority of these were Volunteers and could not compare in calibre with the magnificent French legions. As Commander-in-Chief the Duke of York knew this better than anyone; but his hope and expectation was that weight of numbers, if overwhelming enough and shrewdly handled, could carry the fight. To swamp quality with quantity was Britain's best - only - hope. But while this numerical strength was diffused across the length and breadth of the country the balance of advantage stays with the invader. Thus it was Frederick's intention to weld the pick of his scattered multitude of local defence units into a unified 'disposable force' that could be integrated into a proper field army.

Although the main focus of invasion lay on the other side of the Strait, the threat against Britain was peculiarly dangerous because it was hydra-headed; the enemy could, at least in theory, strike from different quarters against any number of objectives. The Duke of York explained the problem by way of a preamble to a long memorandum on defence presented to the Cabinet.

> At the commencement of this war, the dominion or influence of France extended over the ports from Brest to the Texel - a relative position unknown in any former contest and which exposes the frontier of Great Britain to invasion from Land's End to the northern extremity of Scotland.[9]

Almost a decade previously, in the course of a disastrous two years, Britain had watched in dismay as the armies of revolutionary France routed the ramshackle alliance that included her own expeditionary force and swept into the Netherlands and Holland. Soon the Netherlands as a separate entity had vanished, digested into the French departmental structure, and Holland in her new guise as the Batavian Republic had become the most docile of French vassal states. It was now Napoleon's intention to exploit as never before the potential of this extended front to keep up the pressure. The Brest squadron was a perpetual menace, as much to Ireland as mainland Britain; Britons anxiously recalled the near-success of the invasion attempts on Ireland in 1796 and 1798, both launched from Brest. On the opposite flank at the Texel lay the eight ships of the main Dutch fleet together with a French army 23,000 strong, well placed to threaten Britain's North Sea coast.

Napoleon juggled his pieces with a skilful hand, throwing a continual play of shadows across the Channel. When confronting this type of multiple threat, a commander can be tempted to seek a specious security by putting a guard at every gate. Frederick saw the trap and avoided it. Looking back on the opening weeks of the war, when troops were desperately scarce, he later wrote:

> If the deficiency of troops at that time had not prescribed the necessity of concentrating the force of the country for the defence of its vital parts, I should still have deemed it the wisest conduct to be pursued. Too great a diversion of force is what an enemy has most to desire; and innumerable instances occur in war where the stake contended for had been lost from arrangements aimed at universal protection.[10]

Even when he later had more troops to hand, Frederick stuck to the principle of concentration on the 'vital parts', London and its south-eastern approaches. Apart from the capital the places thought to need special security were few: Edinburgh, Yarmouth, Hull, and, particularly important, Plymouth and Portsmouth, the bases of the Channel Fleet.

When war first broke out in May, Frederick's immediate worry was that the balloon would go up before the country was in a proper state to defend itself. Most of the nation's parishes were still trying to pull in recruits to make up their Militia quotas; the ranks of the Volunteers, though swelling by the day, were still thin and they were not properly trained, armed or organised. The Supplementary Militia had not yet been called out and the Duke's pet project, the Army of Reserve, still existed only on paper. After a few weeks he wrote:

> When I consider that the extensive preparations now in agitation cannot be calculated as efficient in the scale for the next two months....and judging from the publicity which attends every measure in the country the enemy must be aware of this circumstance, I am led to believe that he will strain every exertion to make an attack during the period.[11]

In fact the Duke's fears were groundless, as Napoleon appears never to have considered mounting a *coup de main*. But knowing he was up against a dedicated and cunning adversary with a habit of launching a tiger's spring on unwary opponents, he did well to be on his guard. A surprise attack on a comparatively minor scale might well win the same result as a full-blown invasion, by throwing the defences off balance and then exploiting the consequent panic and confusion. Hence the Commander-in-Chief's first duty was to stitch together a contingency plan to see the country through the critical early period. This entailed simply stationing the majority of available troops between the south-east coast and London and hoping for the best. Within a month he had managed to concentrate a force of 20,000 in Kent and Sussex and another 14,000 in Essex. The coastal counties from Hampshire round to the Bristol Channel could be spared no more than 12,000 between them, while London itself was allotted a garrison of a mere 7,000. As for the other regions, they had to make do with tiny contingents of regular cavalry and local Militia, token presences that would have been hard put in an emergency simply to keep the peace. It was all pitifully makeshift, and, as Frederick admitted, for the time being the fate of the nation was more or less in the sole hands of the Navy.[12]

As the first few months of war ran their course, the Commander-in-Chief was busily working on a more considered long-term strategy. Of the thirteen military Districts into which England and Wales were sectioned, the two in the south-east continued to be his first priority. Each was in the hands of one of the Duke's most trusted captains. Sir David Dundas, suzerain of the Southern District comprising Kent and Sussex, was a long-time crony of his, one of the trusted coterie that had helped him carry through his reforms. Dundas was a well-respected military theorist whose drill manual after the Prussian model was followed by the British army until the 1820's, well after his death. But he was no mere pundit; his experience of active service went back to the Seven Years' War and he had held commands under Frederick in Flanders and Holland where he had acquitted himself capably. The other front-line District, the Eastern, including Essex and most of the rest of East Anglia, was commanded by Sir James Craig who like Dundas was an intimate friend of the Commander-in-Chief, having served on his staff in the Flanders campaign. He had fought with distinction in the American war and was to be appointed to the command of the expeditionary force sent to Malta in the spring of 1805.

As the burgeoning Volunteer movement allied with the ballots to provide him with more manpower, the Duke of York was able to fill the front-line Districts with ever greater concentrations of his best troops. Regions remote from danger could be left to provide their own Volunteer defence and remained only lightly garrisoned with regulars and Militia. The North-Western District for example, comprising Shropshire, Cheshire, Lancashire and North Wales, contained fewer than a thousand and could safely be entrusted to the command of the bumbling Prince William of Gloucester, where his uncle the king was satisfied 'he will be most out of the way'. By the beginning of 1804 Dundas had 32,000 men under his command, 12,000 more than six months previously, while the size of Craig's forces had more than doubled to 29,000. Frederick was still not satisfied. His original aim had been to cram no fewer than 55,000 of his regulars and Militia into the Southern District alone, but the reassuring amplitude of Volunteer enrolment persuaded him to settle for 40,000.[13]

Frederick was convinced that it was on the beaches that Clausewitz's 'bloody decision' should be tested.

> The period of the enemy's greatest weakness would be the moment of his landing and the time he is preparing his artillery and stores to commence his march. There will be no opportunity for manoeuvre. It must be a contest of valour in which every Briton would find his value, and I should therefore look upon 2,000 additional men which could be brought to the beach in the first twenty-four hours as of greater importance than treble that number which might join the army at a later period of the contest.[14]

In order to hit the invading force as hard as possible while it was still embroiled in the muddle of disembarkation, the bulk of the troop strength was located on or within easy reach of the coast. Among them, in the corner of Hythe Bay whose long sweep of beach made it a prime candidate for assault, were based the three regiments, the 43rd, 52nd and 95th, that were to become the illustrious Light Brigade and later the Light Division, training as light infantry under Sir John Moore at Shorncliffe Camp which had been specially set up in response to the invasion threat.

Although calculation might shorten the list of possible landing sites, prophesying the enemy's precise intentions could be no more than guesswork: indeed, it is likely that Napoleon himself was content to leave the final choice of landfall until the last minute.[15] A multi-pronged assault with diversionary attacks was a distinct possibility. Spread versus depth: it was the oldest defence dilemma - to leave no gaps in the defensive line, while retaining the capability to concentrate maximum strength rapidly wherever the enemy happened to come ashore. The Duke of York calculated that Dundas could get 24,000 of his regulars and Militia to any beach in Kent within 24 hours or less, depending on where the landing took place.[16] Dundas himself reckoned that all his troops in the eastern part of the county - that is, the majority of his command - could reach Hythe Bay within only 12 hours. But on the critical first day everything would hang on the tenacity of those first-line units, since they could expect no reinforcements for 24 hours, and then would be joined only by 9,000 local Volunteers. If the landing came in Essex the force assembled to face it on the first day would be significantly smaller than in Kent, and diluted with a proportion of Volunteers.[17]

Whether this first line succeeded in pinning the invader to the coast, or whether he managed to burst through and secure a *logement*, the mobilisation of the entire south-east would continue to roll as planned. Each District had two reserves: the main ones to assemble at Coxheath near Maidstone and Chelmsford plus flank corps at Guildford and Cambridge. Thus on the second day, if things went to plan, Dundas could count on reinforcements of

15,000 regulars, Militia and Volunteers from Coxheath reaching
the coast. In the course of the third day 30,000 more would have
arrived at Coxheath from as far afield as Buckinghamshire,
Berkshire and Oxfordshire. In the meantime contingents from
Hampshire, Dorset, Wiltshire, Somerset and Gloucestershire would
be thronging the roads to Guildford where after three days the
flank corps, 25,000 strong, would be ready to march. They could
be disposed according to how the situation developed - kept in
reserve on the western flank or thrown into the fray where they
were required. In addition Lord Harrington, in command of the
London District, had his orders to detach 15,000 of his best troops
as further reinforcements.[18]

Since speed was of the essence, good communications
counted. The requirement to move troops towards the coast was
served well enough by the main routes that radiated from the
capital - the Dover road, convenient for Coxheath, the Deal road
that branched off it at Canterbury, the road through Maidstone to
Hythe, and that through Tunbridge to Hastings and Rye. What was
lacking was a lateral link to allow contingents to be switched
rapidly from west to east or - less likely - the other way. In the
middle of 1804 the Commander-in-Chief intended to rectify the
deficiency and sent Lieutenant Colonel John Brown - an officer of
engineers we shall encounter again - to survey the southern scarp
of the North Downs from Guildford in the west to Rochester in the
east with a view to making a military road along its lip. Brown
made a rapid survey and presented two projects for a "Chalk Ridge
Communication": one to make a brand-new road and a cheaper
alternative, chosen by the government, to do only preparatory work
that could be left to be completed by gangs of troops in two or
three days.[19] The official documents speak in vague terms about
the precise line of the road and the work done on it. It is clear that
for much of its length the route coincides with the Pilgrims' Way,
the ancient track that runs along the edge of the scarp, and Brown
may have planned to use some sections of the old route which like
all ridgeways tends wherever possible to follow a direct line on
well-drained soil. At other points he obviously intended the new

road to follow existing lanes while elsewhere he mentions the requirement to clear a way through woodland and undergrowth and 'lay fields open', presumably by cutting a way through hedgerows and fences. Where the line of the ridge is interrupted by gaps such as the valleys of the rivers Darent and Mole, he advised that completely new stretches of road be made down into the valley and up to the crest of the opposite ridge.[20] Some work was certainly done on the Communication - the Horse Guards put in a progress report to the Minister a couple of months after Brown made his survey[21] - but how far it got is a mystery.

As London was the goal of the invader, so it was also the pivot of a nationwide mobilisation plan. In magnitude and attention to detail it fully matched Napoleon's own planning. The aim was to funnel a multitude of well over a hundred thousand men into the metropolis from the Midlands, the West Country, Wales, the north and beyond the border, all over a period of three weeks. To add to the difficulties, not a single volunteer would move until the alarm had been raised; only then would Volunteer corps legally cease to be merely local defence units and take their place in a national army. In outline the timetable was to go as follows. While the struggle to contain the invader went on in the south-east, messengers would be spurring their mounts across the country to alert local commanders. Frederick estimated that the alarm would travel at the rate of a hundred miles a day, while a local commanding officer would need another two days to rally his men to the designated assembly point. Once arrived, each corps would be issued with ten days' provisions for men and horses from magazines stocked in readiness by the Commissary General's department. In the meantime the District commander would pass on marching orders to the local Volunteer Inspecting Officers whose job it was to deliver them to corps commanders. Once a corps was on the march, the Inspecting Officers would ride ahead to arrange quartering and supplies en route. Only Devon and Cornwall would have different instructions; they were to converge on Plymouth to meet a possible descent on the base of the Channel Fleet.

To explain further, we can take the example cited by Frederick in outlining his plan to the Cabinet. Leicestershire would be alerted within 24 hours and its forces massed and ready to move after 72 hours. The march to the capital, about a hundred miles, would take four days, so that they would reach their destination a week after the initial summons together with the contingents from neighbouring Rutland, Worcestershire and Warwickshire. Thereafter units would continue to stream in from progressively more distant points so that after a fortnight the capital would have witnessed a mighty river of 95,000 men flowing through its streets, with yet another 30,000 to follow within a week from Scotland and the Borders. Having arrived, they could be disposed according to the needs of the moment - either thrown into the struggle or if the enemy had broken through and the capital was under threat, set to building and then manning the defence works in preparation for a siege.[22]

The Horse Guards planners were constantly looking for ways of sharpening up these arrangements. Early in 1804 the Commander-in-Chief put out a circular instructing each Volunteer corps to designate a number of wagons to be fitted out with plank seats as rudimentary horse-buses - all to be done, he was careful to make clear, at the Treasury's expense. It is doubtful whether a clumsy rustic cart would have the advantage in speed over a pair of human feet, especially on eighteenth-century roads, but protracted bouts of unaccustomed foot-slogging lasting days or weeks would leave unseasoned troops in a state unfit for anything, let alone fighting. Transported by wagon, they could husband their energies for when it would be needed, not to speak of the saving in boot leather. However, some months later a scheme was devised with the intention of actually hastening the Volunteers' progress to the capital. Staging posts were designated at distances of 50 to 100 miles from London in an irregular arc from Guildford in the west through Andover, Marlborough, Burford, Banbury, Daventry, Northampton, Kettering and Stilton to Cambridge. Once a particular corps had reached one of these points, as many as possible would transfer from their own wagons to post-carriages donated by or requisitioned from local citizens. These, lighter and nimbler than farm carts, would convey them at a smarter clip - Frederick calculated up to 40 miles a day - on the last stage of their trek.[23]

Ultimately, however, the speed of response depended on how quickly the invasion alarm could be raised across the country. Luckily, London was connected with the Kent coast by the fastest means of communication then known, the telegraph. This ingenious contrivance had been invented in the early 1790's by a Frenchman, Claude Chappe, and by 1803 its gaunt, gesticulating outline atop high ground was a familiar sight in northern France. Chains of semaphore stations linked Paris with Brest, Strasbourg and Brussels, the latter, significantly, with a brand-new branch via St. Omer to Boulogne. The British were not far behind in developing their own version but while Chappe's machine, a true semaphore, used the various alignments of two jointed arms to encode messages, the British model, invented by Lord George Murray, displayed six pivoting shutters in a rectangular frame. Like the French machine it was often mounted on the roof of a hut whence it was worked by a rope and pulley mechanism into 63 combinations of positions. Britain's three telegraph links were built for the Navy's use and centred on the machine that adorned the roof of the Admiralty building in Whitehall. Thus their Lordships, freed from their predecessors' dependence on post-horses, were able to keep in touch with the bases at Portsmouth, Chatham and the Downs. As far as invasion was concerned, the vital link was the latter, which went via stations at St. George's Fields, New Cross, Shooter's Hill, Swanscombe, Gad's Hill, Beacon Hill, Shottenden Hill, Barham Downs, and Betteshanger to the terminus at Deal, with a branch from Beacon Hill by way of Chatham to Sheerness.[24]

The alarm would initially be raised by Lord Keith's cruisers, watching the enemy coast for the tell-tale signs of embarkation. The message would be relayed by repeater ship in mid-Channel to Deal, thence along the telegraph link. Given good visibility and alert operators, the telegraph could transmit at impressive speed: a message from Whitehall was once received in Portsmouth in ten minutes and another reached Chatham within just two. In the most favourable circumstances, then, it is likely that the government would have the news well before the first enemy wave had landed.

Once the warning had reached the British side it had to be taken not only to the capital but also along the coast and inland throughout the front-line counties. Dundas pronounced himself satisfied with the warning system in his District but Sir James Craig and Lord Keith agreed that arrangements in Essex were less than adequate, and Craig ordered a chain of 16 signal posts to be put up across the county. These were simply flag posts fixed to a church tower or the roof of a hut specially built on a high point, each visible to its neighbours by telescope. Stations would register one of only two signals: a white flag permanently hoisted signifying all was well, to be replaced by a red one for raising the alarm.[25] Keith was particularly concerned that a pair of posts should be positioned within sight of each other on either side of the Thames estuary for rapid communication between Kent and Essex, with that on the Essex bank also visible from the telegraph terminus at Sheerness.

As we have seen, as soon as the word reached London, mounted messengers would speed it across the country. But having reached a particular area it still had to be passed on to thousands of Volunteers in far-flung village, hamlet and farmstead, along poor or non-existent roads. Hence during the summer of 1803 activity could be seen on hill-tops all over the country, with men busily engaged in building rough huts and stacking furze faggots and straw; fire beacons were being made, as they had been to warn of the Armada's approach two centuries before.

In the North Riding the authorities had their arrangements carefully worked out in some detail:

> ....an intelligent, steady sergeant and three men should encamp and be stationed at each place....A telescope to be provided for each post by the Quarter Master General, and one of the men is always day and night to be on the lookout towards the station from which he is to expect the signal, and also to that one to which he is next to communicate. A large stock of furze or faggots....and such as may be expected to produce a fire

conspicuous at ten or twelve miles distance is to be erected at each station, together with three or four tar barrels to add occasionally so as to make a fire that will be visible in two hours; also a large quantity of straw wetted and in readiness to wet, to make a smoke by day. Smoke balls will also be sent to each station with directions for their use.

But the beacons should not be entirely relied on.

Notwithstanding the beacons being fired, mounted messengers are to be despatched in all directions to supply the stoppage of intelligence which might arise from negligence or be occasioned by unfavourable or thick weather.

To pre-empt false alarms each beacon should have a dependable man in charge, who

....is to be perfectly convinced that he is not misled by accidental fire or smoke before he repeats the signal, nor is he on any occasion to leave it, nor is he to fire his own beacon during the day in dark or hazy weather until he distinctly sees the one with which he is to communicate, and until he is persuaded that from that beacon he is to be seen.[26]

But such precautions did not prevent mistakes in an atmosphere tense with the daily possibility of invasion. I have found mention of some half-dozen major false alarms, but there must have been many more. At least one originated with the Navy itself. In September 1803 the signal station at Folkestone took a message that enemy vessels had put out from Calais. A jumpy duty officer on duty misread it as saying that they had left Ostend on a westerly course. With one of the periodic scares approaching its height and the wind in the right quarter for a crossing, the alarm was duly raised. It found General Sir John Moore away from his Shorncliffe headquarters, at Dungeness.

My horse suffered; I galloped him the whole way back. The Volunteers, Sea Fencibles and all were turned out, and very cheerful - not at all dismayed at the prospect of meeting the

French; as for the brigade, they were in high spirits. By the
time I reached camp the mistake was discovered.[27]

In the same month, Chelmsford was given a fright by the sighting
of a night-time fire to the south that was taken for a coastal beacon.
Troops were stood to,

> ....a torch was lighted and every preparation made to convey
> the alarm to all parts of the coast and the interior of the country
> by firing the beacon at Danbury; had which circumstance taken
> place, from its elevated situation the whole kingdom must have
> been thrown into that state of anxiety (though unattended by
> fear) which may be expected when ever the necessity arises of
> resorting to the expedient of testifying the approach of an
> enemy.

Whoever was in command had the sense to wait for confirmation
before doing anything further. His steadiness was justified, as

> ....it was discovered that the country had nearly been alarmed
> by the ignorant and imprudent act of some persons burning a
> quantity of weeds and bean straw.

The Essex 'Herald''s correspondent felt the necessity to conclude
his excited report with a wordy lecture to his readers.

> The many disagreeable consequences and unnecessary alarms
> which have been occasioned by burning haulm and other dry
> substances by night, added to the many cautions which have
> appeared in this and every other paper would be sufficient to
> convince any person endued with common sense not only of the
> necessity of refraining from doing so but also induce them to
> prevent as much in their power, more particularly at the present
> moment, such improper and injurious practices.

Evidently such commotions were not uncommon.

In Northumberland a few months later, another innocent
nocturnal blaze led to the firing of the Hume Castle beacon, so
setting half the Borderland in turmoil and turning the Volunteers of

no fewer than three counties - Berwick, Roxburgh and Selkirk - out
of their beds as the alarm raced eastward to the coast and westward
as far as Liddledale before being called off. Walter Scott, himself
an enthusiastic Volunteer, was at the time Sheriff-Depute of Selkirk
and must have heard many accounts of the episode from participants. When he came to the climax of his novel 'The Antiquary',
set in a coastal town plunged into uproar by an invasion alarm, he
re-created the events with a story-teller's eye.

> ....the windows were glancing with a hundred lights which,
> appearing and disappearing rapidly, indicated the confusion
> within doors. The women of lower rank assembled and
> clamoured in the market place. The Yeomanry, pouring from
> their different glens, galloping through the streets, some
> individually, some in parties of five or six, as they had met on
> the road. The drums and fifes of the Volunteers beating to arms
> were blended with the voice of the officers, the sound of the
> bugles and the tolling of the bells from the steeple. The ships
> in the harbour were lit up, and boats from the armed vessels
> added to the bustle by landing men and guns destined to assist
> in the defence of the place....Two or three light vessels had
> already slipped their cables and stood to out to sea, in order to
> surprise the supposed enemy.

All for nothing, as it transpired early next day. It could have been
worse had not another prudent spirit kept his head.

> If the beacon at St. Abb's Head had been fired, the alarm
> would have run northward and roused all Scotland. But the
> watch at this important point judiciously considered that if there
> had been an actual or threatened descent on our eastern sea-
> coast, the alarm would have come along the coast and not from
> the interior of the country.

Twice in 1805 other stampedes were set off in Yorkshire by the
same thing. In March the 'Lancaster Gazette' reported that one
night:

> ....the inhabitants of Wensleydale were greatly alarmed by the burning of heath at Hamilton, which was mistaken for the beacon on the top of Roseberry.

The locals mobilised in good order and tramped through the night all the way to Thirsk before they learned that their exertions had been in vain. The other incident, in the fraught month of August, set the beacons flaming in the night sky above the south-western corner of the county, bringing out the Volunteers of Sheffield and the nearby area.

> The neighbouring beacons having been lighted, the Sheffield Volunteer Infantry assembled at 8 o'clock.......at eleven we marched towards Doncaster, wagons being ordered to convey us, but sufficient only were collected for about two companies. The rest were ordered to follow and did not arrive till we reached Conisbrough from whence the whole regiment was conveyed in them.

When the corps arrived at Doncaster, they found that the cause of their nocturnal exertions had been

> ....Mr Dixon of Woolley having mistaken a brick-kiln for a beacon, ordering the neighbouring beacons to be lighted.[28]

In view of such episodes, Sir James Craig probably made a wise decision in forbidding the firing of beacons during the hours of darkness to avoid 'the confusion and the terror it would occasion'. Nevertheless such outings were not wholly futile; however grouchily the exhausted participants may have traipsed home afterwards, they could at least console themselves with having done their duty in steady, disciplined fashion.

An enthralling description of an invasion alarm is to be found in two other works of literary imagination, though, like Scott's account, the story has a solid basis in fact. In the pages of Thomas Hardy's novel 'The Trumpet-Major' and his strange epic drama 'The Dynasts', there is a depiction, based on the Dorset lore in which Hardy steeped his creative vision, of an event that galvanised the Dorset coast in August 1805. Hardy sets the scene on the Dorset heathland that often acts as the indifferent witness to his characters' lives.

> Night in mid-August....A lofty ridge of heathland reveals itself dimly, terminating in an abrupt slope at the summit of which are three tumuli. On the sheltered side of the most prominent of these stands a hut of turves, with a brick chimney. In front are two ricks of fuel, one of heather and furze for quick lighting, the other of wood for slow burning. Something in the feel of the darkness and in the personality of the spot imparts a sense of uninterrupted space around, the view by day extending from the cliffs of the Isle of Wight eastward to Blackdon Hill by Deadman's Bay westward, and south across the valley of the Frome to the ridge that screens the Channel.

Here two of Hardy's 'bang-up locals', as the Volunteers were called in Dorset, keep their lonely vigil, scanning the surrounding blackness and rehearsing their orders:

> Whenever you see the Kingsbere Hill beacon fired to eastward, or Black'on to the westward, light up; and keep your second fire burning for two hours.

Then a point of light begins to twinkle in the west towards Blackdon Hill. The watchers set to their duties. 'Fall in, fall in, mate. Straight to the tinder-box. Quick march!' As the alarm gallops from village to village, Hardy portrays the reactions, some fearful, others grimly resolute, the hasty farewells as children and women-folk are packed off inland with whatever they could carry, the fumbling with uniforms and muskets, the abandoned homes, the roads from the coast thronged with those fleeing to safety, and the Volunteers, caked white with summer dust, tramping in the opposite direction. And then with the day's dawning the cause is revealed - not, this time, a fire left carelessly to burn but the appearance of an overdue fishing fleet in Lyme Bay.

It was not the first time that the sighting of a harmless gaggle of ships had thrown the south coast into panic. Two years previously, a young lady visiting Portsmouth found the place in turmoil.

> A great concourse of people on the beach, the Yeomanry out, guns frequently fired, signals made, the telegraphs at work and many sails in sight....On enquiring, I was told it was supposed the French were effecting a landing, as numbers of flat-bottomed boats were seen making towards the shore.[29]

But the enemy flotilla turned out to be no more than a convoy of coasters becalmed off the Isle of Wight.

An amphibious force has to travel light. Since the overriding aim must be to deliver the maximum fighting strength to the landing point, the space allotted to freight other than troops, particularly heavy and bulky items - horses, wagons, artillery, provisions - has to be severely rationed. Napoleon was not particularly concerned about this as a large train would only slow down his full-tilt drive on the capital. In any case, he intended remedying some of these deficiencies after landing:

> I do not need artillery wagons; in the country where I'm going, I won't be short of wagons.[30]

As regards provisions it had always been his habit to leave shortfalls to the French soldier's expert rapacity in foraging, a casual approach that was eventually to be his undoing in the icy wastes of Russia. For a campaign in England he planned to load only a week's supplies by the time these had run out he anticipated that he would be issuing his first decrees from St. James's Palace. Even if events did not fall out exactly on schedule, he foresaw little difficulty in keeping his troops on full bellies in the lush farmlands of Kent as he had done previously on the Lombardy plain.

We have seen that the strategy of delay was intended to confound this confident scenario. However, to capitalise on it to most deadly effect there is a weapon available to a defender desperate enough to use it. Then called 'driving the country', it is

more familiarly known to our own century as 'scorched earth' -
that is, the removal or destruction of all means of subsistence,
particularly food supplies, from the enemy's path to starve him into
surrender or retreat. Though horribly effective, such a self-inflicted
wound was a hard price to pay for victory, rather like that of the
bee employing its sting. However, the government of 1803 was not
the first to consider visiting the rigours of total war on its own
people. During a perilous interlude in the American war, when the
Royal Navy lost control of the Channel, a royal proclamation of
1779 decreed that it should be carried out in the event of a French
landing; and in the 1790's, successive invasion scares had led to a
revival of the idea.

Shortly after war broke out the Addington government
announced its intention of implementing the same grim policy. In
a circular sent out to the Lord Lieutenants they explained its place
in the overall defence strategy.

> If unforeseen and improbable circumstances should enable him
> to make some progress at first, a steady perseverance in the
> same system will increase his difficulties at every step; sooner
> or later he must pay the forfeit of his own temerity. How much
> the accomplishment of this object will be facilitated by driving
> away the livestock and consuming, or, in cases of absolute
> necessity, destroying all other means of subsistence in those
> parts of the country which may be in imminent danger of
> falling into his possession, is too evident to need discussion.[31]

But what was by no means evident was the feasibility of the
operation, since the planners had never seriously considered
awkward questions of logistics. But one man at least had taken the
trouble to conduct his own investigations into the subject. Charles
Lennox, third Duke of Richmond, was a considerable military
expert; he was a Field Marshal, the sixth most senior officer in the
army, and had served as a capable Master General of the Ordnance. He also happened to be a conscientious Lord Lieutenant of
Sussex, and in 1801, just before the end of the previous war, had
called a meeting of county notables and officials to look at the

figures. They showed that the county did not possess nearly enough draught animals even to remove the total stock of grain and forage. Richmond's enquiries revealed other complications hitherto unconsidered. Civilians would have to be packed off to places of refuge, but should the authorities evacuate the inhabitants first or the goods and stock? Common humanity would give first claim on the transport to the infirm, aged and others not able to shift for themselves. But rounding up a dispersed populace would be a protracted business, shortening the time available for the removal of goods and risking their capture by a quick-witted enemy. There would in any case, argued Richmond, be a natural temptation to stave off drastic decisions until the last minute as a false alarm might well lead to premature devastation. The Duke concluded:

> I must confess it appears to me a disgraceful and, I fear too, a dangerous thing to hold out to the country that we must ourselves destroy it to prevent the enemy's getting possession of it.[32]

He subjected the Home Secretary to a bombardment of remorseless logic on the matter, though he did not want the policy abandoned in its entirety. He argued for the removal of horses and oxen only; as a practicable step, this would prevent the enemy from making up his most important inadequacy. Meanwhile others had reached the same conclusion. A deputy Lord Lieutenant of the North Riding admitted:

> I have given no directions about driving the country because, if it is attempted, the loss is certain and the attempt may begin with a false alarm; and in this country it is impossible to starve an enemy. The horses shall be taken good care of and moved away with as many women and children on their backs as they can carry.[33]

The government itself soon began to have second thoughts on the matter and by the end of 1803 the official line had changed to Richmond's way of thinking. Instructions now specified only the removal of draught animals; as for the destruction of property,

....nothing more can be done than generally to recommend its being done when the danger is evident of its falling into the hands of the enemy.[34]

This would be no more than a routine tactical precaution of war; in effect the plan to drive the country had been quietly dropped. Napoleon himself justly remarked:

Were you a nation of half savages, of poor wild mountaineers or of ferocious shepherds like the Scythians, then indeed you might destroy your capital and desolate your country in order to stop the progress of an invader. Even if you were as poor, as wild and as ignorant as the Spaniards perhaps, you might destroy some of your towns and habitations. But you are too rich and too selfish.[35]

If invasion came, the government realised it was liable to face a widespread collapse of public order. Though earlier fears of revolutionary insurrection had been laid and no seditionist fifth column existed in Britain, the crust of civilised order over early nineteenth-century society was paper-thin and frequently broken by eruptions from the lower depths. Whether triggered by mischievous intent or simple panic, a tide of anarchy would threaten to swamp the machinery of mobilisation. Since nothing was better calculated to aid and abet the invader's efforts, the government could not afford to neglect preparations for the imposition of an apparatus of coercion. British governments of the time were by nature ill-equipped for repression, but as the ruthless response to the unrest of the 1790's had shown, they could rise to the occasion when required. Soon after the war began a royal proclamation was drafted, investing the Secretary of State and the Commander-in-Chief and his subordinates with absolute authority over the nation for the duration of an emergency. Copies were printed in bulk and put in store against the day.[36]

But the imposition of martial law would not in itself suffice. Britain's casual system of local government would very likely disintegrate under pressure so measures were taken to stiffen it. In an emergency each hundred or county sub-division would come under the control of a Justice of the Peace, and under him each parish would be administered by a superintendent who was to be a 'gentleman, clergyman or principal farmer'.[37] These local dictators might find themselves having to enforce harsh edicts on their neighbours - requisitioning their property, denying them their cherished freedoms and controlling food supplies. In such circumstances, authority would need the backing of muskets and bayonets. In many places the only armed force available would be small units of Militia and regulars, who would be hopelessly overstretched in an extremity. On mobilisation the Duke of York intended initially to keep a proportion of each Volunteer unit at home for police duties while the rest marched, but on reflection he preferred not to weaken his hand on the battlefield to such an extent, proposing instead that a special constabulary be recruited from the ranks of 'trusty householders'. But the Duke of Richmond for one pronounced himself unhappy about the idea, fearing that posses of citizenry would lack the discipline to do the job properly; far better, he argued, to entrust it to trained men.

In the end it was decided that most of the few volunteer cavalry units, known as Yeomanry, should stay put; amateur cavalry blundering about a battlefield were in any case liable to be a nuisance and would be better employed on local peace-keeping duties. 'Trusty householders' should still be encouraged to enrol as special constables but if they were not forthcoming in sufficient numbers, the strength would be made up from the Volunteers. Whoever was to perform them, police duties were clearly laid down: night patrols, watching alehouses, putting down disorder, jail delivery and guard, keeping important roads open and ensuring the passage of provisions to markets. The Commander-in-Chief underlined the need for an iron hand and urged reprisals if necessary; all foreigners should be closely watched and 'suspicious and turbulent persons secured'.[38]

In the matter of internal security the government regarded London as a special case, as its populace was generally supposed to be swollen by a delinquent riff-raff that posed a perpetual

1. A contemporary portrait
of Napoleon in 1803.

2. William Pitt in martial
pose as Colonel of the
Cinque Ports Volunteers.

3. Addington and Napoleon confront each other, the former astride a joint of the roast beef of old England. The cartoon probably originated from the Opposition camp but in its portrayal of a blustering but secretly nervous Addington, reflects a more widespread lack of confidence in him as a national leader. On the left, Pitt makes plain his own reservations.

4. One of the most ferocious of Gillray's cartoons. An anticipation of Napoleon's end at the hands of John Bull.

THE PROBABLE END OF THE INVASION ACCORDING TO GILLRAY.
JULY 26, 1803

5. Admiral William Cornwallis
as a 30 year-old post captain.

6. John Jervis,
Earl St Vincent.

7. John Bull taunts Napoleon from mid-Channel.

8. Probably the best known of all invasion prints. A French fantasy of invasion showing an armada of balloons and a Channel tunnel. A Chappe telegraph is visible left of centre.

9. Napoleon reviews his troops in the Boulogne camp during his visit in July 1804. In the background are soldiers' hutments and flotilla vessels.

10. Napoleon as Harlequin, the stock stage buffoon with his prop, a bat, orders a vainly protesting Dutchman to join the invasion project. The dead Pantaloon seen in episcopal garb probably symbolises the Concordat of 1802.

11. Sir Sidney Smith.

12. Lord Keith enrobed as a
Knight of the Bath, 1816.

13. Sir Home Popham.

14. 'Mr. Francis' a.k.a. Robert Fulton.

15. Schematised picture by an eye-witness of the line-up before the catamaran attack on Boulogne in October 1804. Lord Keith's flagship, 'Monarch', is fifth from the left at the bottom. The 'Immortalité', the frigate of the squadron commander, Edward Owen, is on the extreme left half-way down the picture.

16. Frederick Augustus,
Duke of York.

17. Sir David Dundas in
1809 as Commander-in-
Chief of the Army.

18. A contemporary picture of a shutter telegraph station. Three of the six shutters are transmitting, the remaining three being in the horizontal inoperative position.

19. A contemporary diagram of Chappe's telegraph showing the rope and pulley mechanism and a letter and number key for the various alignments of crossbeam and arms.

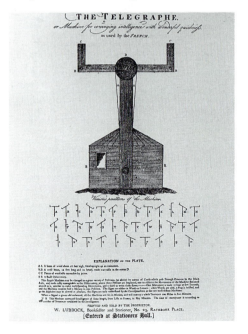

20. The Admiralty and Horse Guards in 1805. The telegraph is visible on top of the Admiralty building to the left.

21. One of several caricatures transposing scenes from Swift's 'Gulliver's Travels' to the invasion crisis. Here the King of Brobdingnag (George III) inspects Gulliver (Napoleon) as his boat is blown about in a water tank.

In case of actual Invasion.

The Deputy Lieutenants and Justices, acting in Chester Ward, desire to recommend to your Parish of the following Plan for the Removal of Women, and Children, and the aged, and infirm, and request you would call a Meeting of your Parish, as speedily as possible, to take into your Consideration the said Plan; and apply it (if necessary) as far as Circumstances will admit.

To lessen as much as possible that Confusion which must necessarily take Place in case of Alarm on the landing of the Enemy,—the following PLAN for the more easy Removal of the Women and Children, and the aged and infirm, from Villages near the Sea Coast to the Place of general Military Rendezvous, is recommended.

The Village to be nominally divided into Stations, where Carts should be appointed to receive the people.

STATION. No. 1. The Parsonage.
No. 2. The Poor-house.
No. 3. The Common Pump ⎫
No. 4. The Pinfold   ⎬ or as the Names of Places may be.
No. 5. The Common Pond ⎭

The Stations to be in such Parts of the Village as are most known and conspicuous; and interfere as little as possible with the Turnpike-road, so as not to prevent the March of Troops, &c.

The Carts to attend at their respective Stations immediately on a Signal given, in the following Order—

CART.—No 1. To attend at Station No. 1. there to wait and receive the People from thence to the House of A. B.
No. 2. To attend at Station No. 2. for the People of the Poor-house only.
No. 3. To attend at Station No. 3. for the People from the House of C. D. to the House of E. F.

and so on, a Cart for each Station. The No. of Carts will of course vary in Proportion to the Size of the Town.

Each Cart thus properly numbered, and the Names of the Owner, and Driver, and the No. of the Station marked thereon, should be provided with two Horses, a Truss of Hay, six Battins of Straw, with a winnowing Cloth, which, by the Help of Poles, may serve as a Covering at Night.

Those who wish to receive the Benefit of this Conveyance, being previously furnished with a Ticket (see the Form) describing their Names, and the No. of their Children, are expected, on Alarm given, to be at their proper Stations, there to wait till the Cart appointed for that Station arrives—To carry there their Blankets, and a Change of Cloaths, bound up in the Coverlid of their Beds, with a Direction on the same describing their Name, and the Parish to which they belong.

All Women (except those who are sick, or near being confined) who usually go out to work at Hay or Corn-harvest, will be considered as able to walk by the Side of the Carts; and Children above 7 Years of Age will not be suffered to ride in the Carts, unless sick or tired.

A Cart to be provided with extra Provisions for a few Days, till the first Struggle is over—to attend at the Station No. 1. as the nearest the Road to S........ the general Rendezvous.

Carts with tilted Covering made of Hoops and Sail-cloth, for those who cannot secure other Carriages for their Families, and are able and willing to subscribe to the Expence of the same. These Carts are intended for the Use of the upper Set of People—but for the helpless sick Poor a Cart of similar Convenience and Comfort should be provided at the public Expence of the Parish, to be paid out of the Poor's Rate.—

The whole to be under the Direction of the Clergyman of the Parish, as Superintendent, assisted by twelve of the principal Farmers, armed, cloathed and mounted at their own Expence, who are to attend as an Escort Corps, not so much to shew a good Face against the Enemy, as to protect their Convoy against domestic Plunderers.

If the Rules of this PLAN are punctually obeyed with common Alacrity, the whole of the Women and Children, aged, sick, and infirm may be removed out of the Town in an Hour's time, after the Alarm is given. Every thing depends upon Regularity, Sobriety, and Subordination to the Superintendent and his Assistants.

FORM OF THE TICKET. No. 1.

A. B. You and your three Children belonging to Cart No. 4.—Driver G. D.—Station No. 4.—as soon, therefore, as the Alarm is given, do you pack up your Blankets, and a Change of Cloaths for yourself and Children, in the Coverlid of your Bed, and fix upon the Bundle this Direction—

No. 1. A. B. Cart No. 4.—Driver G. D.
Station No. 4—of the Parish of N - - - -

Carry also what Meal, and Meat, and Potatoes (not exceeding one Peck) you may have in the House at the Time; but on no Account will any Article of Furniture, or heavy Baggage, be allowed to be put into the Carts.

22. Instructions for coastal evacuation of non-combatants.

23. 'Light Infantry Volunteers on the March' by Rowlandson. A little relaxation from the rigours of military service.

24. 'Loyal London Volunteers preparing for Field day' by Isaac Cruikshank.

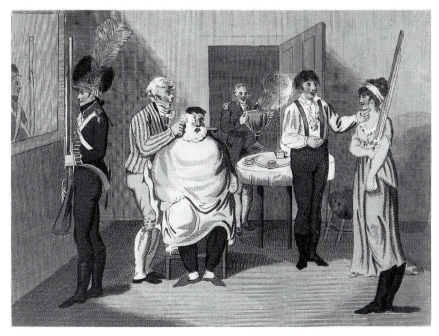

25. City of Westminster Volunteers in camp.

26. Napoleon encounters Pitt manning the battlements of Walmer Castle.

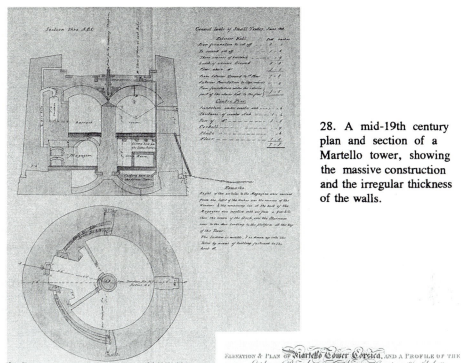

28. A mid-19th century plan and section of a Martello tower, showing the massive construction and the irregular thickness of the walls.

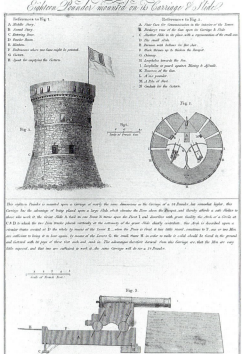

27. Elevation and Plan of the Tower on Mortella Point, Corsica, one of the drawings made after its capture in 1794. The cannon traversing slide pivots at the parapet end whereas that on the British model does so from a central iron post.

29. One of the line of
Martello towers between
Hythe and Dymchurch.
Others can be seen
in the distance.

30. Charles Middleton,
Lord Barham.

menace to law and order. A few years previously a published 'Estimate of persons who are supposed to support themselves in or near the metropolis by pursuits either criminal, illegal or immoral' put the number of such reprobates at 115,000 or about one-ninth of the city's population. This accounts for the fact that previous arrangements for the defence of London show as great a preoccupation with the enemy within as the one without, with plans laid for deploying the Volunteers to crack down on any sign of riot or sedition. As in previous crises Frederick made sure that his commander in the city had his instructions to set up a network of alarm posts 'for the purpose of destroying all unity of action amongst any body of men endeavouring to disturb the public peace'.[39]

Would any of it have worked? Detailed speculation is profitless, and history has demonstrated many a time and oft that the best laid plans of military men have a habit of coming unstuck when subjected to the only test that matters. Lord Cornwallis warned of the effects of exposing soft civilians to the routine hardships that regulars would take in their stride.

> However intrepid their minds may be, unless their bodies have been inured to those hardships from early youth, they will soon sink under them, and sickness will soon thin their ranks and cause a general despondency throughout the country.[40]

It is possible that everything would have collapsed in a welter of confusion and jammed roads, so actually helping the enemy's advance. On the other hand there is good reason for supposing otherwise. Every Volunteer corps was integrated into a command structure that led directly to the Commander-in-Chief himself, who saw to it that all the key figures in the chain of command were professionals, from the adjutant of the local corps through the Inspecting Field Officer to the District Commanders. Ultimately, it has to be said that Britain's best hope of deliverance from invasion lay with the Navy. However, granted the breathing-space denied a future generation in 1940, British planners made the best use of it. If the wooden walls had been breached, it is likely that

Napoleon's progress to St. James's Palace would have met a stiffer resistance than Hitler's Wehrmacht in 1940.

So far we have glimpsed Britain's defence forces largely as statistics - units of manpower to be disposed hither and yon at the bidding of the Commander-in-Chief. It is time to take a closer look at them - how they were recruited, armed and trained, what kind of men they were, and how they might have fared in defending their homeland against the Grand Army.

Chapter Six

The 'Bang-up locals' and Others

When the Addington government began to realise the huge scale of the threat in preparation across the Channel, they determinedly set about a correspondingly sizable expansion in Britain's defensive manpower to match. In doing so they took on a role that combined the functions of a recruiting sergeant with the dexterity of a juggler. The tides of half a century of invasion scares had thrown up a motley assortment of home forces that by 1803 had been pruned but still numbered four - the Regulars, the Militia, the Supplementary Militia and the Volunteers - with the creation of a fifth, the Army of Reserve, in prospect. Thus the year 1803 saw the government trying to run five different recruiting campaigns, using different mechanisms, all operating simultaneously - a nightmarish tangle that posed well-nigh impossible predicaments of co-ordination and timing. To rush at things would be to compound the confusion that was inevitable anyway; to go too slowly was to risk having to fight in insufficient strength. As well, the temper of the country had to be gauged; though there was no lack of fighting spirit about, Britons drew the line at anything that smacked of militarism.

The bedrock of the nation's defence was the Regular army. Addington, sceptical of a lasting peace, had kept it at 132,000 men, three times the peacetime complement maintained in the pre-war years. But a large proportion of these were scattered across the globe wherever British interests required their presence. A further 18,000 were stationed in Ireland, in effect an army of occupation to keep down the sullen populace of that troubled land. That left about 50,000 for the defence of Britain.[1] If the day ever dawned when the beaches and downlands of the south-east had to be contested with the invader, the outcome would ultimately depend on the steadiness of the Regular soldier and the competence with which he was led. If the Regulars were broken the best chance of defeating an invasion would have gone. But no impartial comparison of the quality of British and French troops could supply much comfort to British commanders. A staff officer close to the top later wrote:

> It would have been madness in the British to have risked a general battle in the field, even in such tempting positions as the chalk hills offered. Our troops were not of a quality to meet and frustrate the manoeuvres of such an army as that which Napoleon would have led to the attack.[2]

The British army of 1803 was not the same force that later triumphed in the Peninsula and held the line at Waterloo. By contrast with French troops, many of them toughened by years of campaigning in Italy and elsewhere, their British counterparts were unseasoned. Yet if the army of 1803 was not the equal of what it was a decade later, neither was it the feeble instrument of a decade previously. In 1795 it had gained a new and energetic Commander-in-Chief in the Duke of York, who set about reforming the ills that had set in during ten years of peace-time neglect. There was much that required a shake up: an officer corps grossly deficient in professionalism, a degree of indiscipline that allowed colonels to ignore the official manual and drill their men as they fancied, and the system of purchasing commissions abused to the extent that school children held them. Frederick made a sustained attack on these and other evils; he introduced uniformity of manoeuvre, prosecuted a relentless campaign against indolence and incompetence among officers and began the British army's first programme of staff officer training. A single but auspicious testimony to the new wind blowing through the Horse Guards was the success of the expeditionary force sent in 1801 to conquer Egypt, though it was not until the Peninsular War that Frederick's efforts came to their full fruition.[3]

Another consequence of the new thinking in Whitehall was that in 1803, 50 of the 93 regiments of the line gained a second battalion. Collectively known as the Army of Reserve, these units represented Frederick's attempt at a solution to the perennial problem of recruitment, aggravated by the vast losses from disease in the West Indies. Four years earlier, in 1799, the Pitt administration, casting about for troops to mount a campaign in Holland, in desperation appealed for volunteers from the Militia and was surprised by the enthusiastic response. The significance of this was not lost on the Commander-in-Chief. The new force created by the Additional Force Act, passed in July 1803, provided for 50,000 recruits to be raised within 12 months by ballot. Each recruit was, like a Militiaman, liable only for service within Britain itself. However, the hasty expedient of 1799 was now a permanent fixture; Reserve recruits were allowed to volunteer as Regulars with the inducement of another bounty. Thus, at the same time the nation's defensive strength would be enhanced and the Regular army would gain a plentiful new source of recruits.[4]

In the course of the eighteenth century as Britain and France struggled for mastery across the globe, the large numbers of troops committed to overseas campaigns seriously over-stretched Britain's military capability. At the same time a growing threat of invasion from France itself required more men to be stationed at home. The most straightforward solution would have been to increase the size of the army, but in eighteenth-century Britain this was a political non-starter - parliamentary opinion reflected the intense national antipathy to armies as tools of despots and a drain on the public purse. Hence the emergence of the Militia, a territo
ially-based infantry force intended strictly for home defence. It was much cheaper than the Regular army as it was disembodied when not needed, and, being administratively separate from it, was constitutionally blameless.

The Militia was born by Act of Parliament in 1758, in response to the military disasters that marked the beginning of the

Seven Years' War. It continued to survive, on local enthusiasm rather than official support, until the outbreak of war with revolutionary France when the government was forced to address the problem of home defence with a new seriousness. The most important innovation of this period was the adoption of Lord Cornwallis's scheme for a Supplementary Militia to reinforce the existing body. By 1803, after 40 years of slow, halting growth, the Militia had evolved into a sheet-anchor of the nation's defence.

The Militia of 1803 was very different from the idea contemplated by its original proponents. Its ranks were filled not by the respectable property-holders they anticipated but the types who usually gravitated towards soldiering - the poor, the feckless and the criminal. But the Militia's chief weakness when compared with the Regulars lay not so much in the calibre of the rank and file but in the officers. Here too, the reality was remote from the original idea - an officer corps composed of men of standing in the local community, who would serve out of a sense of obligation. Some of this description could be found, but they were very much in the minority. There was also a sprinkling of capable professionals but the types too commonly found in the unreformed Regular army - juveniles, the elderly, the indolent and the absentees - were even more representative of its sister force. With decent officer material perennially at a premium many regiments struggled to find a full complement and had to do with what they could get.[5]

Both the Militia and the Reserve were raised by ballot. With the renewal of war being only a matter of time, the government activated the Militia ballot in December 1802. Three months later, using a phased mobilisation scheme outlined in the Militia Act of 1802, they called out the 'old' Militia, to be followed shortly afterwards by the Supplementary body. The ballot itself, organised in each parish by the churchwardens and overseers of the poor, was, to put it mildly, a curious process. To begin with, a list of men between the ages of 18 and 45 who were eligible to be balloted was posted on the church door; but by no means all men in the parish within that age range were included. There was a long list of exempted occupations, from peers of the realm down to seamen and Thames watermen. The ballot was universally feared; it could take a man away from his family, his trade and his locality for long periods, and everyone naturally tried to avoid it. Contrary to what one might expect, the regulations did not make this too difficult. A man who found his name drawn - a lotman, as he was called - had several legitimate ways out. He could pay a fine that gave him exemption for a stated period or produce a substitute - someone to serve in his stead - which gave exemption outright. The less well-off were helped by obliging clauses in the legislation that provided for subsidies from official funds to help pay for a substitute and gave an immediate discharge to poor family men. These latter provisions were devised not out of concern to remedy inequity but to keep the parish rate as low as possible by ensuring that it would not be burdened with the expense of maintaining poor men's dependants while they were serving in the ranks.[6]

If this appears to be a perverse means of going about the business of conscription, the reason is that conscription was not its real purpose. The entire proceeding was a gigantic fiction; no-one, from His Majesty's Secretary of State to the parish official, expected a lotman to serve in person. All recognised that the object of the exercise was to use parish officials as recruiting sergeants to raise men by any means they liked to employ. Consequently the ranks of both the Militia and the Reserve were filled almost wholly by volunteers who took a bounty to enrol as substitutes. Of a total of nearly 42,000 men who had entered the Army of Reserve after nine months of recruiting, fewer than 3,000 were balloted men.[7] At one time the Middlesex Militia boasted one solitary lotman in its entire complement of over 4,500; so rare a specimen was he that when his discharge became due the Lord Lieutenant put in a special request to the Home Secretary to keep him on as a curiosity.[8]

The few unlucky lotmen who found their way into the ranks were there because they were too poor to buy themselves out. Such was the fate of the man known to posterity as Rifleman Harris, who began the adventurous military career recounted in his memoirs when, as a shepherd boy on the Dorset downs, he found himself balloted for the Reserve. Harris's ageing father, who would be left to tend his flocks on his own,

> ....tried hard to buy me off, and would have persuaded the sergeant of the 66th that I was of no use as a soldier from having maimed my right hand [by breaking the forefinger when a child]. The sergeant, however, said I was just the sort of chap he wanted, and off he went, carrying me (amongst a batch of recruits he had collected) away with him.[9]

Whether or not men like Harris ended up following the drum often depends on the readiness of their betters to help them out financially. Sometimes a local fund would be set up for the purpose, subscribers being variously moved to dip into their pockets by charity, reluctance to lose labour or maintain a poor man's family on the parish rate while he served his time, and unease about social discontent. For those who could afford it, all kinds of societies and clubs existed to provide insurance against being drawn, some operated quite openly by the local authorities anxious to avoid the fines levied for every recruit short of the quota, others by private enterprise. The principle was always the same: a large number of small premiums created a fund to buy substitutes for the unlucky few whose names came up. The operation of no fewer than three ballots in the course of 1803 - for the Militia, the Supplementary Militia and the Reserve - combined with the exemption from all three granted to those who joined the Volunteers, created a desperate scramble for substitutes. Many and ingenious were the fiddles born of the search for these increasingly elusive and expensive creatures. It was a seller's market, and there was money to be made out of providing a scarce commodity. One Mr. Pearce of Hackney ran a steady business for 12 years as a recruiting sub-contractor supplying Tower Hamlets Militia with substitutes at £2 10s a time - that is, until the officers got together and threatened to reject the lot unless they received their cut of £20. Private insurance societies thrived, often on an extensive scale. Several were based in London, where substitutes were easily found among the metropolis's human flotsam, with networks extending into the Midlands and beyond where they were scarcer and could be sold at a handsome profit.

As the price of substitutes went up and up, with demand in many places far outpacing supply, men tempted to join up found that they could sell their services for a sum several times greater than the Regular army's standard recruiting bounty of £7 12s 6d, and indeed for more than many a labouring man could earn in a whole year. By the end of May 1803 the price of a substitute in many places had risen to between £20 and £30; nine months later it had reached the £60 mark and above. By the end of 1803 the usual 5s premium charged by a Lichfield insurance society had gone up to £1, and about the same time the going rate for ballot insurance in Scotland, where the Militia was even more unpopular than in England, was between one and two guineas. The situation was ripe for exploitation, with endless possibilities for every kind of chicanery. Insurance companies would charge exorbitant premiums to provide decrepit recruits. Men would enlist as substitutes, take the bounty and disappear. This was such a common trick in London that the Militia regiments there were forever holding ballots to stem the tide of desertion. In desperation, some Home Counties Lords Lieutenants took to marching each new intake out of the county as soon as they had been enrolled. The more brazen absconders would enlist, take the bounty, desert, then repeat the trick for as many times as they could get away with it, a routine known as the Grand Tour.[10]

Mr. Pearce and his kind who made money by buying and selling substitutes were known as crimps. Although not strictly legal, crimping was not exactly illegal either, and while it was ritually denounced on all sides as parasitic profiteering, everyone knew that without the middleman the system would collapse. All kinds of people engaged in crimping on a part- or full-time basis - parish officials, all ranks in the regulars, Militia and Volunteers, and many others. Fiddles of all sorts abounded, particularly the practice of holding back the commodity to get a better price. The ins and outs of crimping could be labyrinthine beyond belief. A

Warwickshire official told the story of a substitute engaged for the county Militia by a corporal for a ten-guinea bounty: the corporal sold him to a sergeant for £18; the sergeant then passed him on to a 'crimping publican' who got 27s 6d for him from a parish officer. The substitute was eventually engaged for £40 by a parish officer at Lapworth, who offered him fifty guineas if he would lend him the bounty money without interest for five years![11]

Yet after its own roundabout fashion, this bizarre network of horse-trading did its work. Within a week or so of the beginning of the war and four months after the ballot had begun, it had delivered to the Militia about 80% of its official quota of 51,000. Recruiting for the Reserve, which began in August 1803, resulted in 22,500 enlistments within the first month, though thereafter the supply began to give out, so that by the end of the year the new force was still some 15,000 short of its designated complement of 50,000 and the government decided to suspend recruiting.[12] Yet despite the shortfalls, it is hard to imagine any workable alternative at that time that would have answered the purpose so well. All the same it was true, as many alleged, that the ballot and all its concomitant trafficking was largely to blame for the scanty harvest brought in by the Regular army's recruiting parties. Even the most simple-minded rustic who was tempted to go for a soldier would see the sense in avoiding the Regulars. Recruiting sergeants offering the fixed bounty of £7 12s 6d, later raised to eight guineas, could not possibly compete with those on offer for the Militia and the Reserve. They also gave other self-evident advantages: no service overseas, with its decidedly odds-on chance of incapacity or death from disease, and a fixed term of service - five years or the duration of hostilities, whichever was the shorter - as against regular service which was quite simply for life.

When Pitt returned to office in May 1804 he was confident that he had a scheme to revive the Reserve and at the same time restore the balance of recruiting in favour of the Regulars. Having studied the figures, he decided that there was no sense in perpetuating a sham and by the provisions of his Permanent Additional Force Act of June 1804, the ballot was swept away. Instead the Act laid down that each parish should find a quota of recruits within a 20-mile radius of the same county or up to 10 miles into an adjacent one. There was a fixed bounty for the recruit, lower than that for the Regulars, a bonus of £1 to the parish for each one brought in and a £20 fine for every one short of the quota. Pitt anticipated that the Act would raise an initial 31,000 men over the next 15 months: they would be amalgamated with the Army of Reserve and Supplementary Militia, all of whom, 79,000 men in all, would constitute what was to be called the Permanent Additional Force. Thereafter the intention was to raise an annual quota of 13,000 to replace those who, it was hoped, could be persuaded by an additional bounty to volunteer for the regulars.

It was a singularly misconceived piece of legislation. The ballot could at least deliver the goods if the price was right but in attempting to do away with the old venalities, the new measure made recruitment virtually impossible. Parish officers, lacking the cash to buy recruits, had no other means of inducement at their disposal; the recruiting boundaries were too confined; and a one-guinea bonus was no incentive to try and surmount the restrictions. It was also badly timed; so much balloting had taken place that even with inflated prices the pool of potential recruits had temporarily dried up. Despite the government's protestations of innocence, everyone took it for granted that the Act's real object was not recruitment at all, but the £20 fine. Known to one and all as the '£20 Act', it proved a dead letter from the beginning. Instructed to raise a first quota of 20,000 men within four months, all that the nation's parishes could muster was a grand total of 778, the best result the Act ever managed to obtain. At the end of 1805 the results were examined: 25 counties had not furnished even a single man, and £1½ million in fines was outstanding on a shortfall of 90,000 men. Although a manifest fiasco, the Act was to outlast both its author and his administration until it was repealed in 1806.[13]

Living in an age that has grudgingly accepted the principle of emergency mass conscription, one reader may wonder why, with the ultimate emergency on their hands, the governments of the day did not save themselves much trouble by simply outlawing substitution and forcing balloted men to serve in person. One explanation is the average Briton's fierce and long-entrenched aversion to soldiering, a prejudice that has persisted almost to within living memory. Even the honest poor considered it the most degraded of trades, regarding the man who donned the red coat as lost to decent society. Despite all the routine obloquy of the ballot as a fraud, no-one seriously questioned a Briton's right to avoid such a wretched fate if he could.

Another reason lay in the changing nature of society. As Britain entered deeper into an era of economic transformation and increased productivity, military service came to appear a distraction from the main purposes of people's lives. And yet as the invasion cloud darkened the land, Britons did not funk their duty. But they did it on their own terms, as civilians in arms.

Wednesday October 26th 1803 in London dawned autumnally misty. By eight o'clock the greensward of Hyde Park was unusually thronged for such an early hour. Around the park's boundary blocks, of red, regularly spaced, indicated troops drawn up by company in close column. Shortly after nine o'clock a signal gun boomed out of the mist, the columns dissolved and formed a line two deep. A few minutes after ten, the signal gun spoke once more, an expectant hush fell over the crowd and the troops drew themselves to attention. As a 21-gun salute from the cannon of the Honourable Artillery Company crashed across the glades and thickets, His Majesty the King entered in his carriage from Kensington Palace. He stepped down, a tall figure, now slightly bent and stout in his 60th year, mounted a waiting horse and preceded by his Life Guards made his way along the Carriage Road. At his back rode the Duke of York and four more of his sons - the Prince of Wales being a conspicuous absentee, sulking at Carlton House over his father's refusal to give him high military rank - the royal womenfolk in carriages, with a gaggle of emigre Bourbons and staff officers bringing up the rear.

The king had come to inspect his Loyal London Volunteers. He took up a position facing the line, 12,400 muskets were brought to the 'present arms' and the bands struck up 'God save the King'. As His Majesty made his way along the line the mist began to clear.

> We do not remember to have seen a sight so grand and delightful. The whole of the ground to the rear of the royal train was covered to the summit of the hill with women elegantly dressed, interspersed with Volunteers and officers in uniform.

The inspection completed, volleys were fired and 12,400 throats gave forth:

> ....three English cheers, hats and hands waving in the air, drums beating and music playing God Save the King.

The proceedings concluded with a march-past and when, at twenty-past one, the king left for Buckingham Palace, he

> ....was followed by a vast multitude of people who rent the air with their cheers and huzzas.

Two days later a similar event was enacted, this time with the 14,000 Volunteers of Westminster, Lambeth and Southwark mustered, and again the morning mist lifted providentially on cue for the event.[14]

The Hyde Park reviews were only two, if the grandest, of innumerable Volunteer parades and reviews that became a familiar feature of British life in the course of 1803. The king himself, always readily stirred by the call to arms and eager to play his part in the preparations to repel the person he invariably referred to as the Corsican usurper, busied himself doing the rounds of the Volunteer camps. With 380,000 Volunteers in arms by the end of the year, the most unmilitary nation in Europe found itself wearing a strange new military guise. Up and down the land, particularly on Sunday mornings after divine service and during the long summer evenings, awkward squads would turn out in untidy phalanxes on green and common and in market-place and town square, fumbling with muskets and pikes to the barking of drill sergeants. Clusters of uniforms made a dashing display at social gatherings. Nowhere was the new style more *de rigeur* than in the metropolis.

But the Volunteers, whether in London or elsewhere, were far from being all show.

> Every town was in fact a sort of garrison, [wrote George Cruikshank, the caricaturist] in one place you might hear the 'tattoo' of some youth learning to beat the drum, at another place some march or national air being practised upon the fife and every morning at five o'clock the bugle horn was sounded through the streets to call the Volunteers to a two hours drill from six to eight, and the same again in the evening, and then you heard the pop, pop, pop of the single musket or the heavy sound of the volley or distant thunder of the artillery.[15]

Even places far from immediate danger were animated by war-like bustle. The scene in Edinburgh is depicted by a lawyer practising in the city:

> Edinburgh like every other place became a camp....We were all soldiers, one way or another. Professors wheeled in the college area; the side-arms and the uniform peeped from behind the gown at the Bar and even on the Bench; and the parade and the review formed the staple of men's talk and thoughts....The parades, the reviews, the four or six yearly inspections at Dalmahoy, the billetings for a fortnight or three weeks when on 'permanent duty' at Leith or Haddington, the mock battles, the marches, the messes - what scenes they were! And similar scenes were familiar in every town and in every shire of the kingdom....any man of whatever rank who was *not* a Volunteer or a local militiaman had to explain or apologize for his singularity.[16]

Small boys like the eleven-year-old Cruikshank fascinatedly observed this new ferment among their elders and, as small boys will, imitated it with equal gusto. Cruikshank fondly recollected:

> ....my brother....who was my elder by three years, formed one of these juvenile regiments and appointed himself the colonel. We had our drum and fife, our 'colours' presented by our mammas and sisters who also assisted in making our accoutrements. We also procured small 'gun stocks' into which we fixed mop-sticks for barrels....with a tinge of black-lead to make 'em look like *real* barrels. The boys watched their fathers drill; and 'as the cocks crow the little one learns', so we children followed in the steps of our papas and we were ready for inspection quite as soon as our elders, and could march in good order to have *our* 'Field-day', from Bloomsbury Church to the fields where Russell and Tavistock Squares now stand.[17]

The gestation of Britain's first Volunteer corps in 1794 was brought about by prevailing climate of repression rather than the threat of invasion. The movement was founded by government adherents to mobilise patriotic support for a reactionary united front against the new revolutionary cancer, and provide a cheap paramilitary force to intimidate potential trouble-makers and deal with outbreaks of unrest.[18] In 1803, however, the seditionist bogey was moribund, while the menace across the Channel lowered as never before. The response at the outbreak of war was a nationwide avalanche of offers to form new Volunteer corps that took an embarrassed government completely off guard. Thereafter it never really recovered its footing, and the ensuing series of ill-coordinated lurches in official policy were to present its critics with an unending supply of brickbats. The root of the problem was the multiplicity of defence forces, forcing the government into a desperate balancing act, with one eye on the ballot quotas and the other on the number of Volunteer enlistments. Left hand and right worked diligently against each other, with inducements like exemptions from the ballots and pay allowances - two different scales - being granted to Volunteers while at the same time a stop was maintained on the formation of new corps to allow the ballots time to do their work. To compound the confusion there passed through Parliament the first British mass conscription measure of modern times, the Levy En Masse Act. This directed Lords Lieutenant to draw up lists of men between the ages of 17 and 45 for military training, who would be liable in an emergency to be drafted into Regular and Militia battalions. In the event, the size of Volunteer enlistment made it a dead letter even before it was enacted, its sole effect being to thicken the fog that already surrounded the government's intentions.[19]

As distracted ministers struggled to master the situation - in two years Parliament passed no fewer than 21 Acts dealing with manpower matters - they were faced with the burdens not only of regulating and training the new Volunteer behemoth, 380,000 strong by the end of the year, but issuing each of its members with a firearm. The Ordnance Board, which was responsible for supplying weapons to all the armed forces, was by no means caught out by the outbreak of war. Although it had stopped buying arms from the gunmakers when hostilities ceased two years previously, it had stockpiled a large reserve of 160,000 muskets. However, these would not go even half far enough to meet the new demand. Like the Churchill government in the same predicament in 1940, its predecessor of 1803 was reduced to rather desperate suggestions to drill with anything to hand that looked like an offensive weapon; as the Home Secretary wrote to one Lord Lieutenant:

> Your Grace, I am sure, will agree with me that a good fowling piece with a bullet mould properly adapted to it, a powder flask and ball bag, together with a dagger or bayonet contrived to screw into the muzzle upon occasion will prove a very efficient equipment for brave and zealous men determined to defend their country.

But whereas the Home Guard of 1940 were content to practise with wooden rifles and garden tools to face the might of the Wehrmacht, their forefathers of 1803 raised a chorus of outrage at the government's advice to drill with the pikes of which the Ordnance Board had an oddly limitless supply. Evidently the average Briton did not regard the pike as a fitting weapon for defending his own backyard, and in the view of one Lord Lieutenant,

> I fear the prejudice against this sort of weapon is so great that the idea of being supplied with them will do harm.[20]

Other siren voices from the shires joined in the warning that unless proper firearms turned up soon, the Volunteering spirit would evaporate.

> The zeal is cooling, [was the word from Pembrokeshire] and I firmly believe that in the course of a month the greater part of the whole will go to the right about.[21]

The Volunteers of Northumberland were:

> ....likely in point of discipline to be no more than a name, as the greater number were without any arms whatever.[22]

With the Amiens peace and the abrupt end of Ordnance Board contracts, the Birmingham gun trade which produced the vast majority of the army's small arms had laid off large numbers of workmen and now needed time to regain a war footing. To provide a stopgap, the Board hastily cast about for other sources of supply. Its agents combed Europe to contact dealers and managed to make contracts for half a million pieces, though fewer than 300,000 materialised, and many of these were found to be useless. However, by early 1804 the gun trade had managed to gear itself up and was busily turning out parts and finished weapons at maximum speed. To supplement the output the Board set up a workshop of its own in the Tower of London, where its armourers assembled weapons from privately manufactured parts. As they took delivery of their new Brummagem pieces, the Volunteers could now at least regard themselves as properly Kitted out for the job.[23]

Most Volunteer corps were born out of a public meeting of some kind. In rural areas, where kinship and political connections facilitated such business, some person of consequence, usually the Lord Lieutenant himself, would summon together all the local men of standing. In towns and cities, where social distinctions counted for less, it fell to prominent citizens to call an open meeting in a public hall, church or inn. In the first flush of exhilaration it was a matter of local self-respect for a corps to make itself independent of the official allowance scheme, a high resolve which could only be realised if men of means were prepared to dig deeply enough into their purses to meet the considerable expense involved. But in the end many were forced to swallow their pride and apply for the allowance. A want of funds caused the stillbirth of many embryo units and continued to dog many of the survivors, who found that cash problems did not end with the initial kiting-out. Indeed, the greater the zeal of a particular corps the higher the running expenses, as frequent drills and exercises wore out uniforms and equipment more quickly. Some corps found their continued existence dependent on indulging richer officers who were prepared to fork out contributions to the regimental coffers. On the other hand a few corps were so well set up that they were able to afford such luxuries as the new-fangled Baker rifle, fancy uniforms, regimental bands, and bonuses for the rank and file on special occasions.[24]

The new national appetite for amateur soldiering stirred even the most unmartial spirits. Gentlemanly physiques, though strangers to exertion, were gamely put to the test.

James Brougham and I recently joined the Bloomsbury Associ-ation, [wrote a young Scottish advocate recently arrived in London] and for ten days past have been drilling most indefati-gably, going from Northumberland Street up to the Foundling Hospital Ground twice every day. I have been at it three hours this morning, and my hand shakes so that you see I cannot write.[25]

Even Charles James Fox, passionate anti-militarist and derisive gadfly of the whole Volunteer system ('theatrical, ostentatious foppery....fit for nothing but to be put on the top of a hill to be looked at') did his stint - but only as a private - in his local unit. By contrast, his long-time adversary William Pitt, moodily kicking his heels out of office, found an absorbing new métier. In his capacity as Warden of the Cinque Ports he plunged into the task of concerting the defence effort on the part of the coast most exposed to invasion. His tall, lean, uniformed figure, perpetuated in prints of the day, became a common sight as he journeyed from his seat at Walmer Castle along the Kentish and Sussex coasts. He succeeded in raising three battalions of Cinque Ports Volunteers and, as their colonel, proceeded to drill them energetically. In addition he saw to the raising of the local quota for the Army of Reserve, besides organising the Sea Fencibles to man a flotilla of 170 gunboats for the defence of the coast from Margate to Hastings. Pitt's relish for his new role as military suzerain is evident in his letters:

> We are going on here most rapidly and, in proportion to our population, most extensively in every species of local defence both naval and military, and trust I shall both add very much to the security of essential points on this coast and set not a bad example to other maritime districts.

Early in September he wrote:

> Before the long nights we hope to be very well prepared to receive them, both afloat and ashore.[26]

Many other grandees played a similar role with a similarly new-found gusto reminiscent of the medieval warlords who had been their distant predecessors.

> I hope soon to be able to converse with you, [Thomas Grenville wrote to his brother, Lord Grenville] and the chief object of these lines is to learn from you what is the present state of your military labours, and whether in a few days I shall find you at Dropmore, or shall only hear of you with your flying squadrons among the woods and defiles of the Chiltern Hills.[27]

But zeal was sometimes in more plentiful supply than aptitude; it was said of Thomas Erskine in his capacity as colonel of the Law Association Volunteers that he was lost without a card to remind him of the words of command, and was not very sure of himself even with it in his hand. Another lawyer, Lord Ellenborough, soon to become Chief Justice, was useless on the parade ground without chalk marks on his boots to indicate left and right.[28]

It was inevitable that the upper classes would take the lead in the Volunteer movement, particularly in rural areas, where social distinctions were at their most clear-cut. It undoubtedly never occurred to anyone in Buckinghamshire - certainly not to the clan itself - that anyone but the Grenvilles, the shire's undisputed political masters, would run the local force from the family seat at Stowe, with Lord Buckingham appointing his brother Lord Grenville as lieutenant-colonel, and other family members assuming commands in various quarters of the county. Even in towns it was often though proper to invite a local magnate to assume command, though officers in urban corps were usually drawn from the prosperous business and professional class. Most of those in the Sheffield Volunteers for example, came from manufacturing and business families, often involved in the town's thriving metal trades, with a smattering of attorneys, bankers and the like.

One may ask what impulses stirred so many Britons to step forward and take their place in the new amateur army. The atavistic tribal urge to defend hearth and home against Boney's hordes was certainly a prime impetus, but as in all such mass movements, motives could be many and various. For the upper classes and the more prosperous echelons of society, a sense of social obligation beckoned, indeed could not easily be denied, as a Yorkshire mother warned her son who was away from home in Scotland:

> I know not what must be done in that regard, for as your father's health puts his personal service out of the question, you become the immediate object and have been repeatedly asked for....God knows how it is to be honourably avoided.

His sister gleefully rubbed it in:

> You are enjoying yourself amazingly just now, but as soon as
> you return home, I assure you, you will not be quite as much
> at large, as you must volunteer yourself for the defence of your
> country and learn all the exercise and command the Brandsby
> Volunteers.[29]

But Volunteering also offered certain attractions that part-time
soldiering has always supplied for the better-off: it gave an
opportunity to cut a dash in a uniform, as is evident from the many
portraits done at the time of Volunteer officers self-consciously
decked out in spanking-new full regimental fig. It also injected a
novel diversion into the ennui that often lay heavy on the provincial
society of the time. More generally, especially in towns, the local
corps was as much a focus of communal identity and pride as of a
wider patriotism. But one may doubt whether all labouring men,
artisans or poor tradesmen shared the gung-ho spirit of their
betters. The tub-thumping of parsons' sermons and the plethora of
'loyal papers' intended to convince them of Boney's fiendish
designs on a conquered Britain may well have played their part in
gingering up the lower orders, but it is likely that instinctive or
prudent deference to the urgings of social superiors and the
prospect of escaping the ballots figured at least as large. After a
day's toil in field or workshop, many a company at drill must have
presented a similarly forlorn sight to that encountered one August
evening by a young lady in Hampshire:

> ....the men exercising in their surock frocks - the poor crea-
> tures looking both tired and awkward and not inspired by
> martial ardour. However, everybody is a soldier here, whether
> they like it or not.[30]

Such reluctant warriors would have had to console themselves as
best they could with their ballot exemptions, the shilling allowance
in the pocket, and perhaps some conviviality in the alehouse when
drill was over.

In the Regular army, authority was backed by the awesome writ of the Articles of War, with brutal punishments routinely meted out to transgressors. On the other hand, except in the event of invasion, Volunteers only became subject to the full rigours of military discipline while on occasional stints of permanent duty. But in the general run of things it was inconceivable that citizens freely tendering their services to their country should be kept in order by methods used for bridling the brutish, despised soldiery. Hence the problem of enforcing discipline among amateur part-timers could be a ticklish one. In corps drawn from rural areas discipline was hardly a problem, since officers were drawn from the landed classes and the rank and file were labouring men; in many cases a landlord often raised a unit from among his own tenants and dependants. But the situation was different in towns, where the old social patterns counted for a great deal less and a large artisan and trading element cultivated a sturdy independence. Here there might be little social distance between officers and men and, even if it existed, it might not necessarily be deferred to.

Examples of mutinous Volunteer behaviour unthinkable in the Regulars are not hard to come by in the official records. Mass resignations from the West Wratling Volunteers in Cambridgeshire, made 'in a very abrupt and disorderly manner', were followed by a refusal of those left to attend the weekly drill or go on permanent duty, and a propensity to 'behave themselves in an irregular and unsoldierlike manner'. In despair, their captain submitted his own resignation together with the rest of the officers and requested that the king disband the whole company.[31] In Cheshire the Nantwich troop of Yeomanry similarly refused either to attend drill or go on permanent duty. Their colonel sorrowfully concluded that

> ....having lost that honest enthusiasm which at one time
> animated them, [they] have refused to agree to any proposal for
> the good of the regiment that is likely to give them trouble.[32]

Another commanding officer was reduced to impotence when his company, the Evershot and Sydling Volunteers, en route to

Weymouth for a spell of permanent duty, got as far as Dorchester and, fed up with foot-slogging along Dorset lanes, refused to a man to take another step further. There was nothing he could do but order them back home and dock the lot of them their marching guinea.[33]

Among soldiers alcohol has traditionally been the most deadly solvent of discipline and, this being a hard-drinking age at all levels of society, it is not surprising to find Volunteer officers having to cope with its effects. It was a cask of ale smuggled on to the exercise field that was the cause of an unseemly fracas among the Ely Volunteers one day in April 1804. When the colonel noticed a man tippling in the ranks, the ensign in charge merely retorted, 'They ought to have it, it is customary'. The colonel then tried to manhandle an argumentative private, who squared up to him saying, 'Meddle with me if you dare'. Retrieving the shreds of his dignity before it was too late, the colonel left the job to a sergeant and departed the scene pursued by a chorus of drunken jeers - 'Goodbye, Brackenbury, who cares for Brackenbury!' Firing their muskets in the air, the company retired to the ale-cask for more liquid refreshment. Rather unwisely, the colonel later sent a lieutenant to retrieve the company's drummer together with his instrument. The hapless subaltern found himself up against fixed bayonets and the ensign brandishing a sword, saying 'You shall not have the drum, you shall have my head first'. In the Regulars, this conduct would have brought the miscreants to the triangle in short order, with the prospect of being flogged into insensibility. As it was, Brackenbury's only resort was to disband the company.[34]

Faced with a resolute refusal to be impressed by recently-acquired insignia of rank, wise Volunteer officers found themselves having to fall back on what is now known as man-management. On one occasion a bumptious young sprig of a subaltern in the Sheffield Volunteers learned a lesson in this particular art the hard way. To enforce silence in the ranks, Lieutenant Thomas Ward marched his men round and round the Doncaster Corn Market until at length two browned-off privates walked away, ignoring his threats of extra guard duty, while the rest complained bitterly that they were all being punished for the offences of a few. Ward found that neither the company captain nor any of his fellow officers would back him in his predicament. It fell to the colonel to deal with the situation. He paraded the company and addressed them in a carefully conciliatory manner; mildly rebuking them for disobedience, he did not deny their right to complain, even admitting the possibility that Ward had been in the wrong: 'for if I really had done wrong, it was their duty to obey, and afterwards complain of injustice'. Ward, sensible man, took his cue from his superior.

> Before dismissing them from private parade, I said to the company, 'From what the colonel has said, I hope that some of you are convinced of the impropriety of your conduct, and will never again be guilty of the same fault. It was never, however, my intention to punish the innocent who are perhaps with reason a little dissatisfied. I therefore give you a guinea as a pleasant plaister to salve the sore feet which you mentioned. If you are satisfied with my conduct, give me three cheers', which they accordingly did, and invited me to drink with them at the Old George that evening.[35]

Volunteers could be quick to voice their grievance at the most trifling slight to their dignity; when the adjutant of the Oxford corps ventured to rebuke the mustered regiment for sporting velvet neck stocks instead of the vilely uncomfortable standard leather issue, the response from the ranks was swift: as the 'Political Register''s correspondent indignantly wrote:

> Would you believe it, sir, the *gentlemen* Volunteers took fire at this remark, and, jealous of any encroachment on their ridiculous privileges, vociferated from on all sides in the genuine spirit of a democratic rabble, 'Velvet, velvet'.[36]

Another officer's unfortunate manner provoked an embarrassing mass absence from a parade of the Dover Volunteers when Pitt arrived to inspect them accompanied by his brother the Earl of Chatham. It appeared that the corps could no longer stomach the parade-ground language of one Major Shee, who

....in addressing them when in the field....so far lost sight of
the gentleman as frequently to swear at the corps, and had even
descended to the use of the very extraordinary and degrading
epithet of 'damned scoundrels'.

Confronted by the threat of mass resignation, the Major

....appeared sensibly affected on this occasion and apologised
handsomely. 'I request you therefore to bury what has passed
in friendly oblivion!'.[37]

A single out-of-order remark by another officer was enough to
spark off a long-running wrangle which was to divert the citizenry
of Bath during the summer of 1804. The incident occurred one
Monday evening in July when the town corps was assembled for
inspection parade. An ensign, George Norman, noticing James
Higgo, a lodging-house keeper,

....talking loudly and marching carelessly and unsteadily, said
to a sergeant major, 'That fellow is drunk, damn him, turn him
out, he can't march three steps right'.

The remark was loud enough to be overheard in the ranks, and
Higgo, who 'felt the indignity that was offered him', retorted in the
authentic voice of the uniform-hating Englishman

You are an impudent puppy, sir, you think because you have
a long sword, a long coat and a cocked hat, that you may insult
persons equally respectable as yourself, but I'll not be insulted
by any of you.

The commanding officer, Colonel Strode, tried his best to make the
peace, appealing to Higgo's better nature and even offering to
convey his apology to the ensign to save his face for him, but the
mulish Higgo insisted that the first apology should come from
Norman. In the circumstances, Strode decided that he had no
choice but to discharge the bloody-minded lodging-house keeper.
That was only the beginning. Thirty-nine members of the company

passed a series of resolutions affirming their loyalty to their
captain, regiment and country, but demanding that Strode recon-
sider Higgo's dismissal or they would resign. The malcontents did
not leave it there; they took their grievances to their fellow
townsfolk by circulating two broadsheets: 'Incontrovertible Facts
in Defence of the Fifth Company' made a forthright statement of
Higgo's case, while the other, addressed 'To the Officers of the
Loyal Bath Volunteers', was a stiff lecture to those persons on the
proper respect 'which should ever be shown to men who sacrifice
their time to the public weal'. The bemused Strode sought the
assistance of the Lord Lieutenant, but it took a letter from no less
a personage than the Home Secretary, read out to the assembled
company, finally to bring about the collapse of the mutiny.[38]

All these incidents seem to pale into insignificance compared
to the mayhem that flared on the streets of Chester in December
1803. It was sparked off when a Navy press gang took a seaman
who happened to be a member of the town's Volunteer corps.
When some of his fellows threatened to free him, the pressed man
was put into Northgate Jail for safe keeping. By evening a crowd
of Volunteers some four hundred strong had assembled in uniform
outside the jail demanding his release and, when the Navy refused
to hand him over, proceeded to storm the building. When a major
of the corps appeared and threatened to shoot the first man to try
and enter, he was seized with cries of 'Down with him!' and
'Break his sword over his head!'. The turnkey hurriedly gave up
his captive, who was chaired through the town 'amidst shouts of
exultation and triumph'. The mob, drunk with success - and very
likely alcohol as well - went on to break up the press gang's
rendezvous. The magistrates were, as usual in these situations,
helpless, and had to send for the Militia to restore order.[39]
Although this episode might seem to confirm the predictions of the
jeremiahs who claimed to detect in the Volunteer movement a
sinister potential threat to the established order, in fact this was no
Volunteer insurrection but rather an example of the old British
custom of the impressment riot - and a rather tame specimen at
that, as no-one seems to have actually been killed.

Although the organisation of the Volunteers was strictly speaking Home Office business, it behoved the Commander-in-Chief to see to the creation of a proper command structure and acquaint himself with the reliability of each corps in order to weed out those that could only be entrusted with local police work. Accordingly corps were brigaded where practicable, while isolated units were grouped into battalions and regiments. From the half-pay list the War Office appointed Inspecting Officers to each Military District with the rank of lieutenant-colonel, whose task it was to inspect each corps at two-monthly intervals and report on its effectiveness to the Horse Guards. By the beginning of 1803 their reports spoke of a reassuringly high level of training and discipline in many quarters of the kingdom.[40] However, an Edinburgh lawyer, himself a keen Volunteer, put his finger on a weakness that would undoubtedly have told against his colleagues' effectiveness on the battlefield.

> ....their drilling was universally vitiated by the essential and obvious defect of their not being moved in large masses....It was all single battalion drilling and useless shows: the work of each week being the same with that of the week before. Except as police, the foot gentlemen were useless.[41]

Battlefield tactics of the day required troops to be deployed in immaculately straight, evenly-spaced lines two or three deep, and the purpose of contemporary drill manuals was to reduce the complicated routines involved into sequences of robotic movements that could be instilled into the simplest ploughboy. Such lines were several battalions long and much practice was needed to achieve precise co-ordination particularly at the advance, otherwise bulges and gaps could be exploited by enemy cavalry and skirmishers or by the French-style columnar attack, specifically designed to punch holes in the opposing line. Units not trained in these routines were not to be depended on in battle, and no amount of drill, sham fights and shooting competitions would do anything to remedy it.

In wading through the thickets of enactments and circulars concerned with raising troops for defence, you begin to experience a certain fellow-feeling for distracted Lords Lieutenant who plied the Home Secretary with peevish plaints from beneath mountains of paperwork. Did the government want Volunteers or not? Should they complete the ballots before enrolling them? Which Volunteers were administered under what Act of Parliament? Yet some understanding should also be due to the Addington government in the unparalleled task it had to set itself, to expand the nation's defensive capability to well over half a million men within less than a year. The official target for enlistment was eventually fixed at 300,000, but initially there was no way of predicting the scale of the response or its effect on the ballot quotas. Add to this the primitive nature of the official machinery and it was little wonder that everyone from churchwarden to Home Secretary should find himself at sixes and sevens. Yet though the workings creaked alarmingly under the unaccustomed strain, the nation managed to muddle through; by the end of the year 1803, as we have seen, the ballots had done their work well enough, while no fewer than 380,000 Volunteers were at their weekly drill. On the whole it is doubtful if a better result could have been achieved. Critics had no real practicable alternatives to offer. The opposition in Parliament called for an expanded Regular army backed up by static local defence units, but this was to ignore political and military realities. For good or ill, the exotic hotch-potch that was Britain's defence forces, cobbled together by the Horse Guards planners into an approximation to a national army, was the best hope of prevailing. But defensive capability does not reside solely in manpower. Fortifications, cunningly placed, can offset weaknesses in human fighting material, and ramparts and ditches were to play their own, vital, part in British plans to stop the Corsican in his tracks.

Chapter Seven

Towers Along the Steep

When Britannia ruled the waves in the age of sail, the British would often refer to their Navy as 'the wooden walls of England'. The expression carried a larger meaning than one might think. Besides signifying the nation's sentimental affection for the Service, it betokens the instinctive defensive stance of a tight little island and the confidence with which it entrusted its security to a few tens of thousands of ruffianly tars. Britain's faith in her wooden walls also implied the redundancy of the kind made of brisk and stone; the brick confident affirmation that rang in the lines of the poet Campbell spoke for the nation:

> Britannia needs no bulwarks,
> No towers along the steep.

The British suspicion of armies extended to all things military; like soldiers, fortresses seemed a useless expense. Neither the invasion scares of the Seven Years' War and the American war nor the relentless hostility of revolutionary France had done much to change British minds on the subject. The exiguous selection of elderly piles that adorned Britain's south-east coast in 1803 certainly gave no evidence of a national enthusiasm for fortification. Landguard Fort, defending the approach to the estuaries of the rivers Stour and Orwell in Essex, was, according to Sir James Craig, fit only for demolition. The medieval castle at Dover, strengthened and modified to take modern cannon, stood guard over the town and harbour. At Deal, Walmer and Sandown were castles of less antique design, built by Henry VIII to protect the

Downs. A small fort further east at Sandgate, another Henrician legacy, was in dire need of repair. Another of Henry's forts at Tilbury together with a large redoubt at Sheerness protected the approaches to the Thames and Medway, while on the right bank of the Medway a line of earthworks enclosed Chatham dockyard. Two other important installations, the Deptford dockyard and the Ordnance Board's arsenal at Woolwich, had no defences whatsoever. The capital itself could boast one solitary medieval fortification in the form of the Tower; otherwise it lay wide open to the invader.

Unlike most of his compatriots, the Duke of York did not regard this situation with indifference. His experience in the Low Countries had convinced him that carefully-sited fortifications could be a nation's salvation:

> Thrice during the last war, the fate of the Netherlands was decided by battles in the field, whilst in former times when protected by fortresses, little impression could be made after the most signal victories.[1]

Frederick argued that more fortifications in the south-east would greatly enhance the workings of his strategy which was, we remember,

> ....to impede the march and thus gain time on the invader should he not be defeated on landing....

and particularly so against an army under-endowed with artillery.

> One of the greatest advantages to be derived over an enemy who must come inadequately prepared with artillery is the opposing his progress by strong posts upon the most direct advantageous lines to the capital and which, he having no immediate means of reducing, must throw him into the most embarrassing difficulties.[2]

Sensitive to the prejudice against spending on defence works, Frederick, far from urging the transformation of south-east England into a vast armed redoubt, pitched his demands low - the fortification of important anchorages, a few other strategic points and those parts of the coast where landings were possible. But he made the mistake of pressing even this modest case with more vigour than was wise in a British military chief.

> I am afraid [he wrote to his ministerial master] that I have been understood as having recommended a system of permanent works for the defence of Great Britain.[3]

However, the most awkward obstacle in the Duke's path, against which he was forever barking his shins, was an antique quirk of British government whereby ordnance and fortifications were the responsibility of a separate department of state, the Ordnance Board. The Board was presided over by the Master General, who was a member of the Cabinet. In 1803 the office was held by the second Earl of Chatham, the elder brother of William Pitt.

> It is a cruel thing at this time [opined Chatham's predecessor, Lord Cornwallis] that so important a department should be placed in hands so incapable and improper.[4]

Though Chatham lacked not so much capacity as application, the remark was just enough; intelligent but indolent, the second Earl added no lustre to his father's august name. However, slack though his grip might be on his own province, he was diligent enough in guarding against trespassers. Any defence work classified as a 'permanent fortification' came under his charge and was, he adamantly insisted, solely the Board's business. Furthermore, Chatham's priorities were not those of the Commander-in-Chief. Strangely, in view of what was happening across the Channel, the Ordnance Board's almost exclusive preoccupations at this time, from which they were loath to be distracted, were fortification projects at Portsmouth and in Ireland.[5]

Although London, the enemy's main objective, was innocent of man-made defences, Nature had not left the city completely bereft of protection. The situation was set out in a Horse Guards paper.

> The position is cut in two by a great river over which we have several and sufficient passages but which effectually prevents any tolerable communication between the parts of an investing enemy. In the line of our surrounding position, nature has provided a circle of commanding ridges, heights and rising ground which are generally protected by their own steepness, by wood, water or by enclosure, so that the approach of our enemy may be reduced to certain spaces which can easily be strengthened by field works supported by additional bodies of troops.[6]

The areas of high ground referred to are the sandy ridge to the north on which Highgate and Hampstead are situated, and the Norwood hills to the south. A defensive ring around the city incorporating these features had been traced during the previous invasion scare by Lieutenant Colonel Brown and at the Horse Guards his map was once more unrolled. North of the river, the eastern sector of Brown's line was formed by the river Lea and the marshes that flanked it from its confluence with the Thames as far north as Stamford Hill, where the line turned west to follow the sandy heights through Mount Pleasant, Crouch End, Highgate and Hampstead; thence dropping south to the Paddington Canal, it reached the river at Battersea Bridge by way of Holland House and Little Chelsea. South of the river the line left the Thames two miles upstream at the confluence with the river Wandle at Wandsworth and followed a fragment of river terracing south-east towards Tooting and Streatham; whence it continued along the ridge of the Norwood hills as they trend north-east towards Deptford, at which point it again joined the river.[7]

It was a lengthy perimeter, about thirty miles in all, extending well beyond the capital's outer limits into the surrounding countryside. (At the time, the city gave out to open fields and market gardens beyond Kennington Oval to the south, what was soon to be called Regent's Park to the north, Hyde Park to the

west, and Limehouse to the east, while places like Hampstead and
Norwood were still remote country villages.) To hold every inch
of such a widely thrown line Frederick estimated that he would
need as many as 128,000 men, but it was unlikely that an invading
army would arrive in sufficient strength to invest the whole
perimeter. Instead it was reasonable to assume that the invader
would concentrate his forces on either the south-east or the north-
east sector, depending on where he had made his landing; in either
case, the river presented a formidable obstacle to his deploying
pressure entirely at will. Here the defenders undoubtedly had the
advantage; all three crossings - London, Blackfriars and Westminster bridges - were well within the enclave, so that troops could
easily be switched to whatever front was under attack. But the
existing bridges were too far upstream to be convenient for moving
troops along the eastern front, and particularly for transferring
reinforcements between the Eastern and Southern Districts, which
would entail lengthy detours westward. Crossing points further
downstream were called for. Inside the perimeter an arrangement
for a ferry or boat bridge was made at Blackwall Stairs, while
beyond it another ferry was set up between fortified points at
Tilbury and Gravesend that would be able to take across 12,000
infantry, 1,100 cavalry or 40 pieces of artillery within a 24-hour
period.[8]

The defensive line was to consist of earthworks that could be
rapidly thrown up provided there were sufficient hands available to
dig the ditches and pile up the spoil to form a rampart. In considering the timing of the operation, the Commander-in-Chief had to
ponder the competing claims of preparedness and public tranquil-
lity. Should he disrupt the life of the metropolis by ordering vast
labours that might prove redundant; or instead wait on the event
and risk being caught napping? Calculations were made and,
satisfied that all could be made ready in the interval he could count
on after the initial alarm came through, the Duke ordered all
preparations short of actual construction to be made against the
day, ready to be set in train if it actually dawned.

Accordingly Lords Lieutenant were instructed to draw up registers of gardeners, smiths, carpenters, sawyers, timber merchants and labourers, and inventories of carts, horses and tools, so that men and materials could be mobilised as swiftly as possible, while the positions of the intended works were laid out with stakes. The Commissary General was directed to investigate the supply situation; he was able to report that the city itself could count on three weeks' stock of flour, with a further fortnight's supply in magazines at Fulham, Brentford and elsewhere. The Duke was particularly concerned to find out the available numbers of two essential species of expert, civil engineers and artillerymen; even in the army experienced artillerymen were always at a premium, and instructing men in serving cannon took a long time. At least there was no shortage of guns; the Ordnance Board was able to supply a total of 267, most of which were shipped upriver from Woolwich and stored in five waterside depots for rapid distribution.[9]

The Duke of York saw a positive benefit in leaving construction work until the last minute. Giving people something to do instead of sitting passively awaiting the advancing onslaught would provide

....useful and animating labour to an overgrown population which might otherwise become dangerous and desponding.[10]

On the other hand, freshly-built earthworks lack the resistance to artillery fire of older ones in which the soil has had time to settle and compact, so that a rampart newly thrown up would need to be that much more massive. Moreover, the Duke was aware that a calculated risk is still a risk, as he candidly admitted:

It would be a great relief to my mind had I sufficient grounds to give a decided answer to your Lordship's question, 'Whether what remains to be done can be completed in due time if the works be resumed after the landing of the enemy?' This must depend upon the more or less rapid advance of the enemy - as also upon the regularity and steadiness of the people of the metropolis, whose zeal shall induce them to contribute their labour towards the completion of the works.[11]

In addition to the earthworks around the capital, the Horse Guards had plans to strengthen two natural features on its eastern approaches. One was the river Lea which formed part of the defensive line. As it approached the confluence with the Thames downstream of the great loop around the Isle of Dogs, branch streams and marshes began to proliferate on either bank.[12] The Duke of York intended to make this soggy area even more impassable. John Rennie, one of the new breed of civil engineers, was brought in to draw up plans and it was decided to combine a deepening of the main channel with the construction of dams to allow flooding of the marshy ground on either side. The other project in the Duke's mind was to build a fortified position on Shooter's Hill, an isolated eminence on the main road to the east Kent coast overlooking Woolwich arsenal. But here he ran into one of his several maddening demarcation disputes with the Ordnance Board. In specifying a permanent fortification, he had no alternative but to pass the proposal over to the Board's committee of engineers who promptly shelved it, as usual pleading pressing business elsewhere.[13]

The two front-line Military Districts which lay between the invader and the capital would present him with very different aspects. The flat coastline of the Eastern District south of Orford Ness dissolves into a watery maze of estuaries, creeks and mud flats and, particularly to the south, sandbanks and shoals. Lord Keith assured the Duke of York that the estuaries of the Crouch , Blackwater and Colne, where the French had previously planned to land an army in 1759, were solidly barricaded by the Maplin and Buxey sands and could in any case be closed off by his ships. But he admitted the possibility of landings at certain other places - in Hollesley Bay, on the coastline between Woodbridge and the Orwell estuary, at Harwich and Clacton.[14]

Inland, the low-lying terrain offered few opportunities for fortification. A few miles south of Chelmsford, the designated emergency seat of government, an elevated position for an entrenched camp was found at Galleywood Common,[15] but the possible location of strong points elsewhere, particularly in the vulnerable Colchester area, provoked much head-scratching at the Horse Guards. Another entrenched camp, at Dunmow on the District's western flank, was mooted but never built. However, as time went on the planners ceased to rate the risk to the area as highly as before, as is evident from a progressive diminution in the District's troop strength. This was not because of any fading in the appearance of danger from the Dutch ports - on the contrary, invasion scares emanated more frequently from Holland than France; but the overall intelligence picture told a different story, showing Napoleon concentrating his main effort on his new harbours south of Gris Nez that looked across the Strait to Kent and Sussex. All the same, the possibility of attack could not be wholly eliminated; the area might still figure as a target for a diversionary thrust from the Texel, and it seemed prudent to keep a force there large enough for an invader to reckon with.

Kent and Sussex afforded Napoleon's flotilla not only a shorter crossing but easier landing. But on the latter score, a study of the map could safely rule out extensive stretches. A seaborne assault needs a clear run to the shore, a generous expanse of landing beach and an absence of natural features that would provide defensive strongpoints and hamper a rapid move inland. A few sections of the south-east coast are almost continuously cliff-bound. Other possible sites are impeded by offshore rocks or submerged by the tide for long periods. Of those remaining, an apparently obvious contender was Pegwell Bay and Sandwich Flats, whose sands seem to reach out endlessly to meet the coast of France itself, and now resound with the howl of hovercraft shuttling back and forth to Calais. Indeed, Napoleon himself later implied that this was his intended landfall;[16] if so, he would have joined a famous company that included a previous emperor, Claudius, St. Augustine and, at least as legend would have it, the Dark Age invaders, Hengist and Horsa.

Yet from the beginning, Britain's defence planners struck this sector from their list of serious possibilities. They did so on the advice of their naval colleagues, who assured them that it was more or less impregnable, being flanked by the Downs. This extensive anchorage sandwiched between the coast and the Goodwin Sands was the base of Lord Keith's North Sea squadron, and the Navy found it hard to imagine a situation when it would not be guarded in strength. The invader would also have to reckon with the ten-mile-long bulwark of the Goodwins themselves, lying athwart the north-easterly course from the main French harbours.

The terrain of south-east England is ribbed by three ranges of hills that lie diagonally north-west to south-east, roughly in parallel. The chalk formations of the north and south Downs have as their coastal flanks respectively the cliff-lines from Folkestone to South Foreland and west from Beachy Head. Between them lies the High Weald, which reaches the Channel near Hastings. None of these heights would hold up a determined enemy advance for long. The plump contours of chalk downland with their thin tree cover offered no snug defensive positions. The Wealden country, on the other hand, though broken and thickly wooded, lacked the consistency of height to pose a really formidable barrier. But the defenders had to make the best use of what the terrain offered and decided to concentrate on holding the line of the north Downs. This made strategic sense; wherever an invader landed, he would have to negotiate this final rampart before falling on the capital and in so doing, would seek the routes into the London basin through the gaps in the ridge. In the summer of 1804 Lieutenant Colonel Brown was sent to survey the terrain for defensive positions. He earmarked 13 between Dorking in the west and Sevenoaks in the east, located either on the southern scarp of the chalk guarding the through passages or a few miles south on the Wealden hills.

Brown's main concern was four main roads that passed through the Downs on their way from the coast to the capital, and he selected locations that stood the best chance of holding out longest for the siting of redoubts, each to hold 400 troops.[17] However, important though these gaps were, none was as vital as

a passage to the east in the angle of the Downs as they turn south-
east, through which the river Medway finds its way into the
Thames estuary. The Medway gap demanded attention for several
reasons. Within it was situated a key river crossing at Rochester
and one of the Navy's principal dockyards at Chatham. It was also
the only position along the invader's way to the capital that, if held,
would put him in anything like a predicament as, lacking a pontoon
train, he would be forced to seek a passage over the next bridge
upstream at Maidstone and so expose a flank to counter-attack.
Once the Medway was forced, the last chance of holding off a
siege of London would have gone.

Until quite recently it had been possible for an invader who
attained the Medway gap to strike a blow without having to cross
the river at all. Chatham Yard, on the right, southern bank of the
river, was considered so vulnerable that at the beginning of the
Seven Years' War it was decided to protect the whole complex of
yards and basins with a cordon of fortifications. These, the
Chatham Lines, were erected on the high ground to the east, and
by 1803 extended in a dog-toothed arc for a mile and a half from
Gillingham Reach round to Chatham Reach. They comprised a
single length of ditch and earthen rampart with the usual projecting
bastions to give flanking fire, though at the southern end where the
ground steepens, the defences clustered more densely with a thicket
of works centred on Fort Amherst, a brick-reinforced redoubt.[18]

Fortifications like those at Chatham, built of earth without
benefit of masonry or brick revetting, commended themselves to
economy-minded governments, but in the long run they were a
poorer investment since they were prone to the wear and tear of the
elements. Consequently, when they were needed, hasty work had
to be put in to restore them to a serviceable condition. This was
found to be the case by the Ordnance Board's chief fortification
expert, Brigadier General William Twiss when he looked over the
Lines in 1803. However, he reported that if sufficient labour was
provided by the army, they could be put in 'a tolerable state of
defence' by the end of the summer.[19] But Twiss's brief was not
to examine the Lines merely as a passive defence. The Com-

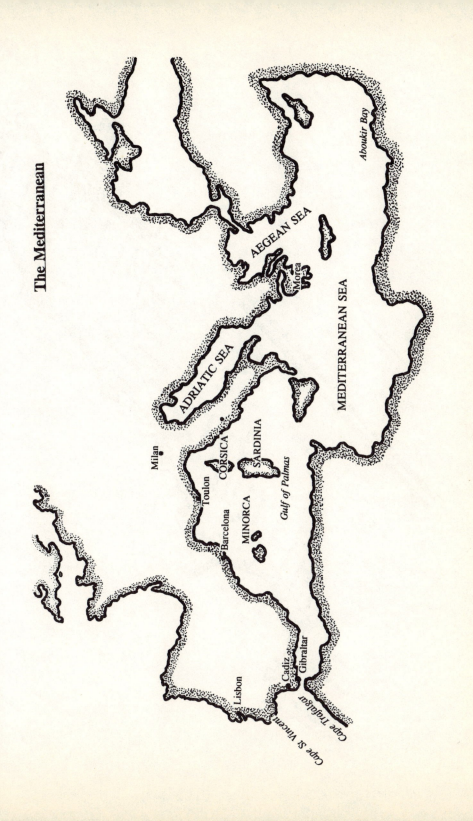

The Mediterranean

Aboukir Bay

AEGEAN SEA

Morea

ADRIATIC SEA

MEDITERRANEAN SEA

Milan

CORSICA

SARDINIA

Toulon

MINORCA

Gulf of Palmas

Barcelona

Lisbon

Cadiz

Gibraltar

Cape Trafalgar

Cape St. Vincent

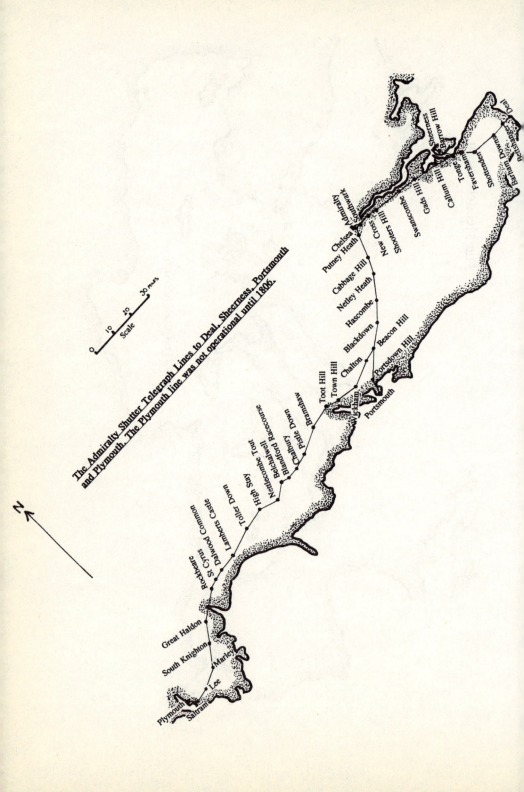

The Admiralty Shutter Telegraph Lines to Deal, Sheerness, Portsmouth and Plymouth. The Plymouth line was not operational until 1806.

Scale
0   10   20   30 mls

N

Admiralty
Chelsea
Putney Heath
Cabbage Hill
Netley Heath
Hascombe
Blackdown
Chalton
Town Hill
Toot Hill
Bramshaw
Pistle Down
Chalbury
Blandford Racecourse
Nettlecombe Tout
High Stay
Toller Down
Lambers Down
Dalwood Castle
St Cyrus Common
Rockbeare
Great Haldon
South Knighton
Marley
Lee
Plymouth
Saltram
Southwark
New Cross
Shooers Hill
Swanscombe
Gads Hill
Callum Hill
Tonge
Faversham
Shottenden
Barham Downs
Betteshanger Deal
Iron
Sheerness
Barrow Hill
Beichalwell
Wickham
Portsmouth
Portsdown Hill
Beacon Hill

mander-in-Chief had conceived for them a new strategic role as a bridgehead covering a pontoon bridge to be thrown across the Medway. Thus capable of reinforcement, they could function as a sally port well-placed for mounting sizeable counter-attacks against the advancing enemy.[20]

To take advantage wherever possible of the terrain inland made sense but it was on the coast where fortifications would count most. In order to make a tenuous toehold into a secure *logement*, an amphibious force must quickly seize a harbour as a bridgehead for the rapid build-up of reinforcements, heavy weapons and supplies. Only in our own century has a successful operation managed without one when in June 1944, the Allied Expeditionary Force towed its own breakwaters - the chains of massive concrete caissons called Mulberries - across to the Normandy Coast. For the role of supply port Napoleon would certainly have had his eye on Dover, the biggest harbour on the Strait and within sight and cannon-fire sound of the French coast - with a glass on the White Cliffs, you could, on a clear day, easily see the Boulogne army encampments. Not surprisingly in view of its position, Dover had over the centuries accumulated a number of defensive works. Its chief fortification was its most elderly, the Norman castle commanding the harbour, town and the road to London. This ancient edifice, ill-suited to the age of gunpowder, had been subjected to drastic modernisation. The moat had been dug out to double its original depth and the spoil piled against the curtain wall to make ramparts and batteries. The towers in the wall had been cut down and filled with rubble to make solid gun platforms and their bases banked with earth. Over a hundred pieces of artillery were ranged along its walls. Elsewhere, later works had been erected on each side of the harbour entrance to protect the approach, including Henry VIII's Archcliffe Fort, perched on the western edge of the cliffs overlooking the town.

Apart from Dover's potential value to the invader as a supply port, it was to figure large in the Commander-in-Chief's overall plan in a three-fold capacity: as a base for the Navy, a mobilisation point for the local Sea Fencibles, and an enclave, similar to the

Chatham Lines, from which to strike at the enemy's rear as he advanced inland. In its latter role, the intention was to supply and reinforce it by sea, so that whatever the situation on land, Dover could continue to hold out as an independent redoubt. As such it would put the enemy in a cleft stick - whether to divide his forces to neutralise the threat or risk forays against his rear.[21]

The thorny problem of Dover's defence lay not on the seaward but the landward side. As the cross-Channel traveller can see, the harbour lies in a valley interrupting the wall of the famous chalk cliffs. To the west the chalk rises steeply to the Western Heights, a flattish ridge some 360 feet high. This feature, overlooking the harbour and town below, was the key to its security. If British forces could hold on to the Heights, even with the harbour and castle lost, their artillery would still be able to rain plunging fire on targets below, making both harbour and town untenable. If on the other hand the French managed to seize them they could, even with their light field guns, overwhelm the defences below well enough to gain control of the harbour or at least deny its use to the defenders.

More likely than an attack on Dover from the sea would be an assault from the landward side following a landing at a convenient point further west, in which case there was nothing to prevent the Heights being seized. The obvious answer was to fortify the position with a large-scale work, something that had long been pondered without result. During the American war the Ordnance Board had bought a large acreage of land for the purpose, but by 1803 it still lay innocent of the sappers' attentions. A rapidly erected entrenched camp on the site now seemed best to fill the gap, and the Duke of York pressed the Board for one large enough to hold a garrison of five or six thousand troops. Brigadier General Twiss was brought in by the Ordnance Board and delivered his verdict; the security of the Heights could not be guaranteed by anything less than 'a respectable fortress' or a network of independent redoubts toughened with brickwork - both long-term, expensive projects.[22] Soon the Cabinet had authorised a vast scheme of fortification that still lay incomplete when Napoleon departed for his final St. Helena exile. Its labyrinth of overgrown and crumbling ditches and ramparts still greet the wondering gaze of the modern visitor, a surreal monument to an earlier age's faith in the arcane art of fortification.

Grand projects for the future were all very well, but they did nothing to allay present apprehensions. Unabashed by the dismissal of his project, Frederick continued to insist on the necessity for some kind of temporary defence to relieve the Heights' nakedness. He proposed a simple earthen rampart, which soon materialised, since Chatham was content to classify it as a fieldwork and leave its execution to the Horse Guards.[23] Although it was better than nothing, everyone was aware that for the indefinite future the insecurity of the Heights was an embarrassment that had to be lived with, reassuring themselves as best they could by rehearsing the problems facing an enemy advance on Dover along the coast:

> ....from the strong nature of the rest of the coast, no landing could be effected or surprised but at a very great distance from the town, viz, in the Downs or beyond Folkestone: in both cases many difficulties may be encountered.[24]

Thus an army landing in, say, the Romney Marsh area and intending to move on Dover would have to negotiate the flank of the north Downs as it approached the sea near Folkestone. It was on this high ground that the defenders could best hope to block such a thrust, and strong points were designated there.

Of all the potential landing places on the coast of south-east England, none preoccupied the planners more than the coastal flats between the north and south Downs and the Weald as they approach the sea. Once shallow lagoons, centuries-long labours had worked their transformation into prime pasture-land. All offered perfect landing for a multitude of shallow craft, but it was Romney Marsh, the easternmost of these reaches, that gave the best combination of advantages, with the shortest crossing and the easiest approach to the capital. On the coast, long expanses of beach sweep down to the shingly snout of Dungeness from Hythe to the east and Rye to the west. Inland, wide, lonely - and indefensible - reaches of grassland dotted with grazing herds of sheep and gridded with drainage ditches stretch out to the faint pencil-line in the distance indicating the low cliff of the Marsh's boundary.

When anti-invasion planning was first seriously gone into at the Horse Guards during the 1790s, it had been decided that the way to pre-empt a descent on the Marsh was to return it to its primeval state by opening the three main outfall sluices on the Dymchurch sea-wall and flooding it with seawater, so cutting off all access to the interior. On first thoughts this seemed feasible enough as much of the Marsh lies below the level of the average high tide, but further investigation revealed considerable snags. Even when it was first broached, questions had been raised about how long inundation would take, and it had been found that three or even four tides - 36 to 48 hours - would be required. Subsequently it was discovered that only the western part of the Marsh would be thoroughly flooded even at the highest tides. Then there was the dilemma of timing, particularly acute in view of the consequences of contaminating prime pasture land with salt water. To act too quickly would risk doing damage in response to a false alert and by the time the mistake had been discovered, the harm would very likely be irretrievable, as even flooding the ditches alone would ruin the soil. Any delay, on the other hand, would risk the capture of the sluices.[25]

Although Pitt succeeded in gaining the grudging permission of the Commissioners of the sluices to modify them for inundation, by 1804 there was little enthusiasm left for the idea. Hence, when an alternative scheme came up, it attracted keen attention. Its author was the ubiquitous Lieutenant Colonel Brown. Brown was a Scot who had served as an officer of Engineers in the West Indies and Ireland and seen active service on the Helder expedition before his appointment as Quartermaster General at the Horse Guards in 1801. The Duke of York evidently had a high opinion of his abilities, subsequently entrusting him with responsibility for the topographical department and the command of the Royal Staff Corps, a unit raised for the Helder expedition to provide the army with a corps of engineers independent of the Ordnance Board. From the outbreak of war he was the Horse Guards' chief fortification expert.

In the summer of 1804 Brown had a hectic programme. After his excursions along the north Downs, he was sent to the coast where he went over the ground levels on Romney Marsh and confirmed that flooding would not work. Whilst on the Marsh he examined its eastern flank defences near Hythe, where the coastal cliffs retreat inland and follow the ancient shoreline. The high ground gave defensive positions overlooking the Marsh's eastern corner but, in his judgement, security would be much improved by the excavation of:

> ....a cut from Shorncliffe battery, passing in front of Hythe under Lympne heights to West Hythe....being everywhere within musket shot of the heights.

But he had a more ambitious scheme in mind, of which this would form only a part. He suggested an extension of the water barrier:

> ....along the rear of Romney Marsh, under Lympne and Aldington Heights, by Hurst, Balington, Ruckinge, Wearhorn, Appledore, under the heights of Oxney Isle and join the river Rother above Boonsbridge, thus in a manner cutting off Romney Marsh from the country, opening a short and easy communication between Kent and Sussex but, above all, rendering unnecessary the doubtful and destructive measure of laying so large a portion of the country waste by inundation.

Brown referred to his project as a 'cut' and when it eventually materialised it became known as the Royal Military Canal. Indeed, a canal is what it looks like, at least to the casual eye, and after completion it was actually in use as a commercial waterway for over a century. But it is more accurately described, in sapper's jargon, as a 'wet ditch': the tell-tale signs that this is no ordinary waterway are the kinks in its course, occurring regularly every half-mile or so, that allow enfilading fire to be directed along the channel. Hugging the base of the cliff-line that limits the Marsh, the canal would seal off 30 miles of coastline from the interior - and any invader who landed there - thus in effect creating an island. Brown calculated that an excavation nine feet deep would be needed, tapering from a width of 60 feet at the top to 40 feet at the bottom. Shelter for the defenders would be provided by a rampart 35 feet thick heaped up from the spoil taken from the excavation, and behind that, a military road was to be laid to speed deployment along its front.[26]

The plan won the immediate backing of Sir David Dundas and the Duke of York, who secured Pitt's approval within a week of its being submitted. To avoid the longeurs of Ordnance Board involvement, the canal was designated a fieldwork. John Rennie was appointed chief engineer and construction work was to be carried out by a detachment of Brown's Royal Staff Corps together with labour supplied by Dundas from troops stationed in the vicinity, though Rennie might bring in navvies if he thought it necessary. Some time in the next few weeks the decision was made to extend the canal beyond Brown's original line, across Pett Level, the adjacent area of reclaimed marshland. This prolongation, using sections of the Rother, Tillingham and Brede rivers, would give the advantage of a secure eastern flank position at the high ground at Cliff End.

The essential preliminary was to prevail on local landowners to surrender the desired acreage. Pitt himself, as Warden of the Cinque Ports, went to Dymchurch armed with a crop of persuasive arguments setting out the financial advantages of the project, shrewdly calculated to appeal to his listeners' pockets. They were probably unnecessary; no doubt relief that the new scheme made flooding redundant was enough to carry the day.

The prompt inauguration boded well for the completion of the canal by the projected date of June 1805. Work began on October 30th, but the onset of winter brought spells of rain, snow and freezing temperatures; sometimes the workings were awash, at others the ground was too hard to work. Squabbles broke out, largely due to a hazy demarcation of responsibility that allowed ample scope for Rennie and Brown to tread on each other's toes.

In particular, Rennie's habit of bemoaning the incompetence of the army and the civilian contractors did not make for happy relations.

> This day [Brown wrote in his diary in February 1805] in consequence of Mr. Rennie's interference, I came to a full explanation with him respecting his orders and interference on the work - after which he departed in a huff for London.[27]

Rennie also contrived an altercation with Brown's superior, General Brownrigg, over his scale of charges, which took the general rather aback.

> 'Why, this will never do. Seven guineas a day! Why, it is equal to the pay of a field marshal.'

Rennie was unabashed:

> 'Well, I am a field marshal in my profession, and if a field marshal in your line had answered your purpose, I suppose you would not have sent for me.'

> 'Then you refuse to make an abatement?'

> 'Not a penny' was the engineer's reply, and the bill was grudgingly paid in full.[28]

By the end of May 1805 only six miles of the canal had been started, and according to Rennie,

> ....not a twentieth part of the whole was executed and that in a slovenly manner.

The time had come for the intervention of higher authority, and in June the obstreperous Rennie was relieved of his responsibilities. Brown was put in charge to finish the work already begun and find another contractor to complete the rest. But Brown had had enough of civilians; as he wrote bitterly to his chief,

You have already had sufficient specimen of civil engineers,
contractors and surveyors, and we have no reason to look for
better treatment from amongst that description.[29]

He succeeded in convincing his superiors that the rest of the job
could be done better and cheaper by the army alone. With the
arrival of better weather, Brown took on more labour and tried to
make up for lost time. However by the month of August, when
Napoleon was poised to embark his legions, the work was nowhere
near completion.

Together with the Royal Military Canal and the Western
Heights, the most enduring and familiar of all the relics of the
invasion scare of 1803-5 are the Martello towers, those squat
shapes that still sit like a giant's up-turned flower-pots along the
shoreline of Kent and Sussex. But the origins of these familiar
denizens of the English seaside scene lay far away on foreign
strands. In a sense, the story begins in February of 1794, when
British forces trying to capture an anchorage in the Gulf of San
Fiorenzo on the island of Corsica found themselves up against
some stiff resistance from an unexpected quarter. Commanding the
approach to the Gulf was an ancient round tower, one of many to
be found dotted along the island's coastline. Sited on the headland
of Mortella Point, it had a garrison of fewer than 40 and was
equipped only with a couple of 18-pounders and a 6-pounder
mounted on the roof. Six months previously, it had been easily
overpowered after a two-hour bombardment by a ship of the line.
Now reoccupied, to the surprise of the British it put up a stout
resistance to the combined battering of a 74 and a 32, showering
them with a brisk output of heated shot from its guns. Eventually
considerable damage and casualties forced the ships to break off,
while the tower continued to hold out against a further two days'
steady pounding directed by Major General David Dundas and
Lieutenant General Sir John Moore before it could be overrun.[30]
Before evacuating the island four years later, the British took the
precaution of blowing it up; but we know a great deal about it as
the besiegers, curious and impressed, examined it with some care.

Several contemporary drawings and a wooden model of it still
exist. They show an elegant wasp-waisted elevation resembling a
chess-board castle piece, 40 feet high, with a diameter at the base
of about 45 feet, a wall 15 feet thick and an entrance door several
feet above ground level reached by a ladder.

Although the Mortella Point tower roused much interest,
structures like it had long been a familiar sight to the British in the
Mediterranean. Since prehistoric times, watch towers known as
Corsair or Saracen towers had been built along many parts of the
Mediterranean littoral to give warning of the approach of pirates,
often by means of a beacon on the roof. The British themselves
were particularly acquainted with those on the island base of
Minorca, and the Ordnance Board subsequently adopted the basis
of the design - circular configuration, massive walls, flat roof,
entrance door well clear of the ground - for a number of towers to
defend the Channel Islands, put up during and after the American
war. Then, within a few years of the siege at Mortella Point, there
was a minor rash of tower building on various far-flung shores
where the British flag flew; more to an improved Ordnance Board
specification on Jersey and others in Capetown and Simonstown in
Cape Colony, Halifax in Nova Scotia, and Minorca.[31]

It was four years after Mortella Point that the first proposal
was made to build towers on the British mainland. Its author was
Major Thomas Reynolds, who was employed on the first of the
Ordnance Board's mapping surveys of Kent and Essex. This would
certainly account for the circumstances that stirred his first
thoughts:

> In the course of my rides along the coasts in question, I have
> observed with regret that neither the situation nor construction
> of most of the batteries established for its defence will allow us
> to place much dependence on their efficacy.
>
> ....it behoves us to consider of some other means of resistance
> more calculated to produce the effect desired, viz, of preventing
> the enemy from settling in any bay, harbour or roadstead, or at
> least to oblige him to abandon his craft when landed. Now,

> there are no works that appear to me likely to effect this great
> object as a simple tower of brickwork defended by a handful of
> resolute men.

For an outlay that he put at £2,000 per tower, Reynolds argued that
it would supply a defensive capability decidedly superior to the
conventional battery; totally enclosed, it would be impregnable to
infantry assault, while the elevated gun platform would give greater
visibility and enhanced range.[32]

1798 was the year when General Bonaparte decided that an
invasion of Egypt would add greater lustre to his name than the
enterprise against England, and Reynolds' memorandum was filed
away in the War Office. The idea was disinterred in 1803, in
response to the new invasion threat, by William Henry Ford, a
captain of engineers. Ford, who had probably visited Minorca with
the Egyptian expedition in 1800, favoured a square tower on the
grounds that it was capable of mounting more guns than a circular
type. Each side of his model was 46 feet long, enclosing a circular
interior built round a massive central pillar and divided into two
storeys, the upper one housing the garrison and the lower the
magazine, water cistern and storage area.[33] This time, the concept
did not sink from view. It was taken up by Ford's friend and
colleague William Twiss, who passed it on to Lord Chatham, Sir
David Dundas and the Commander-in-Chief himself.

Towers were a stouter form of coastal defence than conventional batteries in any case, but their particular advantage against
a flotilla-borne invasion was readily grasped, at least by some. In
trying to win over a stolidly unmoved Chatham, the Duke of York
wrote,

> Your Lordship will remark from the peculiar description of
> armament with which this coast is threatened...composed of a
> multiplicity of small vessels, that it is highly probable the
> disembarkation of an enemy will be undertaken for a consider-
> able series of time after the arrival of the leading vessels upon
> the coast, which renders the possession of the sea batteries an
> object of great moment.[34]

And to the Cabinet:

> The advantage proposed by these towers is to keep possession
> of the coast defences during the whole operation of this
> landing, and the probable prevention of his disembarking stores
> and either to oblige his bringing artillery against them when he
> has landed, or the leaving us in possession of the bay or
> anchorage which they protect, which would enable us to
> intercept all supplies which might endeavour to follow the
> armament.

The Duke argued the case with vigour. He admitted the expense -
Ford's estimate was £3,000 per tower - but maintained that it
would be offset by a saving in manpower, as towers with their
small garrisons would supply the same defensive capability as large
bodies of troops.[35] It was to no avail. Having received its brief
airing, the tower project slid into the oubliette reserved by the
Ordnance Board for ill-favoured Horse Guards ideas - classified as
permanent fortifications, the towers had to wait their turn for
consideration by the committee of engineers. There the matter
rested, despite the Navy's added support and stirrings of public
interest reflected in a Commons speech by William Wyndham, in
which he pressed for the speedy erection of

> ....what were known to our officers under the name of martello
> towers, so called from the memorable instance of one at
> Martello in Corsica.[36]

(This, incidentally, seems to have been the first public airing of the
term, thus in a sense signalling its debut into the language.)
    Then, abruptly, Chatham relented. But the report put forward
by his engineers was strangely perverse, recommending the
construction of 13 towers as infantry redoubts loopholed for
musketry and flanking existing batteries to protect them from being
overrun. This was to put them to a use completely alien to the
intentions of both Reynolds and Ford, who conceived them quite
specifically as batteries in mutually supporting lines with overlap-
ping fields of fire. In the Board's view a tower was no more

resistant to artillery fire than conventional batteries - a strangely
obtuse reasoning, since Ford saw their special advantage as being
their superior resistance not to cannon but infantry assault.[37]

But a swelling tide of support together with a change of
government combined to sweep aside bureaucratic stonewalling. By
September 1804 Twiss had been despatched to the south-east coast
with instructions to earmark sites for towers specifically as artillery
emplacements. He selected some to cover existing batteries and, in
pairs, to guard the Dymchurch sluices, but most were to serve the
purpose envisaged by Reynolds and Ford, to stand in mutually
supporting lines some 500 yards apart, like the 16 planned for
Pevensey Level and the eight for the shore fronting Pett Level.
Twiss positioned others to plug gaps in already existing defences;
for example the long curve of Hythe Bay from Shorncliffe to the
eastern end of Dymchurch Wall was covered by only three
batteries, and the intervening spaces were to be filled by ranks of
towers. In all, from Seaford to Eastwear Bay Twiss found 88 sites
where a tower could usefully be placed, and put forward a
construction programme to be completed by the end of 1805.[38]
Besides his survey work, Twiss was briefed, together with two
other officers of the Board, to draw up a new design that eventually materialised as the British martello we see today.

> The interior circle of the Tower has a diameter of 26 feet and
> the area at the top is calculated to receive one 24-pounder gun
> and two carronades of the same calibre, all mounted on
> traversing platforms to fire over a high parapet, the crest of
> which is about 33 feet above the foundation. The ground floor
> to contain a powder magazine and cistern with rooms for provi-
> sions, fuel and other stores. The middle floor to lodge a
> garrison of one officer and 24 men, having an entrance placed
> 10 feet above the exterior ground. In this project, the centre
> pillar is solid and a stone staircase is contrived in the exterior
> wall which at that point is so increased in thickness as to render
> it everywhere equally strong.[39]

It is worth adding a footnote on certain cunning features of the
design. It cross-section it was ovoid rather than round, with the

long axis perpendicular to the shore so as to present as narrow a target as possible to the front. The thickness of the wall also varied, with the section on the seaward side most likely to take the weight of fire broadened to 13 feet of solid brickwork, while the landward-facing section incorporated the staircase and windows. On the roof the cannon traversing platform mentioned above eventually materialised as a frame with one end pivoted on a central iron post and the other running on a track built into the parapet, thus allowing the gun within it easily to traverse a full 360 degrees.[40]

Evidently the job was done in some haste, the reason probably being a conference on defence matters held in Rochester in October with Pitt, Camden, the Duke of York, Chatham, Brownrigg, Brown and Twiss present. Ford's square model was considered but finally rejected as being too expensive. The new specification was approved in its stead and Twiss's survey report accepted in its entirety.[41] If we are looking for a moment to mark the birth of the Martello tower in England, the Rochester conference is as good as any, since it was there that its familiar form and place in the coastal landscape was more or less fixed. In the end, the number built was 74, 14 fewer than planned. Of that total, only 26 have survived intact to the present day, the rest, despite their massive construction - half a million bricks set in lime mortar of flint-like hardness - having fallen victim to the ravages of the sea or the hand of later generations. Also still standing, at Eastbourne and in Hythe Bay, are two monster Martellos whose specification was similarly approved at Rochester; mounting 11 guns and housing 350 troops, these are actually full-blown fortresses and were known as Grand Redoubts.

It appears that only one dissenting voice was raised at Rochester, and that was John Brown's. He vented his disapproval in the pages of his diary, incidentally revealing that the Ordnance Board had taken on something of the zeal of the newly-converted.

The expensive and diabolical system of tower defence was finally resolved on to an unprecedented extent, contrary to the

> opinions of the best and most experienced officers in the service; but it was carried by the influence of the Ordnance people - only whose opinions were by no means supported by reasoning. Mr. Pitt from whom one would have expected a decided opinion gave in to that of others and without requiring what indeed would not have been obtained, a satisfactory and well-digested plan of defence. All that was advocated was tower, tower, tower; some large and some small was all the variation proposed by the engineers.[42]

Despite the programme's having received its imprimatur from the very top, the final go-ahead was not given until the end of the year, by which time Twiss's original schedule was well behind-hand. In all, nearly eighteen months had gone by since the Duke of York had first broached Ford's idea to the Cabinet and it was to be nearer two years before work was actually begun, in the spring of 1805. So if Napoleon's *grognards* had stumbled ashore on to Romney Marsh in the summer of 1805, the defenders would have had to deal with them without the benefit of the new works. However, the passing of the crisis and the subsequent victory at Trafalgar saw no cessation of work on canal or Martellos, nor on the Chatham Lines and the Western Heights.[*] The Martello programme was not completed until 1808 while the canal had to await its finishing touches until the spring of 1810. When the radical journalist William Cobbett undertook his 'Rural Rides' around the English countryside in the 1820s, when only the memory of the recently departed Corsican remained, he reserved some of his most scathing invective for the defence works whose beginnings have been described in this chapter. Cobbett vehemently castigated the Martellos, the Military Canal and the by then baroque ramifications of the Western Heights as 'incessant sinks of money' and the follies of spendthrift governments. But this was comfortable hindsight: at the time, things looked different. Though Nelson at Trafalgar gave the coup de grâce to an already aban-

---

[*] A further 29 were built later to a larger, more advanced specification on the Eastern District coastline between Aldeburgh and St. Osyth.

doned invasion enterprise, the British were not to be so easily reassured. The works still stand as enduring monuments to the residual though strong and by no means unjustified fear that Napoleon would one day return to what, as late as 1810, was still being referred to in Parliament as 'his chief and favourite project'.

Chapter Eight

'England is no more!'

At the beginning of the year 1805, Napoleon could afford to contemplate the situation on the Continent with a certain satisfaction. After eighteen months of war between France and Britain, there was little sign of any inclination by the European powers to depart from their sullen acquiescence in a *pax gallica* and join a new anti-French coalition. Austria, the essential Continental equipoise to France, was still licking her wounds from the previous war and showed no stomach for renewed hostilities, while the jackal-like Frederick William of Prussia gave every evidence of compliance as long as France continued to dangle before him the prospect of devouring Hanover. True, there had been rumblings from the east where the young Tsar Alexander I was making a play to advance his influence westward, but Russia was too far away to be taken seriously, at least on her own.

On the other hand, the obduracy of Britain's defiance showed no sign of softening, and Napoleon's new year peace proposal was met with a cold rejoinder from London. As before, land and seapower appeared deadlocked. However, a new card had come into play. Since 1803 Spain, ruled by the unsavoury Manuel Godoy, Prince of the Peace, had been a reluctant vassal of France, bullied into pouring an annual 72 million francs-worth of her American silver into her ally's coffers. In October 1804, without prior declaration of war, a British naval squadron had intercepted the Spanish treasure fleet homeward bound from Montevideo and captured or sank every ship. Though in no shape for hostilities, Spain was stung into a declaration of war, thus placing her navy,

Europe's third largest, at the disposal of France. Napoleon did not attach any immediate significance to this, since the Spanish navy had been allowed to run to seed in the years of peace. Then in the following February, the French ambassador to Madrid reported that the fleet was in an unexpectedly forward state of readiness. Napoleon sent a despatch to his aide Junot, who was about to depart to take up his new appointment as ambassador to Portugal.

> From the Prince of the Peace I expect just one thing - that the Spanish fleets be ready for the great expeditions that I have in contemplation.[1]

Flurries of orders began to issue from the Tuileries, and once more the imperial couriers spurred their mounts along the roads to Brest, Toulon and the invasion harbours, where the sands continued to clog the newly excavated basins and channels.

> There is not a moment to be lost in cleaning up the ports of Boulogne and Ambleteuse; if necessary, use up to 400,000 francs for this. I'm told that 30 or 40 days' work is needed to restore these ports to their previous condition.[2]

Improvements were ordered on the routes linking Paris with Brest and Boulogne and on local roads connecting the invasion harbours. The Dutch flotilla, whose progress south had been halted the previous year, received instructions to start moving again towards its designated port of Ambleteuse, while the Emperor once more took up his compulsive tinkering with the organisation of his flotilla.

The invasion project was on once again, and its architect had at last contrived the definitive plan that he was convinced would penetrate Britain's guard and land his forces on her soil. The grand design is outlined in the orders despatched to Admiral Villeneuve at Toulon and Admiral Ganteaume, newly appointed to command at Brest. Ganteaume was to escape from Brest, take his 21 ships south, break the blockade at Ferrol and, accompanied by the Franco-Spanish squadron there, sail for Martinique in the West

Indies to join Admiral Missiessy, who had departed thence from Rochefort in January. Villeneuve's mission after escaping from Toulon was to proceed west, relieve the Spanish squadron at Cadiz and then rendezvous with Ganteaume in the Caribbean. The combined fleet, which would now comprise 40 ships of the line under Ganteaume's overall command, was to return to Europe and proceed to Ushant, scatter the enemy's squadron off Brest and reach Boulogne between June 10th and July 10th, where the Emperor would be waiting to embark his army for a crossing under the protection of the fleet.[3]

On March 24th, Ganteaume telegraphed to Paris:

> The fleet is ready and can make sail tomorrow evening, but there are 15 English ships in the Iroise and it is impossible to leave without a battle.[4]

Although Ganteaume's command outnumbered the British by six, Napoleon drew back, reluctant to risk a battle before the operation got under way; back came the reply:

> A naval victory in these circumstances would lead to nothing. Have only one aim, to fulfil your mission. Leave without an engagement. That which is to join you has left.[5]

In fact, Villeneuve was still at Toulon. For him, a break-out did not present the same problem, since conditions did not favour the kind of close blockade mounted on Brest. But in any case, to bottle up the French was contrary to Nelson's purpose, which was actively to encourage them to put to sea so as to bring them to battle. More than anyone, Nelson knew the gamble involved in this tactic. His shattering victory at the Nile nearly seven years earlier had not wiped out the evil remembrance of how the Toulon squadron had initially given him the slip, and his subsequent frantic search to and fro across the eastern Mediterranean before he had finally caught up with it at Aboukir Bay. Nelson was convinced - perhaps too obsessively - that another Toulon break-out would prefigure a threat to Sicily in particular, or perhaps Sardinia,

Naples, the Morea or Egypt again, rather than a foray westward towards the Strait. It was an apprehension that Napoleon had taken pains to feed with various feints and specially manufactured titbits of disinformation. Yet the latter possibility always had to be covered, so Nelson took his squadron west in mid-March to show himself in strength off Barcelona before dropping away south-east towards the Gulf of Palmas at the southern tip of Sardinia. Palmas was not the squadron's usual anchorage but had been chosen so as to check any French movement eastward; if Villeneuve did, against expectations, sail for the Strait, it was Nelson's intention that the news of the appearance off Barcelona would persuade the French to swing south of the Balearics to avoid him, thus bringing them unknowingly nearer to the actual British position.[6]

Hence when Villeneuve finally left Toulon on March 30th with 11 ships of the line, only two of Nelson's frigates were there to witness his departure. They shadowed him until the night of the 31st when they lost contact and fell away south to join the main body, but with nothing conclusive to report on the French course. Nelson, now in the same fever of anxiety as he had been in 1798, spent the next ten days checking likely routes to the eastward before he gained intelligence hard enough to convince him that Villeneuve's destination was indeed the Strait. He set a course west in pursuit, battling all the way against headwinds. The French squadron passed the Strait with an easterly wind on April 8th[7]; 17 days later the news reached London, where there could hardly have been a less auspicious moment to deal with a naval crisis.

A Commons Commission of Enquiry, set up in 1802 at the insistence of St. Vincent to investigate abuses in the Navy, had discovered that £10,000 of government money had found its way into the Coutts' account of Lord Melville, then the Treasurer of the Navy, and now the First Lord of the Admiralty and Pitt's closest political crony. The Opposition brought in a formal indictment of Melville that was carried despite Pitt's impassioned pleas and next day the First Lord resigned, leaving the Admiralty without a head. There followed a period of a fortnight or so while Pitt worked frantically to secure the appointment by a reluctant monarch of a not particularly eager candidate to a place that Addington, now Lord of the Council, was demanding for a nominee of his own. Pitt's man, Admiral Charles Middleton, was, unpromisingly, an 80-year-old naval bureaucrat with vastly more experience behind a desk than on the quarter-deck. Despite a long record of great achievement in naval reform, Middleton had never raised his flag afloat. He was not a popular figure either in the Service or outside it, and his eventual appointment as Melville's successor with the title of Lord Barham was greeted with widespread dismay and a general belief that he was no more than a stopgap in the absence of a better candidate. Once ensconced in the First Lord's room at the Admiralty, however, the old man was to lose no time in confounding his critics' expectations.[8]

Although it was now known that Villeneuve had passed through the Strait, the scent thereafter went temporarily cold, and an entr'acte of misty groping ensued as both Barham in Whitehall and Nelson in the Mediterranean strained to puzzle out the picture from cryptic fragments of intelligence. The tension grew all the greater with the secret departure from Spithead in mid-April of a fleet of 45 transports containing 7,000 troops commanded by Sir James Craig. With only a tiny escort of two ships of the line its destination was Malta, and in its progress south could conceivably be running straight into the arms of Villeneuve's squadron. At first Barham suspected that the French objective was the West Indies, and a report suggesting as much had recently arrived from the secret agent in Napoleon's entourage known by the code-name 'l'ami'. But then fresh news arrived indicating otherwise. The British squadron off Cadiz commanded by Sir John Orde had found itself having to beat a hasty retreat on the unexpected arrival of a large force of French ships. It was Villeneuve, and with the spectre of Nelson at his back, he was in a tearing hurry. Although Admiral Gravina, the Spanish commander, had not finished taking on supplies or embarking troops, Villeneuve refused to linger and got underway almost immediately, leaving the Spaniards to catch up as best they could. Orde, who had fallen back on Lagos, believed that the combined fleet was coming north to pick up the Brest squadron and enter the Channel. When Barham received his despatch he was inclined to agree with him, especially in view of the reported movements in Brest. Then more bits of information drifted in to muddy the picture further, and it was not until the end of May that the Admiralty was finally persuaded the French were without doubt en route for the West Indies.[9]

When he first learned that Villeneuve had passed the Strait, Nelson's first guess also was that the British Isles would be his objective, but then he too began to wonder whether it might not be the West Indies after all. Without certain intelligence one way or the other, he was racked by indecision.

> I cannot run very properly to the West Indies without something more than mere surmise; and if I defer, Jamaica may be lost.

Then, on his arrival at Gibraltar on May 7th, he met with a Portuguese squadron commanded by Rear Admiral Donald Campbell, one of the many British officers who took service with foreign navies. Campbell seems to have given him the first reliable news confirming that Villeneuve had indeed sailed for the Caribbean - and was later dismissed for his indiscretion when it came to Junot's ears. Other reports corroborated Campbell's tidings, and finally Nelson made up his mind.

> The lot is cast. I am leaving for the West Indies. Although I am late, perhaps chance will have given the enemy a bad passage and will give me a good one.

He admitted he might well be embarking on a wild goose chase, but,

> If they are not there, the squadron will be back again by the end of June - in short, before the enemy can know where I am.

He tarried only to make arrangements for the secure passage of Craig's expedition, which had just anchored in the Tagus. At 7 o'clock on the evening of May 11th, the squadron bore away under full sail from Cape St. Vincent south-west to Madeira on the first leg of the Atlantic crossing.[10]

In the meantime, Napoleon had produced another bombshell in Europe with his decision to make the Italian Republic a hereditary kingdom and take the crown for himself. A tremor of alarm seized the Austrian court. Since the time of Charlemagne, the kingship of Italy had been vested in the Holy Roman Emperors as a symbol of their hegemony in the peninsula. More concretely, Napoleon as King of Italy would make the entire peninsula more or less a French fiefdom. The Emperor tried, though not very hard, to explain himself to his fellow monarchs; he had only taken the crown after it had been refused in turn by his brothers, Joseph and Louis; it was only a temporary arrangement while the Russians occupied Corfu and the British Malta; thereafter the crowns of France and Italy would never be united on the same head. But the Austrians - and the rest of Europe - only saw yet another step in the apparently limitless onward march of French expansion.

In early April the Emperor of the French began a leisurely journey south to Milan to receive his second crown. It was a triumphal progress, with the imperial couple being fêted along the entire route. But there was no relaxation from affairs of state, particularly the invasion design. From stopping-places along the way - Troyes, Lyons, Stupinigi - a stream of despatches show Napoleon refashioning and elaborating his plans. He pondered the increasing possibility that Ganteaume might not be able to get out of Brest and concluded that it need not entail calling things off. Ganteaume's squadron would serve its purpose by holding down a blockading force of comparable strength, while Missiessy - on his way back from his futile excursion to the Caribbean - would do the same at Rochefort; thus the enemy would not have enough force in reserve to oppose Villeneuve on his return. For the latter, a new set of orders was framed. He should wait for Ganteaume in the West Indies for no longer than 35 days. If he failed to turn up, Villeneuve was to return to Europe, lift the blockades of Ferrol and Brest and then proceed into the Channel.[11]

By early May Napoleon had fixed a revamped timetable, the key elements of which were as follows: if Ganteaume had not left Brest by May 20th, he was to stay put; on his return, Villeneuve was to raise the blockade of Ferrol and arrive off Brest between July 10th and 20th; Napoleon himself would reach Boulogne on July 15th and be ready with all his troops and *matérial* embarked by the 20th. Berthier had been set to work on an embarkation schedule, while Soult was instructed to find out whether 15 days was long enough to complete the process;

> Do not give me a hypothetical reply to this question, but take
> into account all the depots and magazines.

Soult should also impress on the Boulogne flotilla commander Lacrosse the necessity of having everything ready to move within three days.[12]

By now Napoleon had persuaded himself that his plans had thrown the enemy into turmoil. Jubilantly he imagined their anxieties for the fate of the West Indies, India and the East Indies and Craig's expedition as well as Britain itself.

> The English see themselves taken hand-for-hand....They well
> know that 20 ships, swallowed up by the oceans, could appear
> at any time anywhere on their coasts.[13] Confusion among the
> English is extreme; orders and counter-orders. One moment
> they want to abandon Brest for Torbay so as not to be caught
> between two fires and be able to act according to circumstance;
> then that appears to confirm the abandoning of India and
> America.[14]

Decrès, the recipient of much of this over-heated conjecture, was not persuaded, as he pointedly hinted in the roundabout way favoured by the minions of autocrats:

> Though the English ministers may not have divined your
> Majesty's intentions, they have nevertheless been penetrated by
> the London journalists....I read in the 'Sun' of 16 May that it
> is seen as good fortune that the division commanded by

> Admiral Collingwood was not sent in pursuit of the combined
> fleet, since its passage to the West Indies can be nothing but a
> ruse to attract English forces there while it makes a return to
> European seas in the hope of finding itself in superior
> strength.[15]

Napoleon pictured the English system of government, as he thought
chronically riven by faction, cracking up under the strain:

> No government is more wanting in foresight than the English;
> it is a régime preoccupied with intrigue that switches its
> attention to wherever there is rumour.[16]

To compound this supposed perplexity, fragments of disinformation
were planted in the public prints;

> These little stratagems have an incalculable effect on men
> whose calculations are not the result of cool heads but of
> collective fears and preconceptions.[17]

However, the uncertainty supposedly at large in London was much
more perceptible in Paris, where British newspapers were seized
on for up-to-date news of the latest developments. For several
weeks, Napoleon blithely assumed that Britain had sent a squadron
to protect India. It was not until the end of June that he knew
Nelson had gone to the West Indies, hitherto imagining either that
he was still in the Mediterranean or had returned to Britain. He
was still in the dark about the destination of Craig's expedition,
speculating that it might be the Caribbean or the Cape of Good
Hope as well as Malta; and it was by courtesy of the London
'Times' that he first learned of his fleet's return to European
waters.[18]

Villeneuve's squadron had dropped anchor at Fort de France
in Martinique on May 14th. It had not had a good passage; several
ships had proved to be poor sailers and the squadron had to take
off 1,000 sick. Nelson arrived off Bridgetown, Barbados, three
weeks later, having gained more than a week on his quarry. But
where was he to begin searching him out? He was not to know that

at that moment the two squadrons were a mere hundred miles apart. Mistaken reports first led him, to his fury, on a futile foray to the south towards Trinidad, while in the meantime Villeneuve had gone the other way to attack the British islands of Antigua and Barbuda in obedience to supplementary orders recently received. From prisoners captured with a British convoy, he first learned the disquieting news that Nelson's squadron had arrived in the area.

Villeneuve weighed his situation. Missiessy had returned to Rochefort. His new orders containing Napoleon's change of plan instructed him to wait for Ganteaume for a further 35 days. If he had not appeared by then, Villeneuve was to assume his daunting new mission alone, to return to Europe and break two blockades at Ferrol and Brest. Nelson's ships, which he had been told, incorrectly, numbered 14, together with another squadron under Rear Admiral Cochrane already in the area, added up to a force at least equal if not superior to his own. He was sure that Ganteaume would not now appear, and the meagre resources of the French settlements were unable to supplement his own dwindling supplies. There seemed only one prudent course of action to safeguard his mission, and that was to cut short the waiting period and sail immediately for Ferrol. On June 10th the combined fleet held away north-north-east on course for the Azores. Nelson, who had by now discovered Villeneuve's whereabouts, was hurrying north in pursuit when he received word that the Frenchman had once more slipped his grasp and been swallowed up by the ocean. Nelson was not downcast; his anxieties for the fate of the British islands were at an end, and he was steadily gaining ground on his quarry. Guessing that the destination would be Cadiz, he set off from Antigua in pursuit with 11 ships of the line on June 13th.[19]

On May 26th, in a ceremony under the great marble Duomo of Milan cathedral, Napoleon surmounted his Emperor's laurel wreath with the iron crown of Lombardy, bearing its meaningful inscription, 'Rex totius Italiae'. But his attention continued to fix unwaveringly on movements at sea far hence. His servants found that distance gave no respite from the crack of the imperial whip. In the long interval of waiting for news of Villeneuve, Napoleon had drawn up yet more new instructions for him, spelling out in detail various alternative courses of action he could take in combination with the Brest, Rochefort or Ferrol squadrons when he arrived in European waters. To Decrès:

> Impress on the maritime prefect [of Brest] the importance of my being constantly informed of the numbers of English vessels before Brest.[20]

For Allemand, Missiessy's replacement to the Rochefort command, there was also a set of new orders; for the wretched Decrès, toiling at an enterprise over which he had the profoundest misgivings, there was a rap over the knuckles:

> It appears to me that you don't have enough single-mindedness for a great operation. It is a fault that you must correct, since it is the key to great success and great affairs.[21]

> Keep your eyes on everything, [Berthier was urged] go into all the details of rations, spirits, shoes - all the details of the embarkation. You should have it all in your files, properly organised....it isn't a matter of if or but or because. The situation has been anticipated.[22]

The enemy must be beguiled into a false sense of security; hence Ganteaume should restrain his eagerness for sorties into the Bertheaume road; 'What would a battle lead to? Nothing.' Even better, the enemy's attention should be led away from the real invasion plan and the Emperor accordingly sent word to Marmont in Holland to embark a portion of his force and move the Texel squadron out into the Helder.

> My intention will be to lull the English as much as possible about the Brest fleet....and lead all towards Texel.[23]

Thus by the beginning of August, in Barham's words, 'the scent of invasion from the Texel is very strong', though at least one British spy was not deceived:

I am enabled to tell you the truth....all that is done on our coast
has no other object but to mislead the enemy.[24]

Napoleon lectured the uneasy Decrès:

Your mistake is to calculate as if the English are in on the
secret; one should calculate as the Admiralty must; 100,000
men are at Boulogne; seven warships are at the Texel with an
army 30,000 strong, and a fleet of 22 warships lies in the port
of Brest. It could be that Admiral Villeneuve's fleet will return
suddenly to Europe: but it might also go to the Indies or
Jamaica; and what an immense responsibility bears on the heads
of these ministers if they allow three or four months to go by
without sending forces to help those colonies.[25]

But he was too ready to imagine agitation at the Admiralty. True,
the building in Whitehall buzzed with more activity than usual as
messengers came and went while the telegraph on the roof busily
clattered out its cryptic signals. And he had accurately prophesied
the wave of consternation that greeted the news of an enemy
squadron at large in the West Indies; accusing fingers were already
being pointed at Nelson for letting it slip through his grasp. But the
Emperor had sorely misjudged his adversary. The Admiralty's new
incumbent was far from losing his head; Lord Barham knew the
tradition, long ingrained so as to be second nature in every one of
his commanders, that in an extremity there would be an automatic
falling back on the Channel without waiting for orders from on
high.

At the beginning of May, virtually certain news had reached
the Admiralty that Villeneuve was heading for the Caribbean, and
on July 1st it was known that he had arrived at Martinique. The
question now was, which home port would he return to - Cadiz,
Ferrol or Brest? Spain had not only provided Napoleon with more
ships but two harbours at each end of her long reach of Atlantic
coastline, thus increasing the potential for British miscalculation.
Barham, like Nelson, saw Cadiz as the most likely possibility - that
is, until the arrival late in the evening of July 8th of Captain
Bettesworth of the brig 'Curieux', hotfoot from Plymouth. Together

with the latest despatches from Nelson, Bettesworth brought with him a vital item of news. In the course of her passage home, the 'Curieux' had sighted the enemy fleet some 900 miles north-north-east of Antigua and then shadowed it along a latitude so northerly - 33o12" - that it could only be heading for one of the Biscay ports, Brest or Ferrol. Cadiz - and the threat to the Mediterranean - could safely be left out of the reckoning. In the early hours Barham got up, sat down at his desk without bothering to dress and in the space of three hours or so drew up a set of dispositions for intercepting the combined fleet at sea. By nine in the morning the orders were on their way to Portsmouth, while Villeneuve's fleet was still only north-west of the Azores.

Cornwallis, just returned from a spell of recuperation ashore, was instructed to send the Rochefort detachment to reinforce Vice Admiral Sir Robert Calder's Ferrol squadron, which was to position itself 90 to 120 miles west of Cape Finisterre, for a period of six to eight days. At the same time, Cornwallis was to place the main body of his own command the same distance south-west of Brest for the same length of time. Thus whichever port was Villeneuve's destination, the interception would take place so far out to sea that the enemy squadron in harbour would be unable to come to his aid.[26] However, Barham's plan had temporarily left both ports wide open, an opportunity seized by Allemand at Rochefort, who slipped away on July 16th to begin a five-and-a-half-month voyage that took him from the Penmarks in the north to the Canaries in the south, miraculously eluding all British attempts to nail him. But what at first sight appears most risky was the decision to leave only half-a-dozen ships guarding Brest itself. Indeed, Napoleon railed at Ganteaume's unwillingness to obey his urgings to seize the moment.

> I cannot understand Ganteaume's inertia; how is it possible that he who is conversant with all my plans can allow the enemy to disappear without making any kind of move? I foresaw in my orders that the enemy would disappear from Brest. For four days now, it seems that he has gone.[27]

Yet Barham's thinking was fundamentally sound, as Ganteaume himself testifies:

> ....if....we venture into the Channel with only the 22 ships of our force, we would soon be observed or the ships we had eluded would make contact.[28]

The First Lord's plan, in fact, struck a masterly balance of risk and opportunity, with a good chance of bringing on a major engagement as decisive as Camperdown or the Nile. The speed of the British response left an incredulous Napoleon utterly at a loss, a state of mind he was rather more used to visiting on his opponents than experiencing himself:

> The brig 'Curieux' did not reach England until July 9th. The Admiralty could not have decided on the movements of its squadrons in 24 hours.[29]

In the afternoon of July 22nd, 300 miles due west of Ferrol, Barham's plan was vindicated when Calder's squadron sighted a large force approaching from the south-west. It was Villeneuve, at last approaching landfall after a protracted 41-day voyage along an ill-chosen course with contrary winds. Calder, though initially put out to find that his 15 ships were up against 20 of the enemy, did not hesitate to close in. But visibility was poor and much of the ensuing action was fought in patchy fog. For four hours or so ships groped about, straining to distinguish friend from foe, often firing blindly at orange muzzle-flashes stabbing out of the enveloping murk. By nine in the evening, when the two sides drifted apart, there had been no decisive outcome; the British had captured the two rearmost Spanish vessels, while they themselves had had three ships badly mauled.

'A very decisive action', was Calder's verdict in the despatch he wrote the following morning. He was right only in a limited sense; true, he had prevented the enemy from reaching his destination and combining with the squadron in Ferrol - but only temporarily, as we shall see; he had maintained his position, captured a couple of enemy ships and inflicted over twice as many casualties as he had taken. But the enemy fleet, though knocked about, was still more or less intact, and the implicit objective of Barham's strategy had been to neutralise the enemy force, even at the cost of reciprocal damage. Calder, himself sensing that he had not done enough, signalled down the squadron his intention to renew the action next morning. But when day came he thought better of it, and over the next two days, as the sides drifted further and further apart, his resolve was eaten away by the worry that the enemy squadron in Ferrol might appear. After a few half-hearted attempts by both sides to try conclusions, Villeneuve made a tentative decision to take his battered but still serviceable force south to Cadiz. Calder always insisted he had done his duty and, indignant at the fierce criticism that met him on his return home, demanded a court martial. He got one and despite a vigorous self-defence, received a reprimand.[30] By then Trafalgar had been won and Nelson, who in that battle had to complete Calder's unfinished business, had re-affirmed in definitive fashion the hard measure - annihilation, no less - by which Briton's after the Nile and Copenhagen had come to judge victory at sea.

As he began his journey south to Cadiz, Villeneuve met rough weather and decided to hole up temporarily in the port of Vigo. He was beset by troubles: the ships were low on stores; scurvy and dysentery were rife among his crews - he had to land another 800 sick - and he had no up-to-date orders nor any information about the enemy's whereabouts. Gourdon, the commander of the Franco-Spanish squadron in Ferrol, was unable to get out to join him. Villeneuve resolved to make the link-up himself and put to sea on July 31st, luckily while Calder's squadron was being pushed to leeward by south-westerly winds, entering the anchorage at Corunna, situated on the same inlet as Ferrol, two days later.[31]

On July 8th, Napoleon, travelling incognito, had suddenly left Turin, crossed Mont Cenis and hurried north. In less than four days - despite the Empress's insistence on stopping for proper meals - he had covered the same route that three months earlier had taken him several weeks. Once at Fontainebleau he dictated a further set of orders to await Villeneuve's arrival at Ferrol:

> Now that your junction with the Ferrol squadron has been made, you will take action to make us masters of the Dover Strait even if it is only for four or five days.[32]

He was to accomplish this by linking up with the Brest or Rochefort squadron or both, proceed north-about round Ireland and Scotland, pick up the Texel force and so arrive at Boulogne.

> Europe awaits in suspense the great event that we have in train. We are all counting on your bravery and skill.[33]

On August 3rd the Emperor arrived at Boulogne to await the historic juncture. His absence had not hindered the honing of preparations to a final edge of readiness. The ever-industrious Berthier had been juggling figures in the mind-boggling business of matching the numbers of boats and men. In a series of operations, carefully co-ordinated with the coastal artillery and hotly contested by the enemy, Verhuell had managed to transfer a hundred or so of his Dutch flotilla from Dunkirk round Cape Gris Nez to Ambleteuse. In addition to the three main corps - Davout at Ambleteuse, Soult at Boulogne and Ney at Etaples - a reserve commanded by Prince Louis was dispersed at various points in the rear and a special 14,000-strong first assault force was concentrated at Wimereux. It was no coincidence that the latter command was entrusted to Lannes, the toughest nut, foulest mouth and Napoleon's only real friend in the Marshalate. No decision more aptly underlines the force of Napoleon's commitment. Lannes bore the scars of suicidal charges across the River Po and Lodi bridge, and many another desperate action. He was the only man for the job.

The four assembly ports were now crammed with 2,000 craft and their environs with the freight - 93,000 of France's finest, poised for immediate embarkation, together with 2,600 horses, artillery, rations and baggage. The minutest particulars had been taken care of, down to things like disembarkation signalling and the issue of cartridges (to be retained by the captain of each company to keep them dry, and for handing out only before the final run-in). The most significant detail of all had not been forgotten. Napoleon ordered the two corvettes reserved for his personal use to be sent to Wimereux; when Lannes' grenadiers waded ashore onto the beaches of Kent, it would be under their Emperor's eyes.[34]

The day after his arrival, Napoleon reviewed the entire Army of England, lined up along the nine miles of foreshore from Cap d'Aspet to Cape Gris Nez, and watched an embarkation rehearsal completed in two hours. In a similar exercise mounted in the previous month, Ney had managed to get his entire corps of 20,000 with 1,200 horses aboard in less than fifty minutes. The high spring tides were imminent. On August 8th the final instructions were issued.

> The English don't know what awaits them. [exulted Napoleon]
> If we have the power to cross for only nine hours, England is
> no more![35]

Still there was no word from Villeneuve. Then at last, on the 8th, his despatches arrived, telling of the battle with Calder. But it was only to his friend Decrès that the admiral dared to reveal his true feelings, confessing with grim candour that the burdens placed on his head had shattered his nerve.

> I have been made the arbiter of the greatest interests; my
> despair redoubles as more responsibilities are placed on me,
> because I see no prospect of success whatever I do.

On an insistent whining note he rehearsed a catalogue of tribulation: poor equipment, ill-trained crews, inexperienced officers and inadequate stores and provisions. There was a deal of maudlin self-reproach:

I foresaw all this before I left Toulon but I deceived myself, though only till I saw the Spanish reinforcements; then, my God, you had to despair at everything.

The recipient himself did not escape censure: 'Why didn't you listen to me before I left Toulon?'

Anticipating the imperial wrath to come, Villeneuve already had his excuses worked out for throwing in his hand.

If, as I had to hope, I had made a swift passage from Martinique to Ferrol, if I had found Admiral Calder with six ships or at most nine, if I had fought him and after joining the combined squadrons, still with a month-and-a-half of provisions and water, I would yet have made the junction at Brest and given passage to the great expedition. I would be the first man in France....[but] the enemy was warned, he was reinforced, he has dared to attack us in inferior strength, time has been on their side.[36]

As to the future, he could see only doom and disaster.

If I leave here with 29 ships, do not imagine I am capable of doing battle with a force of equal strength; I freely confess it, I am worried about meeting even 20.[37]

Gravina, once past the initial sycophancy, expressed similar forebodings:

I will say to your Excellency that the plan of operations could not have been better thought out; it is divine....At the moment the enemy knows our strength....It is natural that they will dare to do battle with us when we leave and after sending word to the Brest squadron, they will be able to follow and choose their moment for a second battle before we reach Brest and thus destroy our plan of campaign.[38]

Did Decrès impart to his master the full depths of the despondency hanging over the fleet at Ferrol? We do not know, but he probably did not dare. To his ministers, and to the public in the pages of the

'Moniteur', Napoleon elected to portray the action off Finisterre as a French victory. But as each long day of waiting at Boulogne succeeded the next without a sighting of French topsails, his doubts about his admiral's mettle began to grow. 'Villeneuve is a sorry character who had more perception than character.' 'Villeneuve is one of those who needs the spur rather than the bridle.' Lauriston, who commanded the troops with the squadron, was urged, 'Help and encourage the Admiral as much as possible.' Napoleon himself made one final effort to egg him on.

> The English are not as numerous as you think; everywhere they are on tenterhooks. If you appear here for three days, even for 24 hours, your mission will have been accomplished....Never will a fleet run risks for a greater aim and never will my soldiers and sailors shed blood for such a great and noble cause.[39]

Meanwhile the British squadrons, in unbidden collective response to the threat to the Channel, were falling back on Ushant. On August 13th the Rochefort squadron appeared, to be followed next day by Calder and the day after that Nelson, who had arrived at Cape St. Vincent a month previously, heard of the news brought by the 'Curieux' and immediately hurried north. But Cornwallis had no intention of waiting passively on events. He knew that Villeneuve would soon have to make another move, since Ferrol could not long continue to supply such a large concourse of ships, now no fewer than 29 sail. If he were allowed to leave Ferrol and elected to sail south rather than north, he would be free to set about the British merchant shipping in the area unless there was a force in the vicinity formidable enough to challenge him. Accordingly, Cornwallis kept his concentration, 36 ships in all, for only 24 hours; then on August 18th, anticipating an Admiralty order even then being mooted, he once more detached Calder with 18 ships and orders to return south and take up station outside Ferrol. At first sight it seems another foolhardy move; indeed, when Napoleon later got to hear about it when it was all over, he dubbed it 'a signal blunder' - the great unique opening to clinch the grand design that his admiral had muffed. Undeniably Villeneuve now had an overwhelming superiority of force to deal with Calder and Cornwallis in detail.[40]

> What a chance Villeneuve has missed [lamented the Emperor]. By arriving at Brest from the open sea, he could have played hide-and-seek with Cornwallis's squadron or fallen on Cornwallis or, with his 30 ships, fought the 20 English and gained a decided superiority.[41]

In theory at least he could be said to be correct, and his judgement was endorsed by no less an authority than the great naval historian, Mahan. But as we shall see, Cornwallis's perception had by no means gone awry.

We must now widen our focus and bring into view the Continent of Europe and manoeuvrings of a different kind. When Pitt succeeded Addington as Prime Minister in May 1804, he brought with him a conviction that the time was ripe to abandon Addington's cheap defensive war - to end the loneliness of Britain's fight, widen the conflict and take the offensive again. Oddly, Britain's initial partner in an embryonic new coalition had suffered little from France's predatory progress. Russia, though a remote and enigmatic country on the margin of European affairs, was nevertheless edging ever nearer centre stage under her ambitious young Tsar Alexander I. Britain and Russia were all the stranger as bedfellows since they eyed each other's activities in the near East with a suspicion only slightly less intense than their shared fear of Napoleon's own ambitions in that region. Alexander's self-esteem, already raw from Napoleon's off-hand treatment of his pretensions, had been dealt a painful prick by the D'Enghien affair, as the Tsar had appointed himself the patron of the German princes. The negotiations for an alliance proved long and tortuous, largely due to Alexander's posturings as the would-be arbiter of European affairs; even after the signing of a provisional treaty in April 1805, wrangling continued over Britain's unyielding insistence on retaining Malta, and the small print was not to be finalised until the end of July.

Meanwhile the Austrian court had begun to ask itself how long it was prepared to put up with the attrition of its power and influence in Italy and southern Germany before the onward march of French expansionism. After long agonizing, the conclusion was reached that continued inaction would not avoid war but merely postpone it. Accordingly in late 1804, Austria gingerly began to make moves towards mobilisation, drawing as she did so warning snarls from the direction of Paris. Napoleon's assumption of the Italian crown, followed by the annexation of the Ligurian Republic in June 1805, provided the final nudge, persuading the government in Vienna to lend a ready ear to insistent Russian wooings. In late July 1805, the two powers entered into an offensive alliance against France.

Despite the elaborate veil of secrecy thrown over the negotiations for the new coalition, Napoleon was too well served by his intelligence network not to suspect that something of the sort was going on. The likelihood of a new Continental war before the year was out now began to grow by the day. Lively speculation about Napoleon's real intentions continued to mount throughout Europe during the first eight months of 1805. The history books tell us how things eventually fell out: the abrupt abandoning of the invasion project, the breathtaking plunge into southern Germany where, in perhaps Napoleon's most brilliant campaign, he forced the capitulation of an Austrian army at Ulm, took Vienna, inflicted a catastrophic defeat on an allied army at Austerlitz and imposed a humiliating peace on Austria, all before the year was out.

By mid-1805 the route that was to lead to Austerlitz had already been scouted, and the Emperor was as well prepared to strike across the Rhine as the Channel. The planning for a campaign in southern Germany was well advanced, with routes mapped and provisioned and even the likely battlefields pinpointed. Hence as reports continued to come in throughout the spring and summer pointing unmistakably to an Austrian military build-up, Napoleon was not unduly perturbed. Secure in the knowledge that the alternative was taken care of, he continued to hold to the invasion project; it was immeasurably the greater gamble, but promised by far the richer prize.

But the Emperor was nothing if not a realist. As the days of waiting at Boulogne lengthened into weeks, the lowering in the east could not be ignored. France must not lose her head start. In order to get the diplomatic preliminaries to war out of the way, the tone of Talleyrand's notes to Vienna suddenly took on a more menacing inflection. But there was still time to deal with Britain before the stately workings of the Austrian and Russian military machines could produce a threat to France's eastern flank.[42] However, watching and waiting was never the Emperor's strong suit, nor did he take easily to standing idly by while underlings fumbled and prevaricated. At invasion headquarters, the strain was beginning to tell. A sign that the imperial nerves were somewhat a-twitch came on August 7th, when an order suddenly went out to Marshal Bessières to send the Imperial Guard from Paris to Boulogne, followed by just as abrupt a cancellation the next day.[43] Still Napoleon willed his admirals not to fail him; if they could summon up one last access of resolve, the great end would yet become a reality. Further exhortations and entreaties to Villeneuve were pointless as they would not reach him in time to make any difference, but Ganteaume, at the other end of the telegraph line, was still subject to his Emperor's behest. On the evening of August 20th the Brest commander received a message from Boulogne.

> Are you anchored in Bertheaume? Has the courier arrived from Ferrol? I hope you realise the importance of this moment and what I have the right to expect.[44]

Next day, Ganteaume obediently moved his squadron out into the Bertheaume road. The following morning Cornwallis stood in to meet him from his overnight position south-east of the Black Rocks. After forming battle order Ganteaume hesitated and then, seeing the enemy racing in to cut off his retreat, hurriedly withdrew after a desultory exchange of fire into the safety of the Goulet under the land batteries. Thus began, and ended, the Brest squadron's only action in the great invasion drama.

Finally on August 22nd, the news reached Boulogne that Villeneuve had left Ferrol nine days previously. Once more messages sped down the line to Brest. For Ganteaume:

> Admiral Villeneuve is coming to Brest with the intention of anchoring there; do not allow it, but leave together for your destination. There is not a moment to lose. Such is my intention, and I count on your character.[45]

There was a last dramatic appeal for Villeneuve on his arrival:

> I hope that you have reached Brest. Leave, do not lose a moment, and with my fleets united, enter the Channel. England is ours. We are all ready here, everything is embarked. Appear for 24 hours and it will be all over.[46]

But Decrès, the fearful functionary powerless except to entreat, had already guessed the truth:

> ....if your fleet is at Cadiz, I beg you to consider this as a decree of destiny which is reserving it for other operations. I beg you not to order it to proceed to the Channel since in doing so it will only meet with catastrophe.[47]

After five chaotic days getting his ships ready to leave harbour, Villeneuve wrote to Decrès on August 13th, 'I am about to sail, but I don't know what I shall do'. He was possessed by the fear that Calder, reinforced by Nelson, would be waiting for him and for two days sailed west to make a rendezvous with Allemand, frequently distracted by false sightings of enemy forces by nervy scouts. Reports from neutral ships that Nelson and Calder had gone north provided no comfort, only confirming suspicions that his path into the Channel was securely barred.[48]

But Allemand was far away looking for him off Vigo, and Villeneuve at last reached the decision that in effect spelled the end for his Emperor's hopes. The last paragraph of his latest set of orders of July 16th ran thus:

> If your situation has changed markedly as a result of engagements you have undertaken, or of some significant separation of forces, or other events we could not have foreseen....in this case, which with God's help will not occur, we wish that, after freeing our Rochefort and Ferrol squadrons, you anchor preferably in the port of Cadiz.[49]

This was the let-out that Villeneuve must have had at the back of his mind all along - indeed, Lauriston maintained that he was set on it by the time the fleet had left harbour. At any rate, Villeneuve decided the Emperor's case was met. On August 15th the combined fleet turned south-west on a course for Cape St. Vincent, reaching Cadiz on the 20th where Collingwood, soon joined by Calder, promptly sealed it in. It had been as Cornwallis had predicted: 'The enemy are most likely bound for Cadiz or up the Mediterranean.' He had the full measure of his opponent, knowing the desperate state of the combined fleet from prisoners taken during the battle off Finisterre and surmising that it would have problems finding enough supplies at Ferrol for a Channel campaign. He also guessed, shrewdly, that Villeneuve's ignorance about the movements of the British squadron and Nelson's whereabouts in particular, would provide an even greater deterrent to sailing north.

At invasion headquarters the press of events on the Continent bore in ever more remorselessly by the hour. On August 23rd, Talleyrand was directed to send another tough note to Vienna.

> The more I reflect on the situation in Europe the more I see the urgency of making a decision. In reality, I have nothing to expect from Austria's explanations. She replies with fancy phrases and gains time so that I will be unable to do anything this winter.[50]

But even now, the Emperor could not bring himself to face the collapse of what had been over two years in the making:

> My fleet left Ferrol on August 14th with 34 ships and no
> enemy in sight. If they follow orders, join the Brest fleet and
> enter the Channel, there is still time; I will be master of
> England. If on the contrary, my admirals hesitate, manoeuvre
> badly and do not fulfil their objectives, I have no choice but to
> wait till the winter for a flotilla passage.

However, there was no time for regrets:

> ....in this situation, I shall turn to the most pressing contin-
> gency, I will break up my camps....and on September 22nd I
> will have 200,000 men in Germany and 25,000 in Naples.[51]

Next day the die was cast. Barely pausing for some rough barrack-
room language at the absent admiral's expense ('that Jean-Foutre')
the Emperor sent Berthier the routes to Vienna for issue to field
commanders and on the 25th, Murat and Bertrand were despatched
into Germany to locate the Austrian troop concentrations and report
back within a fortnight. The Army of England prepared to break
camp, bid farewell to its familiar home and make ready for the
long trek towards the Rhine.[52]

    Thus Villeneuve dared to do his master's bidding and,
against the odds, broken through or evaded the Royal Navy's
concentrations, it would have been to accomplish one of the great
anti-climaxes of history, since he would have found no Army of
England awaiting him. As the long columns streamed south-
eastward towards the Rhine - seven *corps d'armée* in a carefully
choreographed sweep with the Army of England forming the right
and centre - Napoleon stayed behind amid the semi-deserted
encampments of Boulogne with 30,000 men to conceal his army's
disappearance from watching British eyes.

    Even yet the turn-about did not mean for Napoleon the
cancellation of the invasion, only its postponement sine die, and a
decree specified in minute detail what should be done to keep the
flotilla in a viable state.[53] He finally left Boulogne on September
3rd. On reaching Paris, however, he found a financial crisis that
took a further three weeks to sort out before he could leave for

Strasbourg. On September 26th he took personal command of his army and struck south-east towards the Danube. He was never to return to the Channel coast.

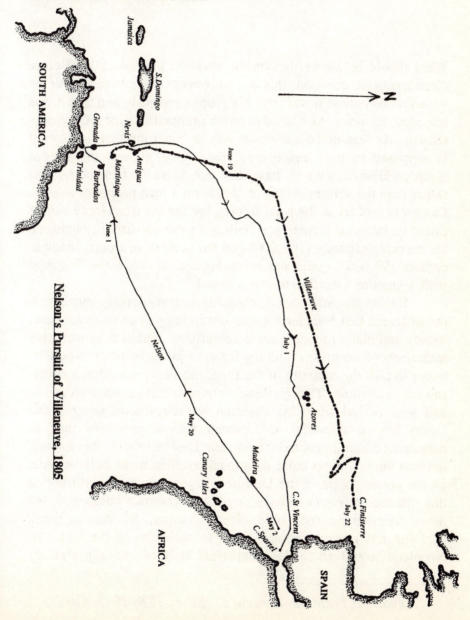

SOUTH AMERICA

Jamaica

S.Domingo

Grenada

Nevis

Trinidad

Barbados

Martinique

Antigua

June 19

June 1

Villeneuve

Nelson's Pursuit of Villeneuve, 1805

Nelson

July 1

Azores

May 20

Canary Isles

Madeira

C.St Vincent

May 2

C.Spartel

AFRICA

C.Finisterre

July 22

SPAIN

N

Afterword

What should be the verdict on the invasion plan of 1805? Before considering the question, this is a convenient place to deal with the view that Napoleon never took his project seriously and that it was intended, all along, as a blind to cover preparations for a Continental war. As was noted earlier, it was an assertion that he himself is supposed to have made more than once, though the French historian Desbrière wisely bases his opinion on the facts of the case rather than the shifting sands of Napoleon's own pronouncements. Desbrière looked at the final figures for the invasion force on the eve of its intended launch, and finding a yawning disparity between the carrying capacity (167,000) and the number of troops ready to embark (93,000), could not bring himself to credit the Emperor with a genuine intention to press ahead.

But on the other hand, credulity is considerably more hard put to accept that Napoleon would unstintingly pour so much time, money and planning into a mere subterfuge. Rather than weighing statements of intent or searching for gaps in staffwork, it would be better to take the measure of the Emperor's correspondence on the subject as a whole. Though there were interludes in the two-and-a-half year period when his attention was elsewhere, decrees and letters by the thousand are imbued with a pervasive tang of passionate commitment to invasion that Desbrière and others would have us think was no more than machiavellian make-believe. And on the precise point of the Desbrière argument, it is worth noting that chaotic staffwork always dogged Napoleon's campaigns but never inhibited him from bold, offensive action. Besides, as Frank McLynn has recently pointed out*, to subscribe to the idea that Napoleon would go to the lengths not only of building a decoy

---

* *Invasion: From the Armada to Hitler, 1588-1945.* (1987).

flotilla but of hazarding the bulk of his naval power on a foray to the other side of the Atlantic and back is to give credence to what must surely rate as the most gratuitous of all exercises in diversion. Common sense surely rebels at any other interpretation than to take seriously what was seriously meant right up to the last minute.

The invasion strategy of 1805 has drawn harsh verdicts over the years, most notably at the hands of Sir Julian Corbett who, in his magisterial study of the Trafalgar campaign, loses no opportunity savagely to berate Napoleon's ineptitude in matters nautical. But first of all, we should consider the feasibility of Napoleon's ultimate objective - to get a large force of ships into the Channel and hold the Strait long enough for the flotilla to make a crossing.

> I do not say that the French will not come.
> I only say they will not come by sea.[1]

Thus spoke Lord St. Vincent in his bluffest vein; but it is worth noting that he was addressing his fellow peers in the Upper House, and the remark has the ring of the kind of morale-boosting public pronouncement, that national leaders feel they ought to make in moments of supreme crisis. We should also bear in mind that there was no great confidence in Addington's capacity to measure up to the emergency and St. Vincent, as his First Lord of the Admiralty, would be mindful of the need to allay the fears of those faint-hearts he contemptuously called 'the old ladies'. For more candid judgements we should turn to less public statements. The received Admiralty line, as laid out in instructions to Cornwallis, viewed invasion as:

> ...a very desperate attempt....likely to terminate in the destruc-
> tion of their fleet if they are able by any extraordinary
> unforseen events to elude your vigilance and thereby make their
> way up the Channel.[2]

But we also have another opinion on the matter, just as weighty.

In considering a subject of this important nature, [wrote Lord Keith] it is fair to look at it from every point of view. I therefore hazard a possible, though not a very probable conjecture which is that a fleet or squadron might get out of Brest unperceived and watch for an opportunity for running up the Downs or Margate Roads, in which case it might be superior to our squadron long enough to cover the landing of any extent of force from the opposite coast.

In such an eventuality:

....by the ordinary channels of communication, it is highly probable that they might be eight or ten days in the Downs before the Channel fleet could be informed and arrive to attack them. Few people who have been in the Channel fleet and will consider this subject well will deny this fact....It will be argued by many that it is a case most extravagantly drawn and that the concurrence of so many circumstances favourable to the success of any enemy amounts to an impossibility. But on a subject which involves the existence of the nation and leaves its dependence on the possible issue of a few days, let us not be lulled into a state of delusive security....The whole case is by no means impossible, nor indeed is it highly improbable.[3]

In one respect, then, Keith is in agreement with his superiors in rating an invasion attempt as a gambler's throw, with the odds heavily stacked against a win. But once a French force managed to give its opponents the slip and enter the Channel, he believed the confusion as to its whereabouts might well prevail long enough for a crossing to be mounted. It is worth noting that the recipient of this assessment was but the Duke of York, who would have to deal with any failure by the Navy, and also that Keith took pains to hint that he was not adverse to his views being generally put about provided they were not attributed to him.

When we survey the Emperor's invasion strategy as a whole, we see on it the unmistakable Napoleonic fingerprints. The heart of his plan, the thrust at a secondary target to tempt the enemy into breaking his concentrations followed by a surprise incursion to knock him off balance, breathes the very spirit of the Napoleonic battlefield. We may observe other features with the same aim of keeping the enemy guessing; the manipulation of the threat from the Texel, the diversionary sortie by the Rochefort squadron, the protracted sojourn in Italy, the dissemination of cooked press reports, the constant insistence on maintaining a cloak of secrecy over all operations. Yet as has often been remarked by critics of Napoleon's maritime strategy, warfare on land is not the same as that at sea, and the riot of error and wishful thinking manifested itself in the Emperor's naval correspondence has often been a sore disappointment to those devotees of the Napoleon of the icy intellect. There were undoubtedly grievous flaws in his ideas, and critics have not hesitated to get their teeth into them; the bewildering changes of plan, the failure to penetrate the subtleties of British naval strategy, the landsman's lack of what a French naval historian called 'a precise feel for the difficulties of the navy'. Yet even on this latter point the blatant miscalculations can blind us to the Emperor's grasp of important realities in maritime operations. Though his deepest instincts were to master and dictate, he fully recognised the limits of his control over events at sea, as he admitted to Villeneuve:

> I have always considered the actions you might take that I cannot calculate and of which I have no knowledge.[4]

In his readiness to allow for the unprophesiable and trust to the initiative of the commander on the spot, the tenor of Napoleon's orders compares quite favourably with that of the British Admiralty. Indeed one could say that in view of his admiral's personality, he was too permissive; Villeneuve's orders laid out no fewer than four alternative courses of action for his return to Europe, including the escape clause that he was only too ready to clutch at.

Two unarguable factors constituted the cornerstones of Napoleon's strategy; first, Britain's navy, for all its size, was always stretched dangerously thin for the multifarious job it had to do; and secondly, communication across large tracts of ocean was a chronically hit-or-miss business. In an age when radio was undreamt of, naval movements, as the previous chapter has shown, often hinged on no more than hunch, conjecture or educated guesswork, and could be decisively affected by chance sightings and intelligence that was inaccurate, went astray or was overtaken by events. Indeed the most reliable sources of vital information for both sides were often chance-met, obligingly talkative neutral merchant skippers. Moreover, as Napoleon realised, sound communications were more important to the enemy than to his own admirals. To be effective, an extensive defensive line has to be well co-ordinated; any muddle or loss of contact would supply the attacker with his hole to wriggle through.

Though long experience had taught the Royal Navy to minimise the play of contingency in its operations, even the matchless Nelson could humbly admit, 'the world attaches wisdom to him that guesses right.' Thus Napoleon was right to lay as much store as he did on hoodwinking his opponents. That he ludicrously over-estimated the effects of his stratagems is undeniable, and the British had long foreseen that guile would be his tool. Yet to anticipate that the enemy will seek to deceive does not necessarily win immunity from his wiles.

> I never had a doubt that, if an attempt to invade the king's dominions at home is meant to be made, the object must be Ireland.[5]

So wrote Lord Melville, and there were others who agreed with him. Such expert miscalculations reveal that the Emperor's machinations had not been so wide of the mark.

Yet for all the opportunities that Napoleon took pains to open up for easing the path of his fleet into the Channel, his mind slid too easily over the key problem, which was the blockade of Brest. Ganteaume's inability to leave harbour without a battle, and his master's refusal to permit him to fight his way out- Napoleon, for all his offensive instincts, could not rid himself of the French navy's long-cherished article of faith that the mission always came first- compromised things from the beginning. The advantages of speed and surprise, the Napoleonic watchwords, leaked away and the Emperor was forced to put back his timetable by several weeks. Then, in the interval after the enemy had located him, Villeneuve's protracted dallyings in Spanish harbours gave the enemy a breathing-space in which to reshuffle his dispositions. Villeneuve was thus confronted with a dilemma that would have given the most ardent spirit pause for thought: either to fight a battle off Brest against an enemy that he correctly surmised would be waiting for him mustered in force across his way, or play an evasive game that would demand a combination of miraculous luck and Nelsonian wizardry.

It was Napoleon himself who pronounced that in war the moral is to the physical as three is to one, and it is ironical that the key role in this, the deepest-laid of all his plans, should have been thrust into the nerveless hands of a commander who was psychologically not up to it. Certainly Villeneuve found himself in a difficult situation. Even if we make due allowance for his fast-ebbing morale, and perhaps a self-serving impulse to touch things up a little so as to make the case for giving up, he paints a sorry picture of the state of his fleet. It is clear that the test of a long-distance operation followed by a battle had proved too much for French and Spanish ships and seamanship. In the circumstances we can well imagine the horror with which Villeneuve must have read the new orders awaiting him at Ferrol, urging him to go north-about around Ireland and Scotland, so as to reach Boulogne from the east. Though notionally a shrewd ploy on Napoleon's part to bypass British concentrations at the mouth of the Channel, there can be little doubt that such a foray would have ended in disaster equal to that which befell King Philip's Armada as it struggled home along the same route in the other direction over two centuries previously.

However, Villeneuve's despatches reveal not only a fleet in disarray but a commander at the end of his tether. Villeneuve's original role had been as subordinate to the more spirited Ganteaume, and indeed Napoleon did not bother initially to tell him the object of his mission, this being confided only to Lauriston, his trusted aide.[6] When the admiral received his new orders at Fort de France, he was suddenly confronted with the awful prospect that the outcome of the whole operation would now rest with him alone. The infirmity of purpose discernible even at Toulon steadily got the better of him until he was overtaken by a paralysis of the will that was impervious to his Emperor's most urgent entreaties. Though diligent and brave, as was to be shown at Trafalgar, Villeneuve had the kind of personality that was simply unequal to the pressures of high command, itemising his troubles with the lugubrious relish of the defeatist and repeatedly rehearsing the arguments against positive action.

Thus we may conclude that Napoleon's strategy came to wreck not so much on the plan itself as on the frailty of the agent who unwontedly found himself saddled with it, though it may be said that the Emperor's failure to take the human factor more fully into account was in itself a defect of his planning.

The vast sweep of Napoleon's invasion ideas and the fact that they were so nearly brought to fruition leads us down one last teasing avenue of inquiry. The 'alternative history' that might have led to the sight of the tricolour floating over the Tower of London in the late summer of 1805, as Napoleon longingly imagined it at the time, and the 'alternative history' of the British people for that matter, can be a tantalising subject for speculation.

'One can always play a parlour game with the might-have-beens of history,' wrote E.H. Carr, 'but they have nothing to do with history.' That may be, but perhaps we owe something to the Corsican's shade to conclude by reflecting at least a little on what might have happened if the Army of England had stumbled ashore on to the Kentish beaches that August, if only because if there was ever a plan devised for a successful descent on Britain, his was it.

However, two factors ought to give us pause in attempting too close a speculation on what might have happened if Villeneuve's fleet had appeared off Boulogne in August 1805. One is the weather. In June 1944, when Eisenhower, after several days' agonizing over meteorological reports, had issued the final go-ahead for the D-Day landings, he sat down and scribbled a communiqué to be released in the event of failure. It is difficult to imagine Napoleon afflicted by Eisenhower's doubts, yet even with his sublime cocksureness he must have known the extent to which the Channel weather would dictate the play. It could have forced a cancellation or, worse, it might have played him false and turned in mid-operation - we should remember the total crossing time was 72 hours - and brought the whole thing to disaster. However, let us assume one of those calm summer spells when the Channel wears a placid face. Even then the different sailing characteristics of the various types of flotilla craft would have presented severe problems of co-ordination, particularly for the contingents crossing at night, making it difficult, if not impossible, to achieve the concentration of strength on the target beaches that was needed to gain the vital initial foothold. As anyone who has ever been involved in such operations will testify, the landing phase of the best-concerted amphibious operation is chaotic, even when launched at short range from landing ships. In the case of the flotilla, making a crossing of perhaps 30 miles before the final run-in, the formations would inevitable drift ever further apart, and so find themselves landing at different times in a scatter of penny packets.

Thus, given even the best-case scenario, it is quite possible that the Army of England would have landed on English soil in such disarray that we may doubt whether it could have pulled itself together properly to fight its way off the beaches. This is the amphibious commander's nightmare, his troops pinned down in detail to be slaughtered where they lay, as happened to the Americans at Omaha Beach, Tarawa and Iwo Jima. Yet let us still suppose that not all cohesion would have been lost, and the *grognards*, perhaps with some parting exhortation from their Emperor still ringing in their ears to inspire them, would have broken through the red line and secured a base on English soil, soon to be joined by Napoleon himself.

From this point on, however, our line of speculation finally takes off into realterra incognita, since the other great imponderable now comes into play, and that is the genius of Napoleon. The

Addington government and the Duke of York had laid their plans as well as rational calculation could make them. But genius is by definition unprophesiable; who can tell what would have been the outcome if only a fraction of the Army of England had been allowed loose in south-eastern England with Napoleon at its head? And, though Britons may have fought dearly for their homeland, we should not forget the remark of Wellington, who was hardly given to overstatement, that Napoleon's presence on the battlefield was worth an extra 40,000 men. It would thus be a pointless exercise to attempt to penetrate that mistiest of might-have-beens, the Emperor's British campaign.

However, we are on surer ground in imagining how Britain might have fared as a satrapy of France, as we have the evidence of how Napoleon treated his real fiefdoms. We need not take seriously his assertion to his British physician on St. Helena that he would have issued instructions for an assembly of deputies to meet in London and allowed them to decide on a constitution of their choice. His record shows too well his impatience with the voice of the people and his habit of dispensing with democratic deliberations when they did not suit his book. He was franker about his more likely intentions when warming to the subject of his reckoning with his favourite *bêtes noires*, the 'English oligarchs'; together with the monarchy, they and their privileges would be swept away, to be replaced by a republic, with all property redistributed on an egalitarian basis among the *'canaille'*, the ordinary people. He was confident that such measures would bind the majority of the population to the French cause, and he may well have been right.[7] Maybe armed resistance may have continued to flicker on, perhaps in the remote hills of the north and west, the traditional refuges of lost causes, with a sick, ageing Lear-like king as its figurehead. Of one thing at least we may be sure: resistance of any kind would be met with a draconian response, as it always did in Napoleon's occupied territories.

The Grand Army never returned to its nursery on the Channel coast. As it followed its eagles across the length and breadth of Europe and beyond at the behest of Napoleon's ever-vaulting ambitions, the neat avenues of hutments that had once been its home fell into dilapidation, while the rows of invasion craft in the sand-choked basins slowly decayed at their moorings. In October 1805, the unhappy Villeneuve emerged from Cadiz to do battle with Nelson in a last despairing attempt to retrieve his honour. The result at Trafalgar was an annihilation of French naval power so complete that it might seem to have extinguished the prospect of invasion for a generation. But neither Napoleon nor Britain saw it that way. As French dominion spread north to the Baltic and south as far as the eastern Aegean, Napoleon fell back on the weapon of trade embargo, his Continental System, in an effort to wrestle Britain to her knees by inches. But he never lost sight of the vision of 1803, to overwhelm the arch-adversary with her own weapons, and in the subsequent years Britain nervously watched the steady resurgence of French naval power in shipyards from Venice to Antwerp, threatening to overtop the Royal Navy's fighting strength and yet retrieve the failure of 1805.

We may conclude with a last intriguing might-have-been. If Napoleon had indeed subjugated Britain, there would have been no British gold on which to build any more Continental coalitions, and no reason for the endless wars and their toll in human misery that were visited on Europe in the course of the subsequent decade. Whether the conquest of Britain could be deemed a worthwhile exchange for perhaps a Europe spared the Austerlitzes, Eylaus, Wagrams, Borodinos and Waterloos that would have gone unfought, each must judge for himself.

References

Chapter One: The Weasel and the Rat

1. Horner, *Memoirs*, i, 217
2. Markham, *Napoleon*, 95
3. Holland, *Memoir of the Rev Sydney Smith*, i, 28
4. Desbriere, *Projects*, iii, 22-25
5. Ibid. 83-84
6. *Naval Chronicle*, ix, 243
7. Malmesbury, *Diaries and Correspondence*, iv, 65
8. Wheeler and Broadley, *Napoleon and the Invasion of Britain*, ii, 37
9. Ibid. 45-46
10. Cornwallis, *Correspondence*, iii
11. Farington, *Diary*, ii, 122-123
12. McCunn, *The Personality of Napoleon*, 297
13. Cockburn, *Memorials of his Time*, 196
14. Wheeler and Broadley, op.cit. 40
15. *Annual Register*, 1803, 418
16. Horner, op.cit. 226
17. see Ashton, *English Caricature and Satire*, 148-241, and Klingberg and Hustvedt, *The Warning Drum*.

Chapter Two: To Leap the Ditch

1. Desbriere, *Projects*, iii, 106-109
2. Napoleon, *Correspondence*, viii, 367
3. Thiers, *History of the Consulate and Empire*, v, 48-49
4. Desbriere, op.cit. iii, 82-83
5. Napoleon, op.cit. viii, 361
6. Ibid. 516
7. Ibid. 499
8. Desbriere, op.cit. iii, 111-112
9. Ibid. 90
10. Ibid. facing p.90 sketches and notes

11. Holland Rose, *Life and Napoleon*, i, 486-488
12. Desbriere, op.cit. iii, 339
13. Ibid. 356
14. Ibid. 566-568
15. Napoleon, op.cit. ix, 122
16. Desbriere, op.cit. iii, 380
17. Ibid. 141-144, 148
18. Ibid. 149-152
19. Ibid. 166-167
20. Ibid. 153
21. Napoleon, op.cit. viii, 359-360, 431-432, 471
22. Desbriere, op.cit. iii, map opposite p.149, iv, 236-237
23. Napoleon, op.cit. viii, 352-353, 473-477
24. Desbriere, op.cit. 427-429
25. Napoleon, op.cit. ix, 23-24, 92, 119
26. Ibid. viii, 386, 532, ix, 85, 90-91
27. Thiers, op.cit. 48-49
28. Keith, *Papers*, iii, 76
29. Desbriere, op.cit. iii. 542
30. Ibid. p.544
31. Ibid. iv, 145
32. Barham, *Letters*, iii, 140-141
33. Napoleon, op.cit. ix, 105
34. WO 30/75, Keith to Duke of York, 29th October 1803
35. Debriere, op.cit. iii, 632-636, 636-638
36. Thiers, op.cit. 85-150
37. Desbriere, op.cit. iv, 3-9
38. Ibid. 109-113
39. *Naval Chronicle*, xii, 248
40. Crawford, *Reminiscences*, 137
41. Napoleon, op.cit.ix, 509
42. Ibid. ix, 216-217, 551-559
43. Desbriere, op.cit. iv, 229, 237-238
44. Metternich, *Memoirs*, i, 28
45. Holland Rose, op.cit. 492-493

Chapter Three: The Wooden Walls

1. Admiralty, *Channel Pilot*, 130
2. see Marcus, *History of England*, ii, Chap.6
3. *Blockade of Brest*, i, 120
4. Ibid. 155
5. Keith, *Papers*, iii, 48
6. Markham, *Correspondence*, 112
7. Barham, *Letters*, iii, 234
8. see Jenkins, *A History of the French Navy*, Chap.2
9. Keith, op.cit. 42
10. Ibid. 53-54
11. *Naval Chronicle*, xii, 414
12. Keith, op.cit. 79-81
13. Napoleon, *Correspondence*, ix, 369
14. Bloomfield, *Kent and the Napoleonic Wars*, 63, 76-77
15. Desbriere, *Projets*, iv, 329, 332
16. see WO 1/924
17. Crawford, *Reminiscences*, 172
18. Keith, op.cit. 68 footnote
19. O'Meara, *Napoleon in Exile*, i, 252
20. Keith, op.cit. 68 footnote
21. Ibid. 76-78
22. Napoleon, op.cit. ix, 272, 285
23. Keith, op.cit. 78
24. Markham, op.cit. 170-171
25. *Blockade of Brest*, i, 65-66

Chapter Four: Two Fiascos

1. *Naval Chronicles*, xii, 250
2. St. Vincent, *Letters*, ii, 395-396
3. McGuffie, *The Stone Ships*, 492
4. Keith, *Papers*, 71
5. St. Vincent, op.cit. 399-400
6. Desbriere, *Projets*, iii, 551-553

7. McGuffie, op.cit. 494
8. Ibid. 495
9. Ibid. 495
10. Keith, op.cit. 72-74
11. St. Vincent, op.cit.406
12. McGuffie, op.cit. 498
13. see Dickinson, *Robert Fulton*, Chap.3
14. Ibid. Chaps. 5 & 6
15. Keith, op.cit. 22
16. Dickinson, op.cit. 165
17. Ibid. 183-185
18. Keith, op.cit. 85
19. *Naval Chronicle*, xii, 313
20. Keith, op.cit. 86
21. Ibid. 88
22. Crawford, *Reminiscences*, 145,
23. Keith, op.cit. 89-94
24. Crawford, op.cit. 147
25. Keith, op.cit. 91
26. *Naval Chronicle*, xii, 330
27. Dickinson, op.cit. 188-190
28. Ibid. 190-192
29. *Naval Chronicle*, xiv, 342
30. Keith, op.cit. 118
31. Dickinson, op.cit. 199

Chapter Five: 'Bonaparte may pass this way'

1. Jesse, *Memoirs of the Life*, iii, 338
2. Glenbervie, *Diaries*, 361
3. Colchester, *Diary and Correspondence*, i, 470-471
4. Desbriere, *Projets*, iii, 79
5. Keith, *Papers*, 17
6. O'Meara, *Napoleon*, i, 353
7. notably by Burne, *The Noble Duke of York*, and Glover, *Peninsular Preparation*

8. WO30/76 Duke of York to Hobart, 25th August 1803
9. WO30/76 ibid.
10. WO30/76 ibid.
11. WO30/76 Duke of York to Hobart, 30th June 1803
12. WO30/76 Duke of York to Hobart, 25th August 1803 and memo 29th June 1803
13. WO30/75 Distribution of Troops in Districts, 1st January 1804
14. WO30/76 Duke of York to Hobart, 25th August 1803
15. Rose, *Napoleon's Last Voyage*, 89
16. WO30/76 Duke of York to Hobart, 25th August 1803
17. WO30/76 ibid.
18. WO30/76 ibid.
19. WO30/71 Camden to Duke of York, 29th July 1804
20. WO30/78 Memo by Brown, 8th July 1804
21. WO1/629 Brownrigg to Cooke, 25th September 1804
22. WO30/76 Duke of York to Hobart, 25th August 1803
23. WO1/629 Duke of York to Generals of Districts, 11th August 1804
24. Wilson, *The Old Telegraphs*, 11-32, 120-132
25. *Naval Chronicle*, xii, 156
26. Home Office Circular, September 1803, quote Ashcroft *To Escape the Monster's Clutches*, 88-89
27. Brownrigg, *Life and Letters of Sir John Moore*, 145-146
28. Ward, *Peeps into the Past*, 81
29. Fremantle, *The Wynne Diaries*, iii, 86-87
30. Napoleon, *Correspondence*, x, 259
31. Home Office Circular, 24th June 1803
32. WO30/70 Richmond to Yorke, 3rd & 21st November 1803
33. Ashcroft, op.cit. 73-74
34. Glover, *Britain at Bay*, 54
35. O'Meara, op.cit. ii, 382
36. WO30/78 Draft of a Proclamation to be used in case of invasion, n.d.

37. WO30/76 Duke of York to Yorke, 12th November 1803 and 30th January 1804. Duke of York to Generals commanding Districts, 27th March 1804
38. WO30/76 Duke of York to Yorke, 12th November 1803
39. WO30/76 Duke of York to Hobart, 25th August 1803
40. WO30/75 Cornwallis to Brownrigg, 29th December 1803

Chapter Six: The 'Bang-up Locals' and others

1. WO30/75 Distribution of Troops in Districts, 1st January 1804
2. Bunbury, *Narrative of Some Passages*,176-177
3. see Glover, *Peninsular Preparation*
4. Fortescue, *History of the British Army*, v, 203-204
5. see Western, *The English Militia in the 18th Century*,
6. Fortescue, *The County Lieutenancies*, 39-40
7. Ibid. 73
8. Ibid. 47
9. *Recollections of Rifleman Harris*, first published in 1828
10. Fortescue, *The County Lieutenancies*, 45-48
11. Ibid. 191
12. Fortescue, *History of the Army*, v, 73
13. Fortescue, *The County Lieutenancies*, 152-156
14. *Gentleman's Magazine*, liii, 975
15. Wheeler and Broadley, *Napoleon and the Invasion*, ii, 105
16. Cockburn, *Memorials of His Time*, 187-195
17. Wheeler and Broadley, op.cit. 106
18. see Western, *The Volunteer Movement*
19. Fortescue, *History of the Army*, v, 198-213
20. Ashcroft, op.cit. 75
21. Fortescue, *County Lieutenancies*, 86
22. Ibid. 86
23. Glover, op.cit. Chap.2
24. Fortescue, *The County Lieutenancies*, 114-116
25. Horner, *Memoirs*, 225
26. Wheeler and Broadley, op.cit. 107-109

27. Fortescue MSS, 188
28. Campbell, *Lives of the Lord Chancellors*, vi, 547
29. Ashcroft, op.cit. 70-71
30. Fremantle, *Wynne Diaries*, iii, 87
31. HO50/97 Keene to Secretary of State, 23rd May 1804
32. HO50/98 Dod to Stamford, 9th February 1804
33. HO50/102 Dorchester to Secretary of State, 7th and 12th May 1804
34. HO50/97 Brackenbury to ? 12th April 1804. Strode to ? 26th July 1804. Strode to Powlett, 8th September 1804
35. Ward, *Peeps into the Past,* 82-83
36. *Political Register*, iv, 718
37. Ibid. 835
38. HO50/119 Statement by Strode and enclosures (no date)
39. Glover, *Britain at Bay*, 44-45
40. Cockburn, op.cit. 197

Chapter Seven: Towers along the Steep

1. WO30/76 Duke of York to Hobart, 25th August 1803
2. WO30/76 Duke of York to Hobart, 4th July 1803
3. WO30/76 Duke of York to Hobart, 25th August 1803
4. Cornwallis, *Correspondence*, iii, 502
5. WO30/75 Chatham to Hobart, 9th February 1804
6. WO30/78 Memo, 'Military positions surrounding and for the defence of the capital', 1803
7. PRO MR1200 'Map of London Defences', September 1801
8. WO 30/76 Duke of York to Hobart, 26th April 1804 and 25th August 1803. Also WO30/71 Gordon to Brownrigg, 26th June 1803
9. WO30/56 Memo, 26th July 1803, WO30/66 Cathcart to Duke of York, 8th October 1803, WO30/76 Duke of York to Cathcart, 15th July 1803, and Duke of York to Cathcart, 26th July 1803
10. WO30/76 Duke of York to Hobart, 25th August 1803
11. WO30/76 Duke of York to Camden, 4th June 1804

12. WO30/76 Duke of York to Cathcart, 12th August 1803
13. WO1/628 Camden to Duke of York, 26th May 1804
14. Keith, *Papers*, 50
15. WO1/628 Camden to Duke of York, 26th May 1804. See also Wood, *Essex and the French Wars*.
16. Bingham, *More Light on St. Helena*, Cornhill Magazine, 1901, 28-29. Also, Glover, *Britain at Bay*, 82
17. WO30/78 Brown to Quarter-Master General, 15th July 1804
18. PRO MR1342 'Plan of Chatham Lines', 18th May 1804
19. WO30/62 Twiss to Dundas, 17th July 1803
20. WO30/76 Duke of York to Dundas, 2nd July 1803
21. WO30/76 Duke of York to Chatham, 12th April 1804
22. WO30/76 Twiss to Dundas, 17th July 1803
23. WO1/627 Duke of York to Hobart, 30th March 1804, and Hobart to Duke of York, 6th April 1804
24. ADM1/4196 Statement by Dundas accompanying plan of proposed Dover defence works
25. WO1/627 Brownrigg to Sullivan, 14th March 1804, WO1/629 Report by Dundas and Brown, 27th September 1804
26. WO1/629 Report by Brown, 19th September 1804
27. Vine, *The Royal Military Canal*, 41-63
28. Smiles, *Lives of the Engineers*, ii, 283
29. Vine, op.cit. 69
30. Ward, 'Defence works in Britain', JSAHR, xxviii, 27
31. Sutcliffe, *Martello Towers*, 22-23
32. WO30/62 report by Reynolds, 7th April 1798
33. WO30/76 'Description of the Tower....' 11th August 1803
34. WO30/76 Duke of York to Chatham, 11th August 1803
35. WO30/76 Duke of York to Hobart, 25th August 1803
36. Hansard, *Parliamentary Debates*, i, 9
37. WO1/783 Report, 26th April 1804
38. WO1/629 Twiss to Morse, 12th September 1804
39. Sutcliffe, op.cit. 56
40. Ibid. 61-79 for a detailed description
41. Ward. op.cit. 31
42. Brown, *Diary*, 21st October 1804

Chapter Eight: 'England is no more!'

1. Napoleon, *Correspondence*, x, 161
2. Ibid. 252
3. Ibid. 182-186
4. Ibid. 261
5. Ibid. 261
6. Corbett, *The Campaign of Trafalgar*, 550
7. Ibid. 89-99
8. Ibid. 69-73
9. Ibid. Chaps. 4 and 5
10. Ibid. Chaps. 6 and 7
11. Napoleon, op.cit. x, various letters, 11th April-8th May 1805
12. Ibid. 346
13. Ibid. 454
14. Ibid. 461
15. Desbriere, *Projets*, iii, 596
16. Napoleon, op.cit. x, 555
17. Ibid. 347
18. Ibid. various letters, 10th May-28th June 1805, Glover, *Britain at Bay*, 81
19. Corbett, op.cit. Chap.11
20. Napoleon, op.cit. 430
21. Ibid. 483
22. Ibid. 571
23. ibid. 556
24. Corbett, op.cit. 227
25. Napoleon, op.cit. x, 505
26. Corbett, op.cit. 181-184
27. Napoleon, op.cit. xi, 22
28. Desbriere, *Projets*, v, 640
29. Napoleon, op.cit. xi, 45
30. Corbett, op.cit. 193-207
31. Ibid. 220-221
32. Napoleon, xi, 18

33. Ibid. 19
34. Desbriere, *Projets iv,* table opposite p.464
35. Thiers, *History of the Consulate and Empire*, v, 375-376
36. Desbriere, *Projets*, iv, 776
37. Ibid. 776-777
38. Ibid. 775
39. Napoleon, op.cit. xi, 87
40. Corbett, op.cit. 247-254
41. Napoleon, op.cit. xi, 161
42. see Deutsch, *Napoleonic Policy* for a detailed account of the diplomatic moves.
43. Napoleon, op.cit. xi, 70
44. Ibid. 106
45. Ibid. 115
46. Ibid. 115
47. Desbriere, *Projets*, iv, 814
48. Corbett, op.cit.255-265
49. Napoleon, op.cit. xi, 19
50. Ibid. 117
51. Ibid. 117
52. Desbriere, *Projets*, iv, 818
53. Napoleon, op.cit. xi, 165-166

Chapter Nine: Afterword

1. This is the most famous quotation of the whole crisis, but I have been unable to find its source.
2. Barham, *Letters*, iii, 233
3. WO30/75 Keith to Duke of York, 29th October 1803
4. Napoleon, *Correspondence*, x, 389
5. *Blockade of Brest*, ii, 95
6. Napoleon, op.cit. x, 185-189
7. O'Meara, *Napoleon in Exile*, i, 349-350, ii, 379-380

Bibliography

MANUSCRIPT SOURCES

Public Records Office

Admiralty 1
Home Office 50
Home Office 51
War Office 1
War Office 30

National Library of Scotland

Journal of Lt-Col. John Brown, 1804-05. (MS 2868)

PRINTED SOURCES

ADMIRALTY: *Channel Pilot*. (1920)
ASHCROFT, M.Y.(ed): *To Escape the Monster's Clutches*. (N.Yorks.CRO. 1977)
ASHTON, J: *English Caricature and Satire on Napoleon I*. (1888)
AUCKLAND, Baron: *Journals and Correspondence, Vol.4*.
AYLING, S: *George III*. (1972)
BARHAM, Charles, Lord.(ed.Laughton): *Letters and Papers, Vol.3*. (Navy Records Society, 1911)
BARROW, J: *Life and Correspondence of Admiral Sir William Sidney Smith*. (1848)
BIGGS, H: *The River Medway*. (1982)
BINGHAM, G: 'More Light on St. Helena', *Cornhill Magazine*. (1901)
BLOOMFIELD, P: *Kent and the Napoleonic Wars*. (1987)
BROADLEY, A.M:*Napoleon in Caricature*. (1911)
BROWNING, O.(ed): *England and Napoleon in 1803*.
BROWNRIGG, B: *Life and Letters of Sir John Moore*. (1923)

BRYANT, A: *The Years of Victory, 1802-1812.* (1944)

BUNBURY, H: *Narrative of Some Passages in the Great War with France.* (1854)

BURNE, A.H: *The Noble Duke of York.* (1949)

CAMPBELL, J: *Lives of the Lord Chancellors, Vol.6.* (1854)

CASTLEREAGH, Viscount: *Correspondence, Vol.5.* (1848)

CHANDLER, D: *The Campaigns of Napoleon.* (1967)

COBBETT, W: *Parliamentary History, Vol.36.* (1803)

COBBETT, W: *Political Register, Vols 4-8.* (1803-05)

COBBETT, W: *Rural Rides.* (1830)

COCKBURN, H: *Memorials of his Time.* (1856)

COLCHESTER, Charles, Baron (ed.Colchester): *Diary and Correspondence, Vol.1.* (1861)

COQUELLE, P: *Napoleon and England, 1803-05.* (1904)

CORBETT, J: *The Campaign of Trafalgar.* (1910)

CORNWALLIS, Charles, Marquis. (ed.Ross): *Correspondence, Vol.3.* (1859)

CRAWFORD, A: *Reminiscences of a Naval Officer, Vol.1.* (1851)

DESBRIÈRE, E: *Projets et Tentatives de Débarquement aux Isles Britanniques, Vols.3-5.* (1902)

DESBRIÈRE, E: *La Campagne Maritime de 1805.* (1907) English translation: *The Trafalgar Campaign*, by C.Eastwick, (1933)

DEUTSCH, H.C: *The Genesis of Napoleonic Imperialism.* (1938)

DEUTSCH, H.C: 'Napoleonic Policy and the Project of a Descent on England' *Journal of Modern History, Vol.2.* (1930)

DICKINSON, H.W: *Robert Fulton.* (1913)

FARINGTON, J. (ed.Greig): *Diary, Vols. 1 and 2.* (1922-28)

FORTESCUE, J.W: *History of the British Army, Vol.5.* (1910)

FORTESCUE, J.W: *The County Lieutenancies and the Army.* (1909)

FREMANTLE, A (ed): *The Wynne Diaries, Vol.3.* (1940)

GARROS, L: *Itineraire de Napoleon Bonaparte.* (1947)

GEORGE, D: *English Political Caricature, Vol.2.* (1959)

GEYL, P: *Napoleon For and Against.* (1949)

GLENBERVIE, Sylvester, Lord. (ed.Bickley): *Diaries.* (1928)

GLOVER, M: *Warfare in the Age of Bonaparte.* (1980)

GLOVER, R: *Britain in Danger.* (1973)

GLOVER, R: *Peninsular preparation.* (1963)

GLOVER, R: 'When London was Last in Danger' *Queen's Quarterly,* (Kingston, Ontario.1940)

GLOVER R: 'The Royal Military Canal' *Army Quarterly.* (1953)

GRANVILLE, Earl: *Correspondence, Vol.1.* (1916)

HANSARD: *Parliamentary Debates, Vols. 1-5.* (1803-05)

HARDY, Thomas: *The Dynasts,* (1903-08)

HARDY, Thomas: *The Trumpet Major*. (1880)

HISTORICAL MANUSCRIPTS COMMISSION: *Various Collections VI* (1909)

HISTORICAL MANUSCRIPTS COMMISSION: *Fortescue MSS*. (1910)

HORNER, F: *Memoirs and Correspondence*. (1843)

JAMES, W: *The Naval History of Great Britain, 1793-1820, Vol.3*. (1822)

JENKINS, E.H: *History of the French Navy*. (1973)

JESSE, J.H: *Memoirs of the Life and Reign of King George III*. (1867)

KEITH, George, Admiral Viscount. (ed.Lloyd): *Papers, Vol.3*. (Navy Records Society, 1955)

KLINGBERG, F & HUSTVEDT, S: *The Warning Drum: Broadsides of 1803*. (1944)

LAS CASES: *Mémorial de Sainte Hélène*. (English Edition, 1823)

LEFÈBVRE, G: *Napoleon, Vol.1*. (1969)

LEYLAND, J.(ed): *Papers relating to the Blockade of Brest, 1803-05. Vols. 1 & 2*. (Navy Records Society, 1898 & 1901)

McCUNN, F.J: *The Contemporary English View of Napoleon*. (1914)

McGUFFIE, T.H: 'The Stone Ships Expedition against Boulogne, 1804' *English Historical Review*. (1949)

McLYNN, F: *Invasion: From the Armada to Hitler*. (1987)

MACKSEY, P: *The War in the Mediterranean, 1803-10*. (1957)

MAHAN, A.T: *The Influence of Sea Power upon the French Revolution and Empire*. (1892)

MALMESBURY, James, Earl: *Diaries and Correspondence*. (1844)

MARCUS, G: *A Naval History of England, Vol.2; The Age of Nelson*. (1971)

MARKHAM, F: *Napoleon*. (1963)

MARKHAM, Admiral J. (ed.Markham): *Correspondence, 1801-07*. (Navy Records Society, 1904)

MEAD, H: 'Martello Towers', *Mariner's Mirror*. (1948)

MEAD, H: 'Early History of the Telegraph', *Mariner's Mirror*. (1934)

MEAD, H: *The Story of the Semaphore*. (1939)

MINTO, George, Earl: *Life and Letters, Vol.3*. (1874)

NAPOLEON: *Correspondence, Vols.8-11*. (1858-70)

NAVAL CHRONICLE, 1802-05.

NELSON, Horatio, Admiral Viscount: (ed.Nicholas): *Despatches and Letters, Vols.4-6*. (1844-46)

NICHOLS, N.H: *Despatches and Letters of Vice Admiral Lord Viscount Nelson. 7 Vols*. (1844-46)

NICOLAY, F: *Napoleon at the Camp of Boulogne*. (English translation, 1907)

OMAN, C: *Napoleon at the Channel*. (1942)

O'MEARA, B.E: *Napoleon in Exile*. (1834)

PELLEW, G: *Life and Correspondence of Henry Addington, First Viscount Sidmouth*. (1847)

PEVERLEY, J.R: 'Brick Cliffs of Dover', *Architectural Review*, (March 1959)

REMUSAT, Madame de: *Memoirs*. (English translation, 1880)

RICHMOND, H.W: *The Invasion of Britain*. (1941)

ROSE, J. Holland: *The Life of Napoleon I*. (1902)

ROSE, J. Holland: *William Pitt and the Great War*. (1911)

ROSE, J. Holland: 'Did Napoleon Intend to Invade Britain?' *Pitt and Napoleon: Essays and Letters*. (1912)

ROSE, J. Holland (ed): *Select Despatches relating to the Third Coalition*. (Royal Historical Society, 1904)

ROSE, J. Holland & BROADLEY, A.M: *Dumouriez and the Defence of England against Napoleon*. (1909)

ROTHENBERG, G.E: *The Art of Warfare in the Age of Napoleon*. (1977)

ST.VINCENT, John, Admiral Earl, (ed.Smith): *Letters, 1801-04*. (Navy Records Society, 1926)

SCOTT, Walter: *The Antiquary*. (1816)

SMILES, S: *Lives of the Great Engineers, Vol.2*. (1861)

STEVEN WATSON, J: *The Reign of George III*. (1960)

SUTCLIFFE, S: *Martello Towers*. (1972)

THIERS, L.A: *History of the Consulate and Empire, Vol. 5*. (English translation, 1845)

THOMPSON, J.M: *Napoleon Bonaparte*. (1951)

TUCKER, J.S: *Memoirs of Admiral the Rt. Hon. the Earl of St. Vincent. 2 Vols*. (1844)

VINE, P.A.L: *The Royal Military Canal*. (1972)

VIVIAN, J.H: 'Minutes of a Conversation with Napoleon', (J. Holland Rose: *Pitt and Napoleon: Essays and Letters*, 1912)

WARD, S.G.P: 'Defence Works in Britain, 1803-05', *Journal of the Society for Army Historical Research*, Vol.28. (1929)

WARD, T.A (ed.Bell): *Peeps into the Past*. (1909)

WATSON, J. Steven: *The Reign of George III*. (1960)

WESTERN, J.R: *The English Militia in the Eighteenth Century*. (1965)

WESTERN, J.R: 'The Volunteer Movement as an Anti-Revolutionary Force, 1793-1801.' *English Historical Review*, (1956)

WHEELER, H.B.F. & BROADLEY, A.M: *Napoleon and the Invasion of England: The Story of the Great Terror*. (1908)

WILSON, G: *The Old Telegraphs*. (1976)

WOOD, R.G.E: *Essex and the French Wars*. (Essex CRO Publications, 1977)

ZIEGLER, P: *Addington*. (1965)

Index